Disclaimers:

This book is a work of fiction; names, characters, places, and incidents are the product of the author's imagination, or used factiously. Any resemblance to actual events or locales or persons, living or dead, is entirely coincidental or intentionally disguised.

Endangered Whitness
  She saw the killers but she can't tell anyone. As the investigation heats up, the clues point to her.
  The killer has his own problem: a serial killer is hunting the killers she is refusing to identify.
  Complicating the investigation is the Police Lieutenant's infatuation with the lady M.E., but there are information leaks from the morgue, and they are helping the killers.
RLH

Endangered Witness

By

R. L. Hegstad

Chapter One

   The squad room was never quiet; even at two
thirty in the morning the place was bustling like a
crazed mob of youths trying to break into a U2
concert. Kurt looked over the frosted line of the
one piece of glass in his shared office; as usual the
guests were in every mode of attire from nude
perverts to tuxedoed Romeos. Using his palms, he
rubbed his face so hard it seemed he was in danger
of removing a layer of twenty nine year old skin.
The casual observer wouldn't know that he was,
figuratively, washing the chaotic pictures from his
mind. When his eyes reappeared from behind his
pinked palms, they blinked in an effort to penetrate
the mysteries of the information displayed on his
'work board'.
   In a habit formed over the years, his hand darted
for his half filled coffee cup. Passing his index and
middle finger through the ceramic handle, he
clutched the other side of the cup with his thumb.
The temperature of the cool cup warned him the
brew was already on the edge of undrinkable. His
eyes, once again still ,riveted to the board in front
of him, he sipped the cold coffee and responded
by turning down the corners of his mouth,

wrinkling up his nose and passing his tongue over his abused lips. He sentenced his cup to a spot was too far from him to repeat the offense.

Kurt Millhouse was a cop's cop, and so was his late father and his father before him, but none of his relatives were as well educated as he. At twenty-nine he had already racked up two doctorates, one in law and another in criminal science, but the paper he treasured the most was his certificate of graduation from the police academy. With the National Guard he had served as a Military Policeman and he had already done a stint at the FBI center at Quantico, Virginia.

The pained look on his face was due to a feeling he had failed to protect someone who was in his care. If confidence were a solid object, Kurt's would look like a thrift store colander.

Three months ago, as a sideline assignment, he had been railroaded into a protection case. Except for the complication that the lady was wealthy, he had thought it was going to be a rather routine piece of cake.

Captain Won had asked him to take charge of the case, mainly because of his education: it was meant to impress the Wentworth family. Kurt's father's reputation would have been enough to dazzle most people, but with some local elections and bond issues that concerned the police department, Won wanted to ingratiate himself to the rich and powerful Wentworth family.

On a freezing and stormy-black October morning, a punishing fall wind was charging down from Canada. Mrs. Thurman Wentworth, Margaret Goldstein-Wentworth, to be more exact, exited from an underground elevator, expecting to see her chauffer in the immediate vicinity, but the sound of gunshots caused her to pivot her head just in time to see a man holding a gun and a figure lying at his feet. Looking up from where the obscured figure lay, she realized the gunman's eyes were not just looking at her, but memorizing her every feature. Later, she realized the yellow hat worn by the gunman had caused her to fail to memorize his features: she was not even sure what race he was. Her husband, Thurman, had insisted she tell the police what she had witnessed. Over Margaret's staunch protests, Captain Won insisted on assigning her some police protection just in case the killer would try to make sure she could not testify against him. Three weeks ago, Margaret was shot twice through the head; she was now a dead witness.

"Making any headway, Sherlock?" Stirring a cup of doctored up coffee; Doris Mercer leaned against the door jam. A red and white swizzle stick was clasped between her chemical stained fingers.

While waiting for an answer, she casually placed
the stir stick between her lips and quickly
withdrew it. With profession curiosity she
inspected the stick.

Kurt smiled and his chair responded with a
complaining groan as he leaned back and tipped
his head to one side, "Taking some coffee down to
your customers in the freezer, Doc?" Kurt had a
real difficult time picturing her as a medical
examiner. With flashing ivory teeth which were set
in a sumptuous mouth beckoning to be captured,
Doris seemed totally unaware how most men
thought of her as the ultimate in femininity, not
sexuality, but reeking with everything that makes a
woman much more prized than the tawdry icons of
movies and television. In an effort to hide his
thoughts, Kurt stretched his neck and flitted his
eyes to again look over the frosted line in his cage.

"Looks busy tonight;" He sighed and returned his
attention to the board. "Guess I can't do much
more damage here tonight." Pausing he leaned
forward and stood up. To no one in particular, he
said, "I just don't get it. "

With a voice that should have belonged to a
1950's torch singer, Doris asked, "Get what,
Kurt?"

His fingertips pushed against his eyelids, he
rubbed them as he spoke. "Ever have the feeling

that an answer is starring you right in the face, breathing on you with its stinking and teasing breath, and it's laughing at you because you don't see it?"

Doris's head jerked as she snorted, "All the time, champ."

Chapter two

With furrowed brow and eyes wide open, he puffed his cheeks as he nodded, "Yeah, guess I'm complaining to the wrong person." In a gesture of fun he addressed a plastic Rhinoceros that owned the left corner of his desk, "Did you ever have that feeling, Mr. Rhino?"

Her childlike laughter escaped from behind the hand she had placed over her mouth, "He probably did have the same problem, but he never got out to have fun, so now he has turned to plastic."

"Okay, okay, I yield!" He started clearing off his desk: he hated clutter. "I'm hungry. What's a good place for you at this time of day?"

Emptying her cup labeled, 'Girl Power', she pointed at Kurt and demanded, "You wait here. I'll be fifteen minutes." She reconsidered, "Ah, make that twenty minutes and I'll take you to my favorite breakfast spot. " Enthusiastically she added, "You'll love it: great hash browns, perfect eggs, and pancakes to die for or live for…you decide."

Kurt laughed so hard he began coughing, "I'll never understand it!" he gasped.

Hands on her hips, the cup dangling from her index finger, she gave a thin lipped smile and asked, "Understand what?"

"Well, in your case two things." He took a deep recovering breath, "How you can ever eat considering what you do down there." He pointed toward the building's morgue. She pretended to bristle, "And secondly, how a gal with your figure could ever be eating anything but diet food."

Smugly, she grinned and gave him a non-flirtatious wink, "Well, Mr. Detective, there is a lot you don't know about me." She turned to go out of the doorway then leaned back and poked her head around the corner. "Twenty minutes." Again she winked, "You'll love the food."

Resigned to his fate, he dropped back into his chair and made a conscientious effort to clear his mind. He was at the point of confusion; it happened whenever a person spent too much time trying to work on any kind of a riddle. Kurt was so far beyond confusion he would have had to look over his shoulder to see it somewhere in the distance. He was now beginning to consider some rather bizarre scenarios. He needed a break, some sort of distraction, but Doris was more than what he had bargained for.

It was now after three a.m. and the morning air was snappy with the sting of ice in the air. The heavy steel lids that covered the city's underground infrastructure were bleeding ghostly wisps of white; thin ground clouds betrayed the warmth laying beneath. Two blocks behind them, Kurt and Doris responded to the sound of the approaching street-sweeping machine. Its whirling brush was overpowered by its snarling diesel spouting noxious black fumes.

Glancing over her shoulder, Doris chuckled as she announced, "If we pick up the pace just a bit, we'll be in the restaurant before he reaches us." She thrust her arm around his elbow and pulled him tight to her, "Come on!" she urged, "We can beat him!" With determined force, she began to drag her reluctant partner.

Upon entering Millie's Place, the first thing he noticed was the ambrosia of bacon, like a cartoon finger it reached out and he softly closed his eyes, better to enjoy the aroma. With a reverent sniff he sighed and inquired, "Why didn't you mention the bacon." Shaking his head he exhaled as he declared, "Oh that… smells great."

A waitress, probably in her mid-fifties, escorted them to a small booth situated at the last window on the street side. Carefully, as if the menus were made of recycled eggshells, she placed them on the table. After adjusting the spacing of the salt and peppershakers, she evoked a motherly smile and asked, "And what can I get you folks?"

Nodding at Doris, Kurt indicated she should go first. She ordered, well done hash browns, bacon, two eggs: sunny side up, and three blueberry pancakes: coffee to come later.

Grinning with approval the motherly waitress turned to Kurt, and cleared her throat, as if expecting him to over order Doris.

After a fake gasp, Kurt flashed a furrowed brow of confusion and smacked his lips. "I'd like two eggs, pouched, side of well done hash browns, and four strips of well done bacon." He paused to make sure he had her attention. "I want the browns crisp on both sides and the bacon should be able to stand out like a pencil."

With a sympathetic smile of assurance, as if to awaken her order pad, she poked her order pad as if to say 'that's that.' With a wink and a nod, she suddenly turned and headed for another table that had just arrived. Faintly, Kurt and Doris could hear their waitress going into her standard routine.

Kurt turned sidewise and faced the window. He could see himself and the counter behind him; the cook had just hung up another order and made a quick glance around the eating area. Plucking another order slip from the aluminum carousel he disappeared into his world of steam and fire.

They hadn't talked much on the way to Millie's, and now Kurt seemed lost for words. In a strange way he was surprised he was here, in this restaurant sitting with Doris Mercer, M.D. By inviting him, she had made the first move, the ball was in his court and now he felt nervous. In a brilliant inspiration of conversation he asked, "Eat here often?"

Doris could sense his nervousness, she felt excited to know he cared enough to be here with her. Fumbling with her eating utensils, she pressed her lips together and nodded, "Every chance I get, which is mainly when I'm covering the graveyard shift." She smirked and said, "Pardon the expression."

Ignoring her joke, he took on a philosophical tone and said, "You know, I think I have you M.E.'s figured out."

"Huh, you do?"

"Yeah, you guys are always eating so you won't have an empty stomach when you up-chuck." He grinned as if he had just made some great scientific discovery.

Sporting a grave expression she spoke as if she had just lost her best friend, "And here I thought our secret was safe for eternity." Like a panther clawing at an unsuspecting prey she countered, "So why do cops like doughnuts?"

"I'm afraid you'll have to ask God that one, but I think it comes with the uniform. Standard issue, you know. Here's your uniform, your badge and by the way here is your craving for doughnuts and coffee."

Chapter three:

Kurt had taken to studying the room; Doris used the opportunity to study him. He had the square jaw of a superhero, apparently built well: muscular but not grotesque. His soft brown hair parted naturally on the right side of his perfectly oval shaped head. The whites of his eyes were clear and featured unusually pale green pupils, that she was sure, never missed anything. He had the reputation of being an incredibly fine detective, he was known to be honest; 'firm, but fair' often how he was described. She knew he dated around but was not locked into any permanent relationship. After her thumbnail evaluating him, she wondered if she would want to change that, or even if she could. Her self-question was interrupted when 'mother' , (displaying a touch of OCD) precisely placed their plates on the table.

Deliberately, Kurt made a show of looking at the display of food in front of Doris. He dropped his jaw and asked, "Are you going to eat all of that?"

"Why? You want some?" she retorted as she placed sliced butter between her hot pancakes. Jerking her head to one side she confided, "I still have two more guys to do. Need lots of food if I want to do the job right." She giggled.

"Okay, you win. But I got to wonder where you put it. "Chomping on a piece of deliciously stiff bacon, he gestured with his knife, "I mean you can't have an ounce of fat on you."

Feigning a pained British expression, she quipped, "It's the up-chucking, you know." With quick jerky nods and a wrinkled forehead, she concluded, "Works every time." She fought back a coquettish laugh.

Throughout their breakfast the two sensed a presence which seemed to be bonding them closer together. Not just the chemical attraction, there, but it was a feeling they had met what some people call 'soul mates'. Later she would say that when she looked at him it was like looking at herself, or herself looking back at her. She wasn't sure if it was love yet, but she knew the fertilized seeds of a friendship had certainly taken root. What fruit it would bear would take time. She felt a wave of sunlight peace as she recalled how her parents had told her that one-day how she would feel.

Chapter four:

  Meticulously, he lined up the thirteen bullets that stood before him. Cocking his head to one side, he studied the way they passively reacted to his scrutiny. He tried rearranging them as if they were soldiers standing at attention waiting for their commanding officer to lead them into mortal combat. Leaning back in his black vinyl second hand executive office chair, he shifted his body in order to avoid the prickly tears which seemed determined to attack him. A grin of childish delight was followed by a sigh of peaceful satisfaction. Cursed with hair that resembled an outcropping of black volcanic rock, his fingers struggled to find a way through the unyielding maze; his eyes darted from side to side as if expecting to find at least one disobedient round of ammunition.

Imitating the bravado of a commanding general, he barked at his obedient pieces of metal and chemicals, "Attention!" Stoically they seemed to stand taller and straighter, their polished copper helmets hiding faces that would have revealed utter compliance. A subtitle bobbing of his head indicated his approval. Leaning forward to select volunteers, one by one he plucked them from their ranks and pontifically placed them into the pistol's magazine: confidant they would perform excellently upon his simplest command, the very thought conjured up past scenes that filled him with a sense of unbridled power.

Somewhere, someone was violating his sanctuary with a sonic intrusion. Breathing deeply to control his indignation, he narrowed his eyes and studied the offending plastic instrument. With the inner desire of a raging bull taking aim to squash an invading prey, violently he shoved the last three bullets into the magazine and slapped it into the handle of the nine-millimeter Rugar pistol.

With an air of disgust, he whirled the squeaking black porcupine in which he was sitting, and attacked the resonating piece of white-molded plastic. He hated telephones when they intruded on his concentration. As a control tactic, he held the villainous intruder at a distance and ran his tongue over his upper denture. "Yeah?" his voice crackled with hostility.

In response, the voice at the other end hesitated. With curiously he listened to the soft, quick breathing, he could almost smell her perfume seeping through the small slots that contained the receiving part of the white telephone. In the background was the sound of street traffic, the sloshing sound of black tires catapulting water in every direction.

From a stifled snort to a booklet's trickle, she began to chuckle, "Caught you in the midst of one of your military rituals, eh?" Her shoulders hunched against the cold, she sniffled and waited for his measured response.

The spell was broken and there was nothing he could do now so he leaned his head back and allowed his eyes to roam over the stark yellow-white ceiling: the porcupine chair pricked his ear. In one corner he discovered the floating remains of a dusty spider's web. "Will dinner be on time?" The words were polite and yet resonated in a snobbish tone.

"Yep…how does ten-fifty sound to you?" While she waited for his answer, her moistened eyes examined the smeared writing and scrawled art in the blue-bottomed phone booth. Warding off the cold, she placed a mitten-covered hand under her arm and danced from one foot to another; puffs of mini-clouds shot out of her reddened nostrils. She wondered if any civic-minded engineer had ever considered heating phone booths: she knew the answer.

Mindful, but unconcerned about her comfort, when he finally replied he joked, "Well, that depends on how many we will have for dinner and what they prefer." He pulled the magazine from his pistol and studied the soldiers waiting for his orders; they were all neatly in place. With a soft breath he puffed a piece of lint from the surface of the blue-black clip.

She coughed lightly and cleared her throat. Furtively she looked out of the plastic paneling that surrounded her: she thought she resembled an ice tray in a glass coffin. "Ah, that will just be one for dinner." The words came out on white clouds as if they had grown to become captions in a cartoon, she paused and said, and "I think the menu is up to us, dear."

Tapping his fingers on the magazine, he frowned at the fingerprints he had deposited. Wiping away the greasy smudges, he considered her cryptic message. *That would be ten thousand five hundred dollars for one hit, and they could choose the means.* It was a low bid, but it was from a 'bread and butter customer' and no frills would be required. "Gosh, Hon, that's okay with me, how about picking up something from the store." He believed she could negotiate a mother bear out of her first born cub. .

Without preamble, she put a smile into her voice and replied, "Sure thing. I'll see you in a bit, dear."
 'Picking up something' meant visiting an arms dealer named Pete Corbin. He was a nice enough guy, if you could get past the battle scars which gave one the impression he had walked into a discharged shotgun, which he might well have done. Whenever he was excited, sounds, like someone gagging on a gargling solution, erupted from somewhere below his collar, easily explained with the knowledge he had an electronic voice box. Somehow, Pete always had the right goods available, anything from a finger size syringe that could deliver an unfelt lethal dosage of one's favorite poison, to a hand held rocket launcher. It was rumored Pete would resist even the most barbaric Arab tortures in order to protect his clients.

Chapter Five:

Outside the grubby-blue and urine stained phone
booth, she felt the cool night air slyly testing the
perimeter of her heavy dark wool Navy pee-coat.
She pulled her collar tightly about her neck, moved
her shoulders closer together, and tugged her
mittens until she could tuck the tops into her
sleeves. Surprised by a sneaky gust of wind
swirling bits of soiled paper and gritty dirt into a
ground cloud of tornado-laidened trash, she tipped
her head toward the chipped and multi-colored
patched sidewalk and held her breath.

Piles of once crystal white snow that now
resembled the filthy fluid pumped out from a
washing machine bordered the street curbs and
clogged the arterial flow of the left overs from last
week's winter blow-in from the lake. At Betty's'
feet, the run-off of the late afternoon rain was
attempting to carry the foamy sludge into a four
foot wide grate which was plugged with assorted
refuse usually found in anyone's kitchen garbage
can. A fair-sized pool was beginning to form.
Searching to her left, she squinted against the
attacking breeze, hoping to entrap one of the

passing taxicabs. A block away she spotted the lights of an approaching cab, mindful of the lake forming in front of her, she hailed the cab and jerked open the door when it stopped. After giving the driver the address of a restaurant two blocks away from Pete's place, she settled back in the cab and enjoyed the warmth of the overheated interior. Swirls of nostalgia rushed at her, they attacked her senses of smell, taste, sight, and hearing. Resting her head on the back of the seat, she looked up at the starless sky and faded back to the days when she was a simple child clutching her text books as she splashed her way down the familiar sidewalks that used to take her to the safe haven of her grade school. She could smell the crisp color of the freshly fallen snow; the smell was a soft pure-white. The flakes would invisibility dissolve on her tongue. Fabrications of divinely created crystals weaved a curtain of beached white chenille redeeming everything as if covering it in a blanket of purity.

"This is the place you're wanting, miss?" The foreign accent had become almost synonanmous with taxi drivers. Bushy eyebrows and a set of tired brown eyes were framed in his oval rearview mirror.

Resenting the intrusion that swept away the serenity she was feeling, she looked out of the window and then reached for the door handle. The door shuddered as it passed over a small pile of wet snow. After paying the cab driver she went inside the restaurant. Ignoring the delicious smells of garlic, oregano, and steaming hot Italian sauces, she made her way out the back door and into a small alley. With the swiftness of smoke rising up a chimney, the stalking wind pushed its way down the walled passageway. *God, I hate this life*! She muttered to herself. *We've made plenty of money and yet we still live like street bums.* With swift, soggy, and purposeful strides she headed for Pete's 'store'.

To Morton Filman, suspicion was like a nagging mother-in-law, no situation was ever satisfactory; there would always be a better way to do something. Without looking, he allowed the heat of his plastic desk lamp to guide his hand to the switch; a stiff click resulted as he pinched the protrusion between his fingers and turned it. The room should have been obsidian black, but instead the faded once red but now a frosty pink' Jesus Saves' sign flashed alternating sets of shadows upon three of the walls in the room. Gingerly rising from his chair, eyes absentminded and unfocused, assiduously he took in his surroundings. The place was a hole that would be avoided by any self-respecting rat, but it was also a place ignored by the police.

Rising up on his toes he stretched and arched his back before slowly walking toward the soot and dirt-encrusted window that had serendipitously created some patterns resembling zoo animals. Caulking that had probably been some shade of white was now weighted down with frequent layers of yellowed and rust-stained goop resembling month old dried out spaghetti. He would have taken in a deep breath but he had discovered that the ambient odors caused him to choke as if someone had stuffed a stale dishrag down his throat. Occasionally, at times like this, ghosts, not creeping in like silent floaty wisps, but demons in wet oil shrouds attempted to grasp him, frantically clutching from some invisible abyss, but tonight, right now, there were no demons; not even a wispy ghost.

Chapter six:

When the sign was not proclaiming the salvation offered by Jesus, he could almost see his reflection. Pulling himself up to his full stature of five foot eight, he sucked in his overabundant gut and pretended he was still the gymnast he once was.

"God help me I enjoy being a contract killer. Even if people didn't pay me I would do it because I have to do it. It's a matter of respect!" He had made this confession more times than he cared to recall and every time he ended up with an involuntary groan for himself followed by a reflexive sigh for the people he had killed. Eventually, the demons would get him, he wondered if they would also get Betty.

Snapping himself out of an altruistic act of contrition, he clapped his hands together and rubbed them as if he were trying to remove a coating of rubber cement, "Well, I guess I had better get ready for—'DINNER'." After cavorting to an imaginary Irish Jig, he headed for the bathroom to shave; it was not for the sake of grooming, although a policeman was less likely to interrogate a well groomed man, it was rather for the purposes of reducing the probability of providing forensic evidence. Next he would stretch out his night gear and pass a hand vacuum cleaner over every inch of the clothing surface. "Sloppiness leads to convictions", he reminded himself.

Chapter eight:

Enrico Angelino was not Sicilian, he was Italian, but everyone knew it was a different thing. He would never be on the inner councils or hold a position of final power, but he was a man of 'respect' and influence. Mr. Angelino was a handsome man, and admired as a 'snappy' dresser. His wife, Cortina, was Sicilian by birth and was reputed to be the real power behind the throne; unfortunately for Enrico, she was a woman of large proportions and had been born with a face people said was about four steps below ugly. She was, in fact, not the power behind the throne, she was not ever very intelligent, but anyone who knew her was immediately overcome by her sweet sunshine disposition. Cortina could make people feel like they were the only important person on this planet. Strangely enough she really felt that way. God had gifted her with a very small portion of ego and a generous share of authentic care for others.

Enrico was proud of her and it is for this reason Enrico had managed to win her hand from an overly protective and devoted father. For many reasons Enrico was faithful to Cortina. He was beyond grateful for the three beautiful girls that she had born for him.

Paulo Ortiz was going to die, not because he had stolen money from the mob or snitched to the cops, but he had made the inexcusable error of seducing Enrico's sixteen-year-old daughter. There would be no discussion, no clemency, and no negotiations: he was a dead man walking. At the price of ten thousand five hundred dollars, it was a bargain basement contract and Enrico ought to know because his primary function with the organization: he procured 'contracts'. Like any purchasing agent he had his preferences, and Tito and Tanya, as he knew Morton and Betty Filman, were among his top three favorites.

For dinner Cortina had prepared a veal scaloppini, penne frigate, a scrumptious green salad soaked in the family's Italian dressing, shredded mozzarella cheese with sliced pepperoni. The Chianti was excellent. Like a scene from any Godfather movie, the family sat at a large table and chatted about the events of the day, but Enrico looked at his oldest daughter and ached for the crime done to her. It was not without her permission, but what does a sweet little Italian girl know at the age of sixteen. The doting father smiled with satisfaction knowing that tonight would be the final sleep for the twenty-two year old Ortiz.

Martina was watching the clock, at ten-thirty tonight she had a rendezvous with Ortiz, and he didn't like it when she was late. She ate with her eyes down cast, she was certain her father did not know of her indiscretions, but she was afraid the shame she masked would be revealed in her quiet, coffee tinted eyes.

   At night, after the passions of the evening were over, she would lie in bed and stare at the pink canopy that draped over the top of her bed. Her father had insisted that a girl of her virtue should have a covering fit for The Virgin Mother: she was not a virgin, but she was in constant fear of becoming a mother. Paulo was so cute with his wavy black hair and his perfect Hispanic features: all the girls said so. No doubt he was a bit too proud, but then he had a lot to be proud about. Besides being a body-builder, he had the sexist eyes and lips that she had ever seen. For months she had fanaticized about going to bed with him and her skin tingled when he finally started showing interest in her. She was convinced every minute she was not with him was a torture to her soul. Martina flipped a look at the six-foot tall grandfather clock standing next to the entrance from the adjoining living room. The large golden

Roman numerals glistened against the muted felt-green background. She watched the hands creep toward the appointed hour. The cherry wood encased guardian of time announced it was now eight o'clock; its bass tones quietly blending into the background of an aria from Puccini's Tosca. She sighed with anticipation.

***

Without turning on any lights, and slinging his gym bag onto a bench to the left of his front door, Paulo Ortiz headed for his cream-colored refrigerator. He jerked open the bottom half, a harsh beam of light shot out and cast his distorted shadow against the kitchen counter and the far wall. After reviewing the contents, he grabbed a tall bottle of V8 juice and unscrewed the top. Thrusting the bottle into his mouth, he allotted himself five large swallows and then returned the container to the original place among a plethora of health food products. While the door of the refrigerator was still open he shifted his eyes up to the wall clock: it was nine fifteen. He had been at the gym longer than usual, that beautiful blond trainer was hard to break away from, she would have made an interesting sideline for him; but for now he had to take a shower before Martina got here. He stared with anger as he recalled how frequently; she was late for their meetings. He didn't believe he should have to take that from anyone much less from a sixteen-year-old Wop who fancied herself as some sort of princess.

Paulo closed the refrigerator door and kicked off his gym shoes. Stripping as he traveled, he made his way to his bedroom and finished undressing for his shower. He started the water. Testing it with the back of his hands; he noticed he would soon need another manicure.

As was his habit, he studied himself in the full-length mirror covering the sliding door to his closet. He turned profile and then raising his arms over his head; he formed the muscles on his back: he was proud of his physique. *I think I should drop this jailbait Wop. She doesn't know anything about the bed anyway.* Moving his face from one pose to another, he studied his grin and thought; *I'll bet that blond knows the ropes.*

With steps reminiscent of a Sumo wrestler, he swaggered toward his waiting shower. Testing the temperature he reduced the cold water supply. Satisfied, he had almost lifted up his foot to step into the perfectly prepared shower when the sound of his door chimes arrested his progress. *Oh, no, the Wop bitch is early!* After taking a deep breath he thought *she must be anxious,* he smiled.

With a towel wrapped around his waist, he sauntered to the front door. As a standard precaution, he looked through the peephole on the door. From surprise, hc jcrked his head back and then looked again; it was the blond from the health club. He shot a quick look at the wall clock; Martina would be here in an hour: if she was on time, which she never was. Unlocking the dead bolt, he opened the door and let it float wide open. Jauntily, he leaned against the door jam and intentionally evaluated the blond from head to foot.

  "Aren't you going to invite me in?" In a nervous gesture she adjusted her handbag. Discreetly she glanced over his shoulder, "Or did I catch you at a bad time?" She ended her sentence with a Cheshire smirk accompanied by a flirtatious batting of the eyes and an appraising look at his physique indicating she approved.

  Adopting a 'man of the world' stance and a 'devil may care' attitude, he pivoted to his left and gave her a sweeping arm gesture that invited her into his lair. If Martina arrived on time or even early, he would just not answer the door. He could 'con' his way out of it later. As for now he was not going to let this fortuitous opportunity slip away. "I've been expecting you." He lied. Nodding his head toward the shower he said, "I was just going to take a shower. Care to join me?" He struggled to display his most confident attitude. Of course she was going to say 'yes'.

She seemed to be giving everything a second thought. She narrowed her eyes as she tightened her lips and deliberately surveyed the surroundings.

With miniscule nods and a thrust of her chin she continued to look around as she said, "Sure, why not." Following Pablo toward the showers, with practiced fingers she began to unbutton her blouse. With confident indifference, he dropped his towel and strutted toward the simulated ice covered shower doors. Having seductively dropped each item of clothing on the floor or draped them over strategic pieces of furniture, by the time she reached the shower she was naked. Before entering the shower, she stopped for the opportunity to provide a brief pose: she too was conceited when it came to her well-sculptured body.

Chapter ten:

Sensing her desire for a compliment, Paulo pushed his lips together and passed his hand over his wet hair, "Whoa!" He paused and jerked his head from side to side. He provided an approving smile as he reached out for her, "I knew you were put together, lady, but, whoa, you're something elsc." Feeling satisfactorily appreciated, she clasped his hand and entered the shower. The warm streams pelted her face as she closed her eyes and felt his wet lips upon her anticipating mouth. Desire was lurking like a crouching tiger; its loins strained anticipating the final pounce, its claws protruding with desire to conquer the soft velvet flesh of its victim.

Even with the shower cascading and a woman of desire in his wet embrace, Paulo heard the meddling sound of the door chimes. At first he thought he would just ignore the intrusion, but then he remembered his nosy neighbors. But it was the possibility Martina would get mad and tell her father: that really scared him. His desire waned and he gently pushed the blond to the back of the shower. She studied his face and said, "Are you expecting someone?"

"Naa…just some business." He replied as he gave her a perfunctory grin. Then slowly he exited the shower stall. To himself he thought, *just my luck, the bitch shows up early. No problem, I'll just get rid of her and move on with my life.*

Without looking through the peephole, he unchained the door and jerked it open, At first he was feeling confused, the guy in front of him was carrying a box of tools and was dressed in the uniform of a commercial plumbing company. With only a towel cinched around his waist and expecting to be addressing Martina, he shook his head as if trying to clear the unexpected scene, "Who the hell are you?" he demanded.

With a confused look on his face the man said, "I'm your cordial plumber!" Nodding his head he repeated, "I'm the plumber. I'm here to fix your clogged toilet." Displaying a set of teeth that were cigarette and coffee stained, the plumber beamed with pride.

The towel-draped Paulo questioned, "You're here to fix the toilet?"

"Yeah, sure, Man." Paulo could not distinguish stupidity from confusion.

With a disgusted roll of the eyes, Paulo shook his head and said, "There is nothing wrong with my toilet, man."

Politely, and compassionately, the man looked at Paulo and replied, "Yes, I know that. But in order to unclog the toilet that is above you, I need to run a snake down your toilet." The plumber changed his tone to one of professionalism, "If I don't get this taken care of, it will back up to your apartment."

Reluctantly, Paulo stepped back and waved the
plumber into his apartment. "I have to leave for a
business appointment in just a few minutes. Can
you be done that soon?"

"Yeah, no problem," was all the plumber thought
it necessary to say. With a surge of resolve the
plumber headed down Pablo's hallway. Executing
a quick right hand turn, he disappeared into the
first bathroom. Paulo stood by the door jam and
watched as the man stuck a long metallic steel
shaft into the toilet bowl. After a few turns the man
seemed satisfied and turned to Paulo, "Where's
your other bathroom?" He slipped a piece of tape
over the trip lock.

Caught off guard, Paulo thought about the blond
in his shower and then thought that it would be an
exciting turn of events; "This way, man." Paulo
turned to the man and gave a knowing grin, "But
be fast, Man, I've got a ---guest in my shower.
You know---."He finished with a nod of pride.

Displaying his palms the man beamed and
promised, "Hey, I'll be fast." The man raised his
eyebrows and   gave a childlike expression of
trustworthiness. Charging into the bathroom, he
turned his head to provide a loud, "Trust me!" he
laughed.

Paulo followed him into the room and noticed the
shower was still running, but he didn't see the

silhouette of the bathing blond. *She must have ducked from sight* he speculated.

   "Thought you said you had a guest in your shower?" the man's eyes were narrowed, almost threatening, if one were to interpret them that way.

   "Sorry, man, but I didn't know who you were so I used the standard excuse." Paulo grinned and smiled benignly." Wish I did have someone there though." They both laughed

Chapter eleven:

   Setting his toolbox on the tile floor of the aged bathroom, the man unlatched the two clips on the side of the box. Deftly, he set the top aside and, from nowhere, the man produced a revolver that looked as if it were eight feet long. To Paulo it looked strange until he realized the object at the end of the pistol was a silencer. His brain struggled to reject the possible threat, but when it finally accepted the situation, Paulo did not know what to do. His mind told him to leave, but his senses said he should attack the man. He did not realize it was already too late. There was a hot feeling somewhere in his body. At first it was like a piece of wood stuck under his skin, then it seemed to be expanding, then it turned hot.

Behind him Paulo heard a woman's voice; "Don't overdo it, Buddy." It sounded like the blond, but it was coming from the wrong direction. "I think the girlfriend is due here any minute. Let's clean up and get out of here." Now Paulo realized the voice was not coming from behind him: it was above him and he was trying to focus on the ceiling, *why wasn't she in the shower?* He tried to clear his head but the hot thing in him was demanding his attention. His mouth seemed dry and his eyelids seemed heavy. He needed to sleep, yes, that would take care of it; he needed to sleep.

"Yeah, but don't forget to get the bullets."

A sense of cold invaded the room; it seemed to attach itself to every molecule of air. Burnt cordite became an unwelcome perfume. The blond picked up a large green bath towel and started to drape it over the body.

The man picked it up and said, "Careful…that could become a signature. Right now they're searching for a killer that always pours flour over his victims, and that is what we are going to do. The right brand is there in the toolbox." He gestured with his head, "Help yourself."

As if she were in a supermarket, she picked up the flour and examined the bag. "My mother always used this brand." After a soft snort and shrug of her shoulders, she asked, "Is there any special way the flour is to be administered?"

"Good, point." He grabbed a pair of scissors from his toolbox and made an angular cut at the top right corner of the bag. "Now, pour it slowly going from head to toe. Try to empty the bag in one pass, but make sure he's completely covered."

Following his instructions, she began pouring the flour over the body of Paulo Ortiz. For a few seconds she could picture the oversized kitchen of her grandmother. The wooden floors, the porcelain lined pots and the iron skillets: the smells of fresh baked bread. Magically, the air became contaminated with a fine white dust." What do I do with the bag?"

"Get closer to the body. If that dust gets thick we could end up leaving a foot print or something." The Plumber began walking around looking to see if they had left any conflicting clues; "Huh...oh, yeah. Give the bag to me when you're done. It has to be folded in a particular way and then inserted between his teeth."

Wrinkling up her nose, she said rather than asked, "What is this sick puppy trying to say?"

Combing the shower for clues, his voice gave a faint echoing sound, "Who knows. "They haven't caught the guy yet, but he wants to get caught."

"Why do you say that?"

"When someone deliberately leaves clues, he wants to get caught."

Hands on her hips, shc held the empty bag in her flour-covered hand. With no intentional effort, her eyes wondered to the shower stall. It was hard to believe just a few minutes ago she was the girl standing naked in that shower, with the man now lying on the bloodstained green and white linoleum floor. "Are we leaving clues?" she inquired.

"Everyone leaves some kind of clues, but only certain ones leave clues as a challenge."

Chapter twelve:

Picking up his toolbox, he hefted it in order to get the right balance. "We leave clues that will lead the investigating detective to another person. He wants clues, so we give them to him, but we make sure they will send him in the wrong direction…at least for a little while."

With a girlish blink and a teasing grin, she said, "I knew that!"

Glancing about the hallway they headed for the front door, whipping spots as they went. Standing at the door they both studied the scene. "Did we forget anything?" He narrowed his eyes as if to better search for errors.

Her full purple painted lips were tightly pursed, "I don't think so." Picking up the pace of her speech she urged, "We better get out of here. Make sure the door is locked."

After using the peephole to see if the hallway was clear, they bolted out of the door, making sure the door pin was activated and the upper lock would catch. At first they pretended to be trying to get into the door and then they sauntered away as if disappointed that no one was at home, while striping latex gloves from their hands.

The plumber took the first set of stairs available; he would go out at the lobby entrance and avoid the garage cameras. The blond walked to the far end of the hallway and took the stairs down to the next floor and then the elevator to the lobby. Having removed his plumber costume, Morton joined her as she came out of the elevator. Outside, as they were making the turn at the end of the block they saw the young Martina heading for the lobby of the hotel. She was not only going to be on time, but she gave them a deliberate glance: like someone trying to recall the name of an old acquaintance.

The hotel wasn't exactly seedy, but it was old and well worn. Its ten stories of red brick had been the pride of the neighborhood when it was built in 1967, but time and the elements had now made the bricks more valuable than the rest of the building. Entering the lobby one could readily see the wood and painted walls had been maintained. Perhaps the antique white paint had too many coats, but in another way it added a sense of history.

A small table-model oscillation fan was pushing about a faint whiff of Lysol and furniture polish. Dressed in a well-creased uniform, the patrolman greeted the two plainclothes detectives as they pushed on the shiny brass bar allowing them to open the etched glass doors. The brass was cold and brittle to the touch.

Kurt Millhouse blew on his hands as he rubbed them together. "Where's the scene--?" Millhouse did a quick read of the patrolman's nameplate, Officer White?"

"Third floor, sir: room 310." His face looked pained as he nodded toward the steps. "You'll have to take the stairs, sir. The elevator is getting its annual inspection." He shrugged and added, "Wouldn't you know it."

Kurt glanced at his partner, John Miller. Born of an Asian mother and a large English father, John was a confusing mixture of white skin with oriental eyes. He might have been called pretty, but on a second thought no one would even consider it. He was six foot four, slim and built with a classic 'V' shape. "Johnny, feel like carrying me up the stairs?" For the benefit of the patrolman, Kurt looked serious.

John sagged and shook his head, "Ah, come on, Millhouse, not again." He turned to address the confused patrolman, "My back is still hurting from the last time." After watching patrolman White's perplexed expression, John slapped him on the shoulder and said, "Gottch'a!"

While the patrolman was rolling his eyes and chuckling, the two detectives started up the six sets of stairs. The old hotel smell had not escaped the stairwell. Pervading the air was a hint of stale cigarette smoke blended with two parts wet, moldy carpet nailed down with brass-plated tacks. Shortness of breath seemed out of place after only six flights, but the two men found themselves taking deeper breaths than they had expected.

"Whoa, that's some set of stairs, Johnny."

"I think it's because we were holding our breath, Kurt."

"Could be, but I think I'm beginning to feel my age."

John wrinkled his forehead and his nose, "Twenty-nine?" Grabbing Kurt by the elbow he turned him in the direction of two officers who were standing in the hallway. The door to the apartment had been decorated with two strips of yellow "DO NOT CROSS—POLICE LINE" tape forming a giant 'X' in front of the door.

Holding up their identification badges, John said, "Good morning, officers."

Kurt grabbed the tape and ceremoniously pulled it from the doorframe. "Charlie, has anyone been snooping around the scene?"

It seemed like every cop in town knew Charlie. He was friendly as well as reliable. At the age of fifty-five he was still a corporal, also due to his affability at the neighborhood bars. "No sir, Detective Millhouse. We just did a little walk through, a careful one and then we called the precinct. I suspect the crime scene boys are right behind you." Charlie paused and then felt obliged to continue, "Ah, the meat wagon, pardon me, sir, the coroner should be on the way."

After slipping on the obligatory latex gloves, Kurt turned to Charlie and said, "Make sure the boys dust the door for prints."

Charlie smiled, "I imagine you'll get half of the residents of this fine establishment."

John snickered, "I'm sure of it." John tilted his head up toward the ceiling and asked, what's the gal's name?"

"Suzan Faulkner, I believe, at least that's what the ID in her purse says. She's covered with white flour, you know." Charlie looked at the other patrolman and then at John, "I don't think we know the name of the man covered in white flour, but he looks to be well heeled, sir."

Kurt and John opened the door and checked it for forced entry; they found no signs the door had been worked. Kurt was in a crouch when he muttered, "It's been a little while since I've heard someone referred to as 'well-heeled'."

John seized the chance to quip, "It means well off financially, Kurt."

Casting an evil eye at John he said, "I don't know why I put up with you. God must hate me," he joked.

"Let's do a quick walk-through before the crime scene crew gets here." Without discussion, Kurt started for the kitchen. "I think the bodies are in here." Over his shoulder he spoke to John as if he were a rookie instead of a ten year veteran, "Remember, don't touch anything until the photo team is done."

"Okay, Dad, I won't if you won't" His actions were inconsistent with his words, not that he was going to touch anything, but his concentration was on the faint outline of a shoe print, possibly a sneaker. He asked himself, *"Why would there be a partial print behind this couch?"* He knew the logical answer, the perpetrator had waited here and some flour had seeped out of the bag, but the explanation seemed too pat for John. Dropping to his hands and knees, he sniffed at the back of the couch, "Hey, Kurt, I think our perp might be a woman." He shouted.

Chapter thirteen:

"Why's that, because of the flour?"

"Na, I think I smell some kind of sicky-sweet perfume."

From Kurt's squatting position in the hallway he looked at each of the bodies, he tipped his head from one side to the other as he studied the flour bags that had been placed in the mouths of the victims. Opening his mouth to respond to John's speculation, he was interrupted by the sounds of a three-man forensics team which had just arrived.

The three men looked for a safe place to put down their equipment, the team leader spotted Kurt and shouted, "Get the Hell out of there, Kurt; we haven't got our pics yet!" Without taking a breath he asked, "How did you get here before us?"

"Just got here, Bruce, and we've been real careful---we haven't touched a thing." Kurt stood up and pointed at John, "John thinks the perp was crouched behind that couch and was a woman."

Ignoring Kurt's sentence, he carefully laid down a piece of butcher paper and then placed a couple of small cases that were filled with his tools of the trade. His eyes quickly swept the scene; he made a face registering confusion. "I don't believe it!" he exclaimed.

"Don't believe what?" John thought Bruce was about to give them a lecture on not touching the crime scene until forensics had finished their work. "We didn't touch a thing."

Grabbing two small bags in which to put some samples, he headed for the shower. Looking under the fingernails of the woman, he muttered, "They told me this was another flour job, but I can't believe he was that busy last night."

"Huh?" Both John and Kurt responded.

"We just came from a case across town. Same MO.: flour, bags, the whole nine yards." Bruce grunted as he changed positions. "The M.E. will have to verify this, but from the feel and look of the bodies, I'd say they were killed at about the same time as the other guy."

"Other guy?"

"Yeah, Hispanic: about early twenties." Bruce chuckled, "The guy just comes out of the shower with a towel wrapped around his middle….gets it in the bathroom."

Kurt looked at John and raised his eyebrows, "Bruce, are you telling us we either have a copycat or the flour guy did two jobs at the same time of day."

"Yep, or he has an accomplice and they decided to diversify."

John curled his lower lip and executed a slight bobbing of his head, "Well, Brusey Boy, you just might have something there." Glancing from Kurt to Bruce, John added, better tell your boys to do an extra special job. We'll need to sort out the inconsistencies."

Having heard hundreds of these admonitions, Bruce considered not even responding. Slowly, he started uncurling from his squat position, wincing as he straightened out his left knee. While shaking out his knee he responded, "My boys always do a good job. Believe me, by now they have come to the same conclusions we have." He placed some evidence bags in a large plastic container. "Nothing different…so far;" Bruce gave them a pacifying grin.

Knowing the pressure on the Crime Scene Team, Kurt avoided any further conflict. "So what's the name on this Hispanic guy?"

"Room was in the name of a Paulo Ortiz, and his driver's pic seemed to match the stiff." Bruce pulled out a large tweezers and tugged the folded flour bag from the mouth of the woman. "We'll leave the rolling to the M.E., and then we will see if we get a print match."

Kurt and John both exchanged a look: they were thinking the same thing.

"We'll get out of your way for now. You'll be done in a couple of hours won't you?" John asked as they retreated from the kitchen.

"Yep, I think so." For emphasis, Bruce paused and said, "Going over to the other guy's place, eh? It's still in your jurisdiction" Without tilting up his face he shifted his eyes to just under his eyebrows. "Ah, you might want the address." Reeling off the numbers, he sounded as if he were giving an address to a cabby.

Kurt and John hustled to be the first detectives on the scene. Taking the stairs two at a time, Kurt chided John, "I'll drive! You old guys are too slow and cautious."

John snorted and said, "Sounds good to me. I'll sleep."

It took them almost an hour just to find the place. "I guess he could have done both jobs, but it's a break from his usual m.o."

"Hey! What about Bundy? Didn't he do three in one day?" John reasoned.

"Okay, you've got a point, but I'm talking time frame." Bruce swung his head to the right as he spotted a parking space: he stopped abruptly. While backing into his claimed space, he continued, "To pull this one off, he would have to have them lined up. First the one: and then rush across town and do the other couple."

Opening his passenger side door, John responded, "He could have had the couple tied up, come over here done this guy and then driven back over to the hotel and killed the couple."

Chapter fourteen:

Entering the lobby of the rooming house where Ortiz lived was a big difference from where they had just come. The lobby was murky and the air seemed to be stained with a thin yellow tint. The pitted phony tile was filled with samples of food, dirt and other foreign substances. The source was possibly explained by the six unisex vagrants that were draped over the lobby furniture. Lying in varying poses they could easily have passed for a group of aspiring actors demonstrating the Stanislavsky method of imitating discarded pieces of fruit.

Ignoring the sleeping desk clerk, they cautiously tiptoed their way to the elevator. Considering the age of the building the two detectives smiled at each other. "Tell me, Kurt, do you think this thing will make it to the top floor?"

"Life's an adventure, old man. Let's go for it!" Kurt stabbed his index finger into the number five. In response the elevator gave a violent jerk and then began its ascent. Smoothly the cables pulled the compartment to the fifth floor and then silently opened the doors.

In a spirit of admiration John smiled and philosophically proclaimed, "They don't make 'um like they used to. See, Kurt, just 'cuz it's old, doesn't mean that it's not still first class." The mid fifties detective proudly strode off of the exemplary elevator.

Scanning in both directions, the detectives quickly spotted the uniformed policeman who was guarding the door to the crime scene: he was jabbering with some lady who gave every appearance of being a woman of commerce.

The footsteps of the detectives caused the patrolman to look in their direction. Attempting to make it look as if he were conducting business, the officer nodded at the detectives and spoke a few quick words to the woman. She responded by touching his arm and smiling then she pranced into an apartment opposite the door to the crime scene.

Holding up their detective shields as if they would ward off the rays from the weapon of some Alien invader, they displayed a visage of understanding. His job was boring, but sometimes they got some good information.

"How's it going?" Kurt inquired.

Not answering Kurt's polite inquiry, and probably seeking to justify his conversation with the 'lady', the patrolman said, "She lives across the hall."

"Yeah, we saw." John retorted.

"She says that last night she happened to see two different gals at the apartment."

"Any descriptions?" The officer sounded hopeful.

"Not really. One was a blond and the other was a brunette. She thinks the second one was Italian. She had seen her here before, but not the blond." Feeling vindicated he waited for the officers to throw him a bit of praise.

"Anything else? Like did she notice the time?"

"I asked her, but she could only recall that her date was late and would have been about nine-thirty, or so." He swallowed. "She couldn't be sure, but the second girl was young and got here closer to ten."

Kurt was making notes, "Must have had her eye stuck to the peephole, huh?"

The officer didn't know how to respond so he said nothing.

John gave the officer a pat on the shoulder and said, "Thanks for the info. If you think of anything else, let us know."

Kurt was studying his notes, "Log us in officer, "I'm lieutenant Millhouse and this is Detective Miller. Okay?"

"Sure thing, detective; are you both from the fifteenth?"

"You bet." John said as he reached for the discolored imitation brass doorknob.

Chapter fifteen:

Enrico grinned as he replaced the receiver. He focused on the instrument as if it had been the very messenger bring him such good news. Ortiz was

dead, good enough for him. Tito and Tanya had
got the job done. Not knowing how close his
daughter, Martina, had come to walking in on the
killers, he was fully satisfied with their work, but
confused by the news Ortiz had been covered in
flour. Tito and Tanya were pros. Not only could he
not understand, but he was concerned: serial killers
get caught, and they usually talked. For his peace
of mind he decided his informant at the police
department must have gotten confused about the
flour.

Martina was late, not just for breakfast, but for
her monthly cycle. She had pounded on Ortiz's
door until the lady across the hall had cracked her
door open to see what was going on. Seething with
anger and humiliation, Martina slinked away into
the shadows of the hallway. Martina wrapped her
arms around herself and waited for almost half an
hour before she decided Ortiz was not home.
Feeling both betrayed and scared with the prospect
of being pregnant, frightened teen-age tears
trickled from her misty coffee brown eyes and
waves of fear rippled through her body like fist
blows to her stomach.

Fully clothed she had lay on her bed, unable to
recall the taxi ride back to her home, she stared at
the virginal pink canopy and tried to shut down her
frantic thoughts. During the long night she

oscillated between consciousness and periods of
fitful sleep. Her tardiness at reaching the breakfast
table was noted, but given second place to the
condition of her tear-swollen face and her
downcast countenance.

Cortina chose to be a patient mother and hushed
those who made gestures or comments, but she
knew something was wrong; she just hoped it was
not the worst. Sensing Martina's fear, Cortina
made comments like there was a lot of flu going
around, and the cold weather and pollution was
making everyone sick. Her little girl was hurting
and she desperately wanted to come to her aid, and
yet, she did not want to hear the bad news that she
sensed would be forthcoming.

Like the persona of a zombie, Martina returned
to her room to prepare for school. She had just
finished repairing her make-up when her private
line started chirping. Reluctant to pick up the
phone and forgive Ortiz for his no-show she
hesitated, but her heart was racing with anxiety.
Plucking the phone from its cradle, she imitated a
calm voice, "Hello." She managed before her dry
throat was forced to try to swallow.

A panting and explosive voice at the other end
said, "Martina, did you hear?"

Another of Marge's pieces of gossip, she thought. Disinterest and disgust couching in her words, Martina slurred, "Heard what?"

"That guy you like, Paulo Ortiz."

Now her heart began to flutter like a frantic bird attempting to escape its captor; "Oh him…yeah, what about him?" Sweat was beginning to moisten her hand, her grip on the telephone tightened. She fought her emotions, not wanting to reveal her true involvement with the unsavory Latino.

In large hot letters the insensitive telphone blurted out, "He's dead!" Margaret continued talking but Martina could still hear the word 'DEAD'. Feeling faint, she lowered herself into an overstuffed chair. She sensed rather than heard Margaret asking, "Can you believe it?"

Martina gasped for air; a cold sweat broke out over her whole body: she could feel herself fading from consciousness; "Got to go, Marge." The room was spinning, "Call you later." The words barely escaped her lips when she fumbled to replace the receiver in its cradle and then her tense body began to shut off the blood to her head. Rapidly she could feel the room beginning to float and a feeling of nausea forcing its way into her fragile body. Then there was a blanket of merciful darkness.

Chapter sixteen:

Slipping her long slender fingers into latex gloves, Doris did a half pirouette as she backed through a set of large swinging doors. On nights like this she often asked herself what she was doing with her life. It had been a long time since she had had any kind of social life, for a while it had been by choice, but lately it had been by habit. The three bodies resting on body-sized stainless steel trays were supposedly related. Kurt had told her they were probably the work of The Baker as they called him, or her. It was Doris' turn to help to solve the riddles plaguing the police department.

The assistant had already prepped the corpses and, except for the gray, greenish appearance, they looked as if they had just come out of the shower, which one of them had. Doris flipped back the courtesy white sheets and studied the two men and one woman. Each had three horizontal bullet holes just above the solar plexus.

Behind her she heard the swishing of the large swinging doors. Briefly her eyes looked up at the stainless steel lamp above the bodies, it wasn't a perfect mirror, but it was good enough for her to be able to identify Kurt Millhouse.

His voice was stiff and pitched as if he were trying to speak in a way which would not offend her three customers. "So, what do you think?" he kept a respectful distance.

Raising her shoulders, she shrugged. "Looks the same on the outside, but we'll have to see what ballistics has to say."

Quietly he stepped up along side of her. Earlier he had seen the bodies, but then they seemed like hurt people, but now they just seemed like three lifelike pieces of discolored plastic. "You know, I just have never gotten used to seeing people like this. They just look like something's missing."

"Something is, Kurt. It is called life."

"Yeah, I know, but maybe there is something else also." Sniffing and batting his eyes to produce more moisture, he said, "Don't these smelly chemicals ever get to you?"

"You get used to them, but not the smell." She squiggled her mouth to one side and narrowed her eyes. "If this is not the same killer, he certainly knows a lot about this m o. I read the prelim on the case and everything looks kosher" She pulled up her mask and reached for a probe. "Let's see what these slugs look like." Behind her, Kurt winced and felt his stomach tighten into something that must have resembled an airsick bag. Sensing his discomfort, she said, "Why don't you wait outside while I finish up here. I have an assistant who can do most of the routine job."

Kurt cleared his lumpy throat and mumbled, "Yeah, I don't want to be in the way." Turning on his heels he tried to walk as casually as he could. Before he reached the swinging doors he heard the sound of a metal slug as it dropped into a stainless steel pan. In his mind's eye he could picture pinkish blood oozing to the bottom of the shiny metal tray. It seemed bizarre to him how many times he had handled slugs that had been cleaned up and how many gruesome corpses he had seen, but he was still bothered by what went on in morgues and funeral parlors. He was certain some shrink would say it was because he was picturing himself lying on the undertaker's workbench: maybe they'd be right.

Doris had to grin at the way many cops reacted to what she did, but when she thought about having to be at some inhumane crime scene she didn't think she would do very well either. In fact, she had been at several scenes which resulted in a torrent of nightmares for several days afterward. Before she was completely done, Jolene came in and stated prepping the bodies from which Doris had just removed three bullets each.

"That a cop... or your fell' a outside!" Jolene shouted above the sound of the surgical saw.

Jolene pulled the jagged disc from its work; it speeded up as it frantically bit into the phantom air. Using the whining saw she gestured toward the hallway, "He looks a bit green about the gills."

Dropping the last set of three bullets into its own dish, she headed for the sink in order to scrub and 'bag and tag' the bullets. "Jolene, he's a cop." Dispensing green soap over her arms she added, "About the other." She hesitated, "It's just too soon to say."

In response Jolene nodded as she returned the eager saw to its work. The frantic whining turned to a loud purr.

Chapter seventeen:

Kurt had purchased some generic coffee from the aging vending machine. It tasted like a combination of all of the other drinks offered by the infrequently cleaned machine. Since it was cold in the hallway he used the plastic cup to heat his hands and divert his thoughts. He took one final sip of the cool concoction and stood up to drop it into a nearby trash bin.

Swishing doors announced the appearance of
Doris Mercer, M. D. She held up the three-bags of
slugs as if they were the daily catch from some
mountain stream. She made a pained face as she
asked; "You didn't actually drink anything from
that machine did you?"

Embarrassed, Kurt shrugged and declared,
"Believe me, I've had worse." But just now he
could not recall where. "It seems to be my lot in
life: cold and or bad coffee!" Unexpectedly, he
found himself looking at her and he liked what he
saw. Something about her seemed to make him
feel peaceful, like laying in a field of wildflowers
on a summer's day, or standing at the top of a high
mountain and inhaling the crisp air as you admired
the surrounding majesty.

Kurt blinked back to reality as he realized she
was grinning while searching his face and asking
"Is something wrong?"

He executed a quick shake of his head and
narrowed his eyebrows as if questioning the
purpose of her question. "Oh! I was just thinking
about the case."

Disappointed, she inquired, "Anything useful?"

"Na, not really, we're still interviewing
witnesses." He studied the evidence bags and said,
"Let me walk you to ballistics. They're always
concerned someone might have tampered with the

evidence. Of course, as always, they are a bit backed up, so I'll see if I can get a rush on these." He shrugged and snorted, "For all the good it'll do me."

"Do you think this flour guy is the same one who killed Mrs. Wentworth in that garage thing?

Pushing the 'up' button on the elevator he leaned against the wall. He raised his head as if he were searching the air for his answer. His eyelids flicked a bit and then he smacked his lips, "Na, I don't see where they would be related, but—"he raise his index finger and continued, "They have taught us to never exclude anything, or any possibility."

The rumbling elevator arrived and the doors creaked open. A smell of cigarette smoke mixed with a pungent perfume exhaled from the interior. Without a word they both hesitated and exchanged looks.

"Want to take the stairs?" he joked.

"Nope, just a few deep breaths"

The elevator car jerked and started its ascent. Together, alone, they could not think of anything to say and yet they both knew they had much to say and even more that would be said. The yellow stained light bulb cast an eerie haze hiding the aged wooden floor of the once emerald green walls. Kurt shuddered as if some misty specter had just embraced him.

Chapter eighteen:

With his feet propped at the corner of his desktop, he slumped in his fabric covered office chair. His eyebrows pinched together as he scrutinized one of the maze colored nine by twelve inch envelopes. Inside them there should be ten thousand five hundred dollars: the price for a man's life. In a gesture of distain, he tossed the envelope on the desk and slid open the drawer to his left. From the drawer he plucked two latex gloves and stretched them onto his hands. With calculated precision he slit the envelope open and slowly spread the contents on top of the desk blotter, then continued to open the envelopes until they were all empty. Using a pen he separated the piles of currency into neat rows.

As if exhausted from the ordeal, Morton Filman stood up and ambled toward a bottle of Black Label scotch. Examining the water glass, he decided it needed one more wiping before he poured an inch and one half in the glass. In a moment he would return to the desk and verify the honesty of the person who had paid him to kill Paulo Ortiz. Not wanting any connection to the one who paid him, he would not leave his prints on the bills. In turn for the merchandise he purchased from the arms dealer, Pete Corbin, Pete would do a one hundred percent exchange for him. Morton was a stickler about details.

 For now he had a different concern. Across the room he watched the changing patterns that the rain made as it slid down his windowpane. His concern was for the daughter of the powerful criminal, Enrico Angelino. The question that kept nagging at him was, did she see him? She seemed preoccupied, and if she did, what could he do about it. Passing his tongue over the inside of his teeth, he worried. Morton didn't like worrying and even more he hated loose ends. He sipped some more scotch and rinsed it around in his mouth. He would see what developed, but if the police connected her to Paulo and she became a threat; *perhaps her grief would become too much for her to bear and she could be 'encouraged' to commit suicide.* Without giving the problem another thought, he returned to his desk and finalized his counting of the cash he had been paid. His eyes scrutinized each bundle as if he were evaluating his own self worth. Every piece of currency gave him weight in the scales that balanced a man's measure of success or failure. Success weighed heavily in the arena of respect.

Dark streets never bothered Morton in fact he liked them. Even now, with a briefcase filled with over ten thousand dollars, he walked with the assurance of a man who was prancing about within the security of a bank vault.

An intermittent wind from the south was pushing about clumpy hands of dark rain that instantly drenched anything it could touch. There seemed to be a presence in the heavy wind that sought to engulf him, it was warm and threatening. He tried to struggle with his reaction, but his labors just seemed to intensify his sensation of blatant terror which was beginning to cling to his body as if it were a water soaked cloak. The sounds of the passing traffic, the whistling of the punching rain and even the country western music coming from a bar across the street began to fade from his hearing as it was replaced by the frenzied beating of his tethered heart.

Morton's expensive leather shoes splashed in the thin layer of water moving over the neglected sidewalk. On impulse he jumped into the doorway of what once was a thriving deli market, but was now boarded up because of the robbery deaths of the last three owners. He clutched the briefcase across his chest. Rain slid down from his water soaked hair. In an effort to abate the stream running into his eyes, he wiped his forehead with the back of his hand. He squinted as his eyes swept the streets and doorways to locate the source of his fear. There was nothing unusual…nothing abnormal.

Gradually he began to rebuke himself for being so paranoid. His feet had warmed the cold water in his shoes, and the clamor of the streets soon overshadowed the nagging of his thumping heart. He had intended to walk to Pete Corbin's place, but now he stepped to the curb and hailed a passing cab: he caught the third one.

With an audible sigh he settled back on the vinyl covered bench seat and mumbled out his destination. He didn't like leaving a trace like taking a cab from his apartment to Pete's but right now he feared for his life and he didn't know why. The four inch wide briefcase was resting on his thighs as he placed his arms and his head on the top of the case. On impulse, he popped his head off of the briefcase and looked out the back window: still nothing. Returning his head to its resting place on the briefcase, he let out a soft moan and closed his eyes.

He had been right to trust his instincts, he was sure of that, but there had been no logic to the sudden anxiety. For a brief time he felt as if he were the hunted instead of the hunter. Was that possible?

Chapter nineteen:

John Miller had always wanted to be a cop. No one in his family had ever been in law enforcement but he had seen enough movies and talked to enough policemen to know he was interested. At college he majored in Criminal Science and took some courses in pre-law. Kurt thought Miller was a natural, but John was still waiting for the day when he was the lead officer who broke the big case. There was no doubt but what he wanted to grab some big headlines; in fact he wouldn't deny it. John's biggest problem was his size and his health. He had contracted tuberculosis when he was young. It never did any serious damage but it seemed to have weakened him and his immune system. His large frame fooled everyone except those who had spent a lot of time with him or visited the personal pharmacy that occupied one corner of his bathroom. Based on his size, people just couldn't understand how he could possibly ever be sick.

Fighting off a low-grade fever, John stood next to a pile of used facial tissues. His sinuses were filled and causing his eyes to itch. His head began to feel like someone had been fishing in his sinuses and had cast a bevy of hooks into all parts of his head. When he finally got home last night, he propped himself up on four pillows and loaded his body with vitamins C, A, and E. He waited until morning before he broke down and took three Chloratrimaton tables: it hadn't helped.

Once again he shuffled the grizzly photos arrayed on the worktable. For the last half-hour he had been trying to figure out what it was nagging at his sensitive mind. Feeling his nose about to drip on the photos, he snatched another tissue from the seemingly endless supply in the flowered box. His red nose semi-buried in the white wad of tissue, he turned to see who was coming into the cubical.

"Man! You look as awful behind that Kleenex as you do in front of it?" Kurt threw his scarf and heavy coat over the back of a folding chair. With a touch of sympathy in his words, Kurt asked, "The croup got you again?"

John pinched his nose and registered an expression of pain. Using his thumb and two other fingers he massaged his throat: then he cleared it. After a quick release of breath, John closed his eyes as he said, "Nope, just a lousy head cold." Following a quick sniffle he asked, "Where you been all morning?"

For effect, Kurt glanced at the clock. "For your information it's five a.m., Buddy. We're not due in here for another hour." Sideling to the other end of the table, Kurt asked, "So why are you here so early? Or should I ask how long have you been here?"

"Sometime after four…just couldn't sleep, Kurt." Jabbing his index finger at the photos he shook his head, "I know there is something wrong about these two murders, but I'll be damned if I can figure it out."

Kurt moved some of the photos so he could better see them. "Well, Johnny boy, maybe you had better stop before you do figure it out and subsequently become damned.

" John rolled his eyes; he had heard that response before. "I know what you mean, it still doesn't make sense. Why two different locations in the same night. So far there is nothing to tie the two cases together, except the style of shooting and the flour."

Stripping another tissue from the bottomless box, John asked, "So it's your take that one of these is a copy cat job?"

"Yeah, I think so. I don't know why, but I'm willing to bet your pension ballistics says that one of those scenes was done with a different gun."

"Come on, Kurt, how could anyone know all of the details of the Baker murders, except the murderer?"

"Good question, but I'm still backing my hunch."
Holding up his palms toward John he stated, "Stay
away from me. I don't want your cold." Kurt
turned and started out the door, "I came in early
because I'm hoping that ballistics has run our
samples. Let's go!"

Grabbing a wad of tissues, John followed Kurt
down the hallway."

John almost ran into Kurt when he suddenly
stopped. "Hear that?"

John gestured at his stuffed Eustachian tubes,
"Can't hear a thing."

Brushing past John, Kurt dashed into their cubical
and snatched up the phone, "Millhouse," he
announced.

"Thanks for the rush." Putting his hand over the
receiver he looked at his red nosed partner. "Tom
has the results, he---" Kurt nodded toward the
phone, "No; Doris didn't tell me a thing. What do
you mean you can't really tell?" In disbelief his
shoulders dropped, he looked at John, and shook
his head. "You mean to tell me that somebody
went through all that trouble? Why not just take
the dammed things." He listened a bit longer and
then said, "Okay, okay. Thanks, Tom." Nodding,
"Yes, I'll talk to Doris." Blindly he replaced the
receiver.

Chapter twenty:

Gingerly John sat his six foot four inch frame into his padded and well-worn swivel chair. "Don't tell me. We don't have to go down to ballistics, and you just lost my pension."

Kurt snorted and dropped to his office chair. Still shaking his head, he licked his lips and said, "Tom said the bullets, all of them, from the Hispanic guy were very skillfully removed, disfigured and then replaced."

"Didn't Doris notice that?"

"He said he doubted she noticed it until after she pulled the bullets out. She did mention it in her report."

"I didn't know anyone could do that."

"Apparently they can—given the right training and equipment." Throwing his hands up in the air he clapped them together as he moved his head from side to side, "What I can't figure out is why go through all that trouble. Tom says the bullets are all nine millimeter, and from a Glock."

"I heard you, Kurt. Why not just take the slugs? Why bother to replace them after you destroy the slugs?"

Shrugging, Kurt said, "To make a statement?"

John dabbed at his nose and answered, "Well, it's been done before, but what kind of statement is he trying to make?"

"Maybe it wasn't the killer who was trying to make the statement?" Kurt leaned close to John. "How well do we know the CSU team?"

"Come on Kurt, the Crime Scene Unit wouldn't have time to do something like that. Not even on the way to the morgue. That's too delicate a thing to do in a moving vehicle."

"All right then, how about the assistants at the morgue?"

"You're leaving out Doris, of course."

Kurt felt a sliver of hot blood begin to rise, but he knew John didn't mean it the way it sounded. Taking a jerky, calming breath he said, "Yeah, I guess I am. But there are others who work down there."

"I know you're right, Kurt. We should check them out, but--" He smiled, "My pension money is on the killer."

"You mean that the Baker did this?"

"I think someone else killed the guy wrapped in the towel and was planning to pin it on the Baker…or introduce reasonable doubt. I'll bet the imitation Baker did the bullet thing just to let the real killer know he knew who Baker was." John acted surprised at what he himself had said.

"Pretty farfetched, John;" He paused to consider, "Do you really think this Baker guy runs around with special kinds of equipment, much less that kind of skill? Besides how would he know there was another killing?"

"Ipso Facto, Kurt. The facts speak for themselves." John attempted to blow his stuffy nose, it just made his eyes water and his ears pop. "That's all I ever got out of law school".

Reflecting, Kurt mumbled, "Yeah, me too." Cocking his head to one side, he got up and motioned to John. "Let's take another look at those photos."

Carefully positioning a small electronic microscope over the picture of Paulo Ortiz, he examined the spot where the blood from the wound had seeped into the flour. "Look at this, John."

John positioned his watering eye over the lens and adjusted the focus. "Yeah, I see what you mean. The flour has been disturbed and then replaced." He turned his head to the side and squinted, "So it was done right there in the apartment."

"There is still the why, Johnny boy. Why?" Rubbing his face with his palms Kurt said, "I wish I could spend more time on this case, but Captain

Won wants me to finish up on that rich, society dame, Wentworth.

"Maybe you could convince him they are connected." John raised his eyebrows and slipped on a mischievous grin.

Chapter twenty-one:

To those who hired his services he was known only as The Actuary, one who calculates risks: a person who knows the most probable way and time of another person's death. It is he who helps the insurance companies establish premiums, and in his case helps certain people, for a price, to collect premium in a more timely fashion. Over the years he had helped people to die from falls in showers or bathtubs, kitchen stools, slippery winter sidewalks, failing car jacks, roof falls, diving accidents, hazardous occupations, hobbies or sports, auto accidents, medication errors, hospital goofs, being in the wrong place at the wrong time, and similar events matching the lifestyle of the victim. The Actuary concluded the most probable way the person would die and simply moved up life's time table so his client and he could benefit from the victim's life or accidental death policy.

He was not known for the speed with which he worked: many of his clients had to wait for six months or more, but his work was so through the event was seldom challenged. For months he would study the subject's habits and tendencies and then in one day he would implement his flawless plan. Undetected, he had operated for over thirty-five years, and the challenge still fascinated him. He felt he was a principled man because he would only take an assignment if the person to be removed was legally untouchable and a proven blight to society.

From all appearances he was a normal man living a normal life. He had retired from a job with a major manufacturing firm and now lived in a sunny community in the Southwest. His wife still taught at a Montessori School and all of their children now had homes of their own. His main company during the day was his two Miniature Schnauzers and a few hobbies. The simplicity of his living, in no way, depicted the millions of dollars he had lying in foreign bank accounts all over the world. What he longed for was to retire with his wife on some tropical island.

The murder of Margaret-Goldstein-Wentworth was the result of a lot of study concerning her tendencies and reactions to certain situations. Born and bred from money she was by breeding very cautious and conservative, but to the point of being obnoxious, a moral bigot and gossip, and had a seamy side business which could make her the target of a wide range of people.

After the morning routine was finished, he put away the vacuum cleaner and poured himself a glass of iced tea. With a copy of USA Today tucked under his armpit, he headed for the sunroom. Behind him he could hear the clip-clip sounds of his Schnauzers' toenails as they loped along behind their master. The three large citrus trees in his back yard provided just enough privacy but did not give the impression of trying to be secretive. California quail darted about as the dogs approached the thirty-inch high back fence. Two rabbits froze and assumed the shape of gray rocks minding their own business. Beads of cool water dripped from the amber glass as he sipped the refreshing iced tea: several drops fell on his newspaper, but quickly began to evaporate. The dripping glass deposited a ring of water as he placed it upon the surface of the glass table.

On page twenty-two he found the article for which he was looking. It was a simple two-column-inch message about a car accident in the mid-west. The article said there were going to be some funeral expenses and the relatives were trying to reach some family members who could share in the cost. They were to call 216-555-7272 and ask for Wayne. Mentally, he nodded to himself and made a note to purchase a disposable cell phone next time he was out.

Setting the paper aside, he bent over and petted his stretched out hairy 'boys', picked up his glass and looked to the west and studied the airplane con trails. Like long strings of frayed white yarn they would begin to unravel against the peaceful backdrop of an azure sky. With a few slow sips, he finished his tea and then plucked his car keys from the rack inside of the dish cabinet.

It was one-fifteen when he picked up his disposable cell phones and called 216-555-2727— the last four number were altered. After two rings, a voice answered, it was only slightly mechanical in sound. Flipping the switch on his scrambler he asked, "Is Wayne there, this is Mr. Purple." He always used a name a color.

The voice at the other end hesitated and then said, "I am sorry, Mr. Purple, but Wayne is not here. Perhaps you could reach him on his e-mail address. It is all lower case, w1442277: it was at aol.com. Shall I repeat it, sir?"

"Yes, please do."

After repeating the address Mr. Purple turned off the cell phone and removed the battery and all interior electronics. Next he picked up another disposable cell phone and adapted it to his computer next; he went online and pulled up the file. He had a new casualty to analyze. He removed the battery from the second phone and took them both to the garage and placed them on his workbench. With both of the phones safely placed inside of a cloth bag, he used a hammer and smashed them into pieces no larger than the top end of a ballpoint pen. Later, after printing out the material, he would replace the hard drive on his laptop computer. The old hard drive would be destroyed.

A Lexmark printer produced a sound reminding him of a colony of bees swarming but couldn't make up their mind where to go. The first pages were beginning to appear when, for the hundredth time he wondered if he would ever meet the man who placed the articles in the newspaper, not that he wanted to; it was just curiosity.

To the soothing background of Mascagni's Intermezzo from the opera Cavalleria Rusticana, The Actuary, Richard W. Price, sipped from a glass of Merlot wine. Wrinkles formed on his forehead as soon as he realized the subject was a woman. He never touched children, and women

had to be some sort of blight on humanity before
he would even consider them. The late Mrs.
Wentworth had easily qualified for that category;
she had developed a habit of employing and
soliciting teenage girls into a life of prostitution.
Plucking the first page from the printer, he turned
the page and began to read. The subject's name
was Doris Florence Mercer; she was a medical
doctor who had become a specialist in forensic
medicine. Although he was not told, the reason for
her termination was to gain the five million dollars
of insurance which had been purchased for her as a
member of a group of physicians: it was what is
known as a Key Man policy. Richard was to be
paid his usual ten percent: that would come to
$500,000.00. He would receive an additional two
percent if he completed the job within thirty days.
On the surface, he didn't like the looks of the job,
but he laid down the paper and thought. *Maybe I'm
just getting too old and too picky to continue this
line of work. It might be time to quit.* The strains
of the music were beginning to end; he picked up
his remote and ordered the compact disc to repeat
the selection. Tomorrow he would begin to find
out about Miss Doris Florence Mercer.

  His thoughts were interrupted by the sharp
sounding barks of his two dogs; they had heard
Thelma, his wife, as she slowly guided their

Cadillac toward a hanging whiffel ball. The ball had saved their garage wall from the otherwise frequent hits Thelma had inflicted upon the unsuspecting barrier.

Chapter twenty-two:

Cortina Angelino was worried. For days now Martina isolated herself from everyone. She came out of her room only to eat and go to school with her friends. Sometimes, for hours she would stay on the phone talking to Marge. Cortina was beginning to suspect her daughter was nursing a secret. She hoped it was not what she thought it was.

For the 'umpteenth time Martina gave herself the home test for pregnancy: the results never changed, she was definitely pregnant. With a tone of understanding, Marge said she knew some girls who had abortions and she could find out where they had it done and how much it would cost.

"Marge, are you sure that no one would know; after all, you know about these other girls."

"Yeah, but they told me. I didn't ask them first."
Marge didn't really care about helping Martina as
much as she liked having Martina indebted to her.
"I think it's going to cost about a grand, Martina.
At least that's what Alice told me it cost, if you
want a good one…you do, don't' you?"

"Of course I want a good one, but how am I
going to get my hands on that kind of money
without my father finding out?"

"What about your mother?"

"Oh, I'm not worried about her, she'd never tell
dad. She would be afraid it might make her look
bad." Martina took a deep breath and continued,
"I have lots in my savings, but I can't get to it."
She was beginning to get depressed.

Marge started speaking, softly and slowly at first,
"Mar, I'm not sure I should say anything, but,
well, Alice told me how she paid for hers."

"Yeah, so what did she do, sell Tupperware?"
There was disbelief in her tone, but she allowed
herself to laugh.

Marge was still serious. No, Martina, she said she
knew some people would pay plenty to go to bed
with a good looking teenager." She gritted her
teeth while she waited to see if her friend would
bite as easily as Alice did. Marge would earn an
easy one hundred dollars every time they used
Martina.

For a split second Martina considered what she had heard, she knew Marge was a bit shady, but she had not suspected anything like this. At school she had heard roamers Marge arranged thing like this, but she had not believed it. "Marge, I thought you were my friend, I can't believe you would even suggest something like that to me."

Struggling to sound contrite, Marge said, "I know how it sounds, Mar, but it's not like one of these guys will get you pregnant." She hesitated and pleaded, "I just thought you didn't want your family to find out you made a mistake. That's all."

Martina balked, true. She couldn't get **more** pregnant and maybe she could get an abortion without her family finding out. "I'm not saying I'm interested." She glanced around the room as if searching for eavesdroppers. "But, if I were. How many times would I have to do—IT?"

A grin followed the glow which had reached Marge's eyes. They always asked the same questions. Taking on a conspiratorial tone she said, "They only have really nice men. Gentlemen, you know. And they're really nice to you. Sometimes they even buy you expensive presents."

Nice young men, gentle, presents, that didn't sound too bad. Pictures of Brad Pitt types worshiping at her bedside: they would be offering her diamond bracelets and softly caressing her flesh. These pictures were more real than sugarplums dancing in her head on Christmas Eve. Even the memories of Paulo Ortiz's violent 'love making' were being vacuumed from her mind. "No lie?"

"No lie, Mar." She paused, "Cross my heart and hope to die. It's true."

"And you said all I need is a thousand bucks…right?'

"Yeah, I'm pretty sure that would do it." Marge sharpened her sales pitch, "You know for a good one." She chuckled, "None of that coat hanger stuff. These are all real docs."

In tentative tones Martina asked, "So, how much can I make each time?"

Marge had done this enough times to know to avoid the specifics. "I just know it's a lot, Martina." She giggled, "It's not like I've done it myself, you know."

Suspiciously, Martina followed up with the question, "Well, if it's so good, why don't you do it?"

Chapter twenty-three:

She was ready for this question, "Well, if I ever get pregnant, I probably will. Think about it, you can't get more pregnant, you get great treatment, and you get the money you need to make your problems go away." Covering her laugh she quipped, "Who knows, you might even enjoy it."

To a pregnant sixteen year old the solution seemed too good to be true. Marge was proving to be a really good friend. She wondered if all seniors were as smart as Marge was. "Okay, if I really want to do this, it's going to have to be fast. Before I start showing, you know." She felt herself getting excited about the prospects.

Marge backed off, "Well, you know I'm going to have to get approval to let you get into this special group. You understand that, don't you? After all, your dad could cause trouble for these people." She was also considering the mysterious death of the old dame who used to front as a lady philanthropist helping troubled girls.

"Forget that, he'll never find out, Marge." Martina looked in the mirror and fluffed her hair. It had been the first time in days she had cared how she looked; now it suddenly became important to her. "I'll be in and out of there before he ever knows a thing." Turning herself to profile she lifted her head and gave herself an approving glance. "Those men will go nuts over me."

"Okay, Martina, I'll see what I can do but, in the meantime, don't say anything to anyone. Okay?" Marjory hung up the phone and shook her head; she couldn't believe how dumb Martina was. She had been one of the easiest to recruit.

When the dial tone hummed in her ear, Martina wondered what Paulo Ortiz would have thought about this turn of events. She also wondered about the two people she had seen leaving his building that night. If the police found out she had been at the apartment that night she would get them off of her back by telling them about the man and woman who were just leaving as she arrived. Replacing the receiver, she held her hand on the phone even as it lay in its cradle. For the first time, she asked herself why, why was Paulo killed? Quickly a rage swept across her face as reality introduced himself and posed the question, *what would your father have done if he had found out about Paulo?* She knew what she had told Marge was true. Recalling her words to Marge she could hear herself saying, 'If my father ever found out about Paulo, he'd kill him.' She had laughed then, thinking it was a remote possibility, but now she knew. He had found out and he had him killed. The rage subsided, she did know where it went, but somehow the fiery inferno of rage had been quenched by lapping waves from the ocean of her father's protective love, and besides, she would now be free to discover a whole new world of feminine power. She released the phone, allowing it to rest in its cradle. Symbolically, she reclined on her canopy-covered bed and slipped into an imaginary world where everything was fully in her control, and all was well.

Chapter twenty-four:

Harold Zane had worked with Pete Corbin for at least ten years after they both got out of the military service. Zane had been the one who carried Corbin out of a firefight. At times Corbin cursed Zane, but most of the time he was grateful for the man's bravery. Pete Corbin was from a Midwest town of six hundred and thirty three people. He had volunteered for the military and ended up in a cavalry unit that dropped into hot spots all over the world. As a fighting man he was respected and feared. After he was released from the service he bought himself a gun shop and did a little weapons customizing on the side. Because of his facial looks, he did very little to expand the business. It was when Harold joined him the shop really took off. Harold was personable and aggressive; he also had connections with some underworld personalities.

It was almost five years ago he started doing business with Morton Filman and his live in girl friend he called his wife, Betty Powers. Harold had a distinct dislike for Betty; she was far too independent to suit him. Every time she left, he would say to Pete Corbin, 'that bitch needs to be put in her place, she's just too uppity. Maybe one day I'll do it.' Knowing how hostile Harold could become, Pete would only nod and grunt.

With this thought in mind he had followed Betty back to Morton's temporary apartment. Not being sure what he wanted to do, he considered going up into Morton's apartment and checking things out, but then Morton had suddenly appeared on the street. Considering the ferocity of the pounding rain, he was surprised to see Morton sloshing his way through the streets. Tracking Morton was easy even when he could tell Morton felt uneasy. Harold laughed when he watched Morton duck into a doorway and waited to see who was following. Harold was already almost a block ahead of Morton and was following him from the front instead of from behind.

By the time he had followed Betty and Morton to the apartment of Paulo Ortiz, hc was convinced they were on the job and somebody was going to get killed. He hoped it would be that sassy bitch, Betty.

Chapter twenty-five:

"I think that this kind of work turns everyone into some kind of a paranoid idiot!" Doris was serious, but she tried to sound as if she were joking. She turned her coffee cup in her hand and studied the words, 'Stanford Medical 1998' the lettering had become chipped from frequent use, but nevertheless she read it for the another time.

Cupping his chin in his hand, Kurt furrowed his brow and attempted a German accent, "Ant ven didt you vurst hab zeezs feelings, mine dear?" he stroked his chin and leaned forward as if to better study his patient.

Doris snorted and combined a chuckle with a shake of her head, "Your accent is horrible, Kurt."

Another brief snort and she became serious, "I think I'm being followed."

Kurt pulled himself into the opposite corner of the couch and pulled his knee up on the cushion as her turned to face Doris. "You're serious, aren't you?"

"Yes, I'm serious!" she expanded her eyes and furrowed her brow. "Some guy is following me."

"What's he want?"

"You're kidding…right?"

"Look, Doris, I don't mean you should saunter up to him and ask him why he's following you, but can you think of any reason why someone might want to follow you." He tried to lighten the conversation by adding, "No doubt you are an attractive woman, but you're not some movie star or a magazine model." Kurt felt he was getting into deep muck and attempted to pull himself out, "Not that you couldn't be a movie star or a magazine model, but right now you cut up dead bodies."

The mud had turned to quicksand: that last comment drew narrowed eyes and pinched eyebrows. "Okay, Buster, I think you had better stop there." She faked an offended face, but soon started to smile. "I know what you mean, but I'm serious. Someone is following me, Kurt."

"Has he spoken to you? Can you describe him?" He thought for a second, "It is a he, I presume."

Her countenance sagged and her voice turned to disgust, "Yes, of course it's a man. He has never talked to me, and yes I can describe him—sort of."

"Okay, go for it; what's he look like?"

Her eyes rolled up to the ceiling and she closed them. "Edward Woodward." Her face looked pained with concentration.

Kurt was confused. "Edward Woodward: the actor?"

"Yes, the one who played, the, ah ah,--"

"'The Enforcer' or something like that;" Closing one eye, he tipped his head to one side and asked, "You're saying that Edward Woodward, the actor, is following you?"

Pushing her lips together into an exaggerated kiss, she sagged her shoulders, "No, Silly, not the actor, just someone who reminds me of him. Except he is sort of blond and maybe a bit shorter."

"Okay," he mocked, "I'm looking for an Edward Woodward type, only shorter and blond." Thrusting his jaw forward he raised his eyebrows to form his expression into one of confusion and interrogation; "Right?"

Assuming an expression of contriteness, she said, "Well, he does!"

"So this guy scares you?"

"I didn't say he scared me. Only that he is following me."

"Why on earth would Edward Woodward want to follow you?" Gently, he grabbed her hand and attempted to look into her eyes, "Do you need protection?"

Flirtatiously, she leaned forward, "I don't know, do I?" With her other hand she brought her coffee cup to her lips and coyly looked over the rim of her cup as she quipped, "It's probably my imagination anyway."

Showing concern, Kurt massaged the back of her hand and looked into her eyes. "I'll look into it, Doris. I don't want to take something like this too lightly." He blinked and mumbled, "There are a lot of kooks out there, you know." To himself he wondered, *perhaps it was really him that they were after. If someone wanted to get to him, they might want to use her.*

Not wanting to spoil their first evening together, she smiled and gripped his hand. She stood up and pulled him to the kitchen table. "I have been dying to have some pumpkin pie with this coffee. Sit down, Mister. You're going to have the treat of your life." She talked rapidly as if to wipe out the words he had just been spoken, "Outside it's cold and the wind is blowing. Nothing like a cup of hot coffee, pumpkin pie and whipped cream topping."

Kurt shifted his eyes to look outside. She was right. The streets were dark and cold; a northerly wind was producing a soft whistling sound as it struggled to work its way into the interior of her warm kitchen. The effect was a contradiction: almost a sinister Currier and Ives.

From half a block away, Richard Price sat in his rental car and opened his thermos of hot green tea. The front window steamed up as he poured a half-cup of tea and then replaced the cap on his Thermos bottle. He would be leaving in just a few minutes, but first he switched on his covered penlight and scanned Doris's file. The man with her must be Officer Kurt Millhouse he noted. He closed the file and put the car in gear. *I wonder if she has told him about me following her.* He hoped she had told him because there was another man who just started keeping tabs on her, and she had not seen him anymore than she had seen Richard during the last two and one half weeks he had been studying her.

It had not taken Richard long to realize she was being targeted just because one of the doctors at the office out of which she worked wanted the insurance money. He would rather have targeted him instead of her.

There was only one car heading down the quiet street: he waited for it to pass. Slowly he pulled out of his parking place and glided up to the stoplight, it turned dirty amber and then a quick grungy red. His wandering mind stared at the light and he began to consider the danger that Miss Mercer might be in. At the time he declined the contract it had not really occurred to him the physician would try someone else, but now he was certain the man following her was doing so for some reason. It could be a rapist, or some disgruntled employee, even someone who didn't like her cutting up some relative's body. The light changed and he checked his rear view mirror before he shifted his foot from the brake pedal to the accelerator. Like the gears in his car, his mind flitted through a series of thoughts; all of them designed to excuse him from being involved. Before he reached the next stoplight he knew he would have to alert the girl and somehow find out what was going on with the man who was following her. For the first time in thirty-five years he found himself being illogical. He was going to have to arrange to meet her.

Chapter twenty-six:

Kurt Millhouse and John Miller exchanged eye-rolls as they waited for Captain Won to finish his phone conversation. It was no secret the Captain was not happy with some of their findings in the Wentworth case.

Captain Won was an ABC, as he referred to himself (American Born Chinese). He looked every bit a typical Chinese and dressed as if he were part owner in a Chinese laundry. His shirts were so white --looking at him made one fear snow blindness. The creases on his clothes were considered lethal weapons. He wore his Bible-cover black hair combed straight back producing an effect of rows of wire pasted to his scalp, strands of gray were beginning to show just around his diminutive ears. Having just concluded a conversation with Mr. Wentworth's attorney, he dropped the wireless phone on his desk and frowned.

"Jesus, Millhouse, you had better be right!" Won drummed his fingers on his desk blotter and took a calming breath. "You're sure the old lady was running a whore house?" Not waiting for an answer he continued, "Teen age girls?" He shook his head, "Jesus, Millhouse, you had better be right."

"You said that, Captain. You saw the report." Kurt gestured at the thirty-page report, the DD-5 crime report, and some photos of the establishment. "Our guess is that it was done by a disgruntled parent, teenager, boyfriend, or maybe her husband found out and got rid of her."

The last comment drew a set of eye-daggers from his boss. "Look, Millhouse, and you too, Miller, I don't want any of that kind of talk around here." Won looked out of his office window which overlooked his working staff, "At least not as a speculation." He corrected himself. He produced a wry smile, "Hell, if it was my wife doing that I'd have killed her myself."

Miller leaned forward, paper and pencil in hand, "May we quote you on that, sir?" His straight face drew a laugh from both Kurt and Captain Won.

Dabbing at his eyes, Won continued, "Okay stay on the case, but be careful who gets any of your findings." Placing his forearms on the desk he changed the subject; "So…what about this Ortiz killing, and the couple from the Essex Arms? Are they both The Baker's?"

Kurt and John looked at each other, each wanting the other to begin, but since Kurt was senior in rank, he was forced to start. "We don't know, Cap?" He shrugged. "The MO seems to be the same, but something is fishy." Kurt picked up the pace of his speech as if he were thinking out loud, "The timing is only **possible**, and I mean just barely. Our dilemma is **why**?" To add emphasis he pounded his fist into his palm, "If they weren't done by the same person—then somebody has been peeking over our shoulder, or the Baker is a cop." Kurt glanced at John and then peered at Captain Won, "No one else would know the details, Cap."

Captain Won looked over at John Miller, "Thoughts?"

"I agree with Kurt, Cap, someone knows every detail. So it is either the same guy, or someone among us." John paused and pursed his lips as he went into deep thought, "Frankly, Cap, I think it has to be someone working with us. I don't think The Baker did both of the jobs, especially considering Ortiz's habit for playing around and gambling. He fancied himself to be some kind of up-coming crime boss." Shaking his head he added, "He was just a punk."

"So you got nothing new after five weeks?"

Kurt opened his notebook and clicked his tongue against the top of his mouth, "Ortiz was making time with Enrico Angelino's sixteen year old daughter." Kurt shrugged and allowed his head to casually take his eyes from one corner of the office to another.

"Oh for God's sake: **no!**" Won slammed his hand down on his desk, "Jesus, Millhouse, don't you ever just have a simple case?" After rubbing his face with his palms, he asked, "There wasn't any sign of a gang style hit… there?"

Miller jumped in, "No, but he would not have deserved a bullet to the back of the head, that would have been considered too good for him. It's possible Angelino hired a freelance contractor for the job and the freelancer got creative and decided to make it look like a Baker hit. **But**, --**But**, that still means the freelancer knows too much about the Baker's MO, Captain."

The Captain rocked back in his plush, but well-worn, brown office chair, it squeaked as he pivoted from side to side. "So?" He looked at the water-stained ceiling and asked, "So, who's our guy?" Won stopped and popped his body forward, "Or— who is telling this guy about the Baker jobs?"

Chapter twenty-seven:

Reflectively and softly Kurt asked no one in particular, "Yeah, who's talking?"

Won stood up, an indication the session was over, "Both of you guys are experienced, so I don't need to tell you how to do your jobs, but I'm getting a lot of heat on this Baker thing, you know." Waving them off he started to sit down, "So, get me some results, huh?"

Like two censured schoolboys leaving the principal's office, John and Kurt exited the office of Captain Won and slinked their way to the department coffee pot. Nodding to other officers and office workers, the two poured in silence: they sipped as they walked back to their office.

Miller was the first to break the silence, "I don't know about you, but I think we got off pretty easy, ---considering."

"Yeah, I suppose so, we could have been French fried and served in an egg roll, but I'm not looking forward to exposing the idiot that's leaking information to some killer. That just never seems to go over well." Kurt scooted back his chair and rested his forearms on his thighs. "And—I hope that it's no one in the morgue people."

"I think both Won and I were thinking about that, but we have to follow the trail wherever it takes us, buddy."

"Okay, let's do that. Where do we start: at the Crime Scene Unit, the Medical team? How about the nosey cops? Or do we just go to the morgue and ask, 'Okay, you guys, who in here has been talking about The Baker case?'"

Miller chuckled, "All good ideas! When do we start?"

Turning serious, Kurt straightened up and ran his fingers through his hair, "Ah, well, let's see. The CSU guys are usually closed mouthed, and none of the cops would know all of the details, except you and me." Kurt looked at John and nodded, "For now we'll assume you're not talking in your sleep."

John mumbled through his doughnut filled mouth, "And I'll assume the same for you, old boy!"

Eager to correct John, Kurt snapped back, "I sleep alone, thank you." John shrugged and Kurt continued, "Okay, let's talk to the Medical Examiners. We'll work backwards and see if someone is just being careless, or is selling information."

"I'm hoping it doesn't turn out to be some cop who is dirty or worse yet, some cop who turns out to be this Baker guy." John skidded his large wooden chair across the ancient tile floor: it screeched. "Got to get a metal tip for that leg:

sends shrills up my spine;" Ceremoniously, John took a big swig of his cooled coffee and made a face, "Whoever makes this coffee should be cited for 'cruel and unusual'. I'll check the logs for the morgue. You want to check on the M.E.'s and their known associates?"

"Why not? I already have two people on the list: Doris and myself." Millhouse sagged and sighed, "You know, the theory you said about Angelino hiring a hit on Ortiz?" John nodded. "I think that could use some checking into. At least we ought to talk to the daughter." Kurt paused and thought, "If we can."

Chapter twenty-eight:

Removing the blood pressure cuff from Enrico's arm, Dr. Bick scribbled a few notes on the form attached to his clipboard. Without looking up, Dr. Bick whispered, "Thanks for the tip, Mr. Angelino. I have your man on the job—now."

Enrico grunted, he didn't like talking in a place where he wasn't sure someone might have planted a camera or a microphone. It bothered him when the electronic age had enabled the manufacture of devices so small and versatile almost anything could be picking him up. Enrico smiled and slid off of the examination table, "Well he did a good job on our barbeque, but he's a good all around handyman."

Understanding Enrico's cryptic language, Dr. Bick nodded as he allowed himself to feel as if he were some powerful criminal underload. After being turned down by The Actuary, Dr. Bick had told Enrico about his debt dilemma and asked for advice, it was then Enrico gave the doctor's name to Morton Filman. "Okay, let's see." The doctor flipped through his pages of checks and numbers. "Mr. Angelino, you still need to cut down on the pasta and drop a few pounds. Your blood pressure is still too high and next time we need to check your prostate. You're well into the danger age now, Mr. Angelino."

Enrico snorted so hard his head popped back. With his left hand he reached out and patted the cheek of the doctor, "Doctorie, I'll outlive you." Nodding toward the door he said, "What I need is a little more Chianti, Doc."

Dr. Bick laughed and wondered, *what does he mean' he'll outlive me.'* "Here, I'll get that door for you, Mr. Angelino." As the pompous criminal disappeared down the hallway, the doctor noticed

he was sweating, not that it was hot, but he had
suddenly developed a bad case of the shakes. His
time to repay his gambling debts was growing
short. He would need some results soon, nothing
fancy like that Actuary guy was known for, he just
needed Doris Mercer dead: she was worth five
million dollars. He estimated his cut would be
enough to pacify his debtors, at least for a while.

  For the last five days, Morton and or Betty were
exercising caution as they followed Doris Mercer
from work to her apartment and back again. Betty
didn't like the idea that Doris was an ME and
worked with the cops, but she even liked less the
discovery Doris was dating a homicide cop. To
Morton it was both a challenge and a thrill, for this
reason he was taking his time and trying to do a
good job. Angelino had referred him, but at the
same time told him he should have made Ortiz
disappear because now his daughter was moping
around, perhaps even on the verge of suicide. He
was most displeased and it was not in Morton's
best interest to have Enrico Angelino unhappy
with him or his work.

  Lying in bed with Betty, Morton quietly
mumbled, "I think that ME gal will have a car
accident."

  Without turning over, Betty said, "What'd ya
mean?" She sniffed to clear her stuffy nose…then

she sneezed; "A car accident? You go'na run her over?"

He propped himself up on one elbow and then laid his head back down on his pillow. "Nope, like the brakes don't work. You know the hill just before she gets to work, well; I think her brakes will give out just as she starts down that hill."

"You don't know anything about cars?" She spoke as if she were questioning his man-hood.

"Spoken just like a woman. You don't know what I know and what I don't know." He fired back. "I know lots of things you don't know that I know."

Unseen, she rolled her eyes and blew her nose, "Okay. Okay. So she has a car accident." She coughed, "Just let's get this thing done. I need a vacation: somewhere where it's warm."

"Hey with this money we can go wherever we want to. How about I get a boat and we go to Mexico?"

"Right now, Hell sounds good. This rat hole is cold. Can't we, just once, get a nice place to work?" Before he answered she knew he would give her the same old song and dance about better times and living high off of the hog, but she was beginning to doubt she would ever see it. "Just once!" she emphasized.

"Sure, Baby, sounds like a good idea. I'm getting tired of these fleabag places too. One day we'll be living high on the hog." After a brief pause he said, "I'm going to see Corbin tomorrow. Somewhere in his shop he must have what I want."

Not wanting to talk, Betty pulled the quilt over her head and closed her eyes. In the crook of her elbow she muffled a cough. *I just can't seem to shake this damned cold, but Morton doesn't want me to go to a doctor. Sometimes he can be a real pain.* With a Kleenex at her nostrils, she took deep painful breaths and fought to go to sleep.

Chapter twenty-nine:

Morton's eyes were open. He looked toward the indistinguishable ceiling and watched as the 'Jesus Saves' sign alternately flashed faded rose and lime green beams about the room. As was his custom, his mind began to feed him a daily portion of fear. Tonight he was once again struggling with his uncertainties about Martina Angelino. Had she seen them and, if pressed, could she describe them to the police? A stab in his gut told him the dose of fear was doing its job. *I got to do something about that dame. This is driving me nuts.* He closed his eyes but the beams of light seeped a new set of colors through his closed lids. *If I touch her, Angelino will kill me.* Out of fear he grinned, *I'll be lucky if that's all he does to me.*

Cuddling up to Betty he pulled back, "Baby, you're really hot. Wow, you're sweating. Bad!" He felt an unexpected invasion into his conscience. "I think I know a doctor we can use. I'll work it out in the morning."

From somewhere under the covers he heard a muffled, "Okay". She shivered.

Chapter twenty-nine:

Martina sucked on her lower lip: the dress just didn't look right. Turning she swished her dress and examined her profile. She looked too young. Of course she was young, but in four months she would be seventeen, practically old enough to be on her own. Tilting her head from side to side didn't help. With frustrated fingers she removed her scarlet dress and tossed it into a pile of other dresses that failed to make her look older and more desirable. Placing balled fists on each of her hips, she scanned her fall-winter closet for another candidate: slowly a pout began to form on her young face. Not finding a suitable selection, she began to think, *what I really need is a <u>new</u> dress, one that is fitting for the occasion.* She fanned out her fingers as she placed them just below her navel, covering her fertile womb.. She wondered: *when will I begin to show?* She was surprised at how the statement made her feel older and more feminine.

"Martina?" The soft rapping on her door was that of her mother.

Martina sagged her body, drifted her eyes upward and tightened her lips: even as she inserted her knuckles between her clenched teeth. "What do you want, Ma?" Every word was weighted with disrespect.

Neglecting to react to the insolence, Cortina Angelino softly announced, "There are some men from the police department downstairs." With nervousness in her tone she continued, "They'd like to talk to you."

At the word 'police' her body stiffened and her throat went dry. Her next words were polite, "What do they want to talk to me for, Ma?" She licked her lips as she struggled to find a way to hide her fear they knew of her affair with Ortiz.

Still standing outside of Martina's door, Cortina said, "They are talking to all of your classmates to find out if any of them have information about someone named, Ordeez."

Knowing that, if the police talked to some of her classmates they would know she at least knew Ortiz, she decided to admit to that, but to play dumb to anything else. "His name was Ortiz, Ma. He's dead. Someone killed him."

"That's what they said." She hesitated. "They're waiting downstairs, Martina."

Trapped! That's how she felt, but she couldn't look suspicious. She had seen how her father had graciously treated the policemen who had come to her home. She felt certain she could do the same. "I'll be right down." Looking at the pile of dresses she was now glad she looked young and innocent in anyone of them. Maybe she was.

Patiently Kurt and John sipped on the iced tea Cortina had forced upon them. She was an affable hostess, but talked constantly. The two officers just sat and smiled while she rattled on about anything that seemed to pop into her energetic psyche. At the sound of Martina's footsteps the officers stood up and greeted her. She looked even younger than the photos they had seen.

Kurt flashed his most innocuous smile and explained, "I'm Officer Millhouse and this is Officer Miller." He gestured toward John and then took a photograph from John's hand. "We are

doing some follow up on the death of Mr. Ortiz."
He held up a picture taken outside of her school.
"We noticed you were in this picture and
wondered if he might have said anything to you
about any problems he was having."

Martina studied the picture as if she were trying
to recall the day it was taken. Selecting a mask of
bewilderment she pushed her lips together and
shook her head, "I hardly knew him, officer. He
came around the school every once in a while, but
most of us were afraid he was dealing drugs or
something."

Smoooth, John thought. She must have learned
from her father. "Yeah, we wondered about that
too, but we also noticed he was a pretty good
looking fella, and thought perhaps he was dating
someone at the school." Giving Cortina a quick
glance he asked Martina, "You wouldn't know if
he was dating anyone, would you?" His look
seemed to be reading her frantic thoughts.

Martina's insides turned to slush. She felt her
heart race, her chest was heaving noticeably. She
was feeling faint. She fought to remain upright as
she blinked and licked her lips. As if in some sort
of trance she faintly murmured, "Sorry. No."

Chapter thirty:

Rushing to keep her daughter from falling to the floor, Cortina grasped her in her powerful arms. As if in desperation, Cortina looked at the officers. The unspoken words shot like light between them. *She knows something.* Struggling to move Martina to a nearby loveseat, Cortina said, "I'm afraid this has been too much for her. Please leave."

The officers knew they had a great opportunity to find out something, but they knew a lawyer would already be at Captain Won's desk before the day was over. "We're so sorry, Mrs. Angelino. Is there anything we can do to help? Should we call an ambulance?" Kurt fired off.

"No! Please just leave." Cortina had turned into a protective mother, a creature far more dangerous than any other known to man.

Kurt and John executed a hasty exit. While briskly walking to their car they exchange words, "Boy, oh boy, the rumor was right. He was dating her alright."

"That's for sure, Kurt. Did you see how she flushed?" Putting his hand on the door handle he stopped to look over the top of the car: Kurt caught his eye. "I wonder if he might have left her with a present."

"You think she's pregnant?" Kurt asked in a loud whisper. He opened his door and dropped into his seat as he said, "Oh, my God!"

"Wouldn't that explain a lot of what is going on here?

"I think it's a reach, John, but I can't dispute your logic. If, and I say if, she is pregnant, then you can be sure her family doesn't know it."

"Kurt, you seem a little dull on this subject. Ask Doris, she'll tell you if the girl is withholding the shocker about a bun in the oven, then her next cover-up will probably be to get an abortion—in secret."

Millhouse waited for John to put the car in gear. Once they were rolling, Kurt mused, "Where will she get the money, John? I know the family has bucks, but just as you said, she will want to do it in secret to keep her family from knowing."

The stoplight in front of them turned yellow and John slowed down in preparation of stopping. Shrugging and turning up his palms, he spoke as if he were tired of the subject. "How should I know? Maybe she'll steal some of the family silver."

Kurt nodded and twisted around so he could look at John. "You know, Miller, you're one smart cookie. I think we should go to her high school and talk to some of her friends, after all isn't that what we told her mom we were doing?"

"Okay, Millhouse, what are you up to?"

"Well, think about it. If she is going for an abortion she'll need money." He paused. "Now I know it's a long shot, but I think she'll tell one of her girlfriends. If we can find out who she hangs out with, we should be able to find out which one of her friends would be the most useful to her."

"So we're going 'rep.' hunting, huh?"

"You bet we are!"

"Why bother?"

"If we can confirm she is pregnant, then we can use that leverage to get her to talk to us about what happened that night. I'll bet she was there."

"You think she killed him?"

"Na, not a chance, but based on the timing, she could have seen the guy who did kill Ortiz."

Blandly John Miller said, "Might work."

Kurt narrowed his eyes and shook his head. *It's better than anything else we have.*

Chapter thirty-one:

As a hole in the wall restaurant, <u>Billy Bob's BQ</u> would not have been Doris's first choice for lunch, but the weather was lousy and the establishment was famous for its barbecued beef sandwiches. The tempting smell of southern cooking hung like the fragrance of an arousing perfume. Boldly the modern-day jukebox was plaintively revealing the story of a cowboy's love gone badly.

The Baker had struck again and Jolene was prepping the body for autopsy, for this reason she was passing time by filling her thoughts with the items on <u>Billy Bob's</u> menu.

Doris responded with a mini-jump when the voice behind her asked, "May I join you, Miss Mercer?"

Baffled, Doris turned and looked up at the man wearing a dark black trench coat. "Do I know you?" She frowned. Her face seemed to register certain hardness as she thought; *he's that Edward Woodward guy.* She glanced toward the door hoping to see Kurt or someone from the department, but no one was there.

"My wife, Thelma told me I should apologize to you, or at least explain why I was going the same places as you were." He pulled a black leather glove from his right hand.

Her lips were thin and tight, her eyes narrowed. "Following me, you mean."

"Well, yes. I suppose you could say that, but actually I was following a man who was following you." It was kind of true. He pulled off his other glove.

She was breathing fast and her body language was that of one who was ready to bolt at any moment; "Yeah?"

From his pocket she produced a business card which read, <u>Richard Price Private Consulting Actuary,</u> "You see I hire out to insurance companies to do specialty studies."

"I know what an actuary does" She glanced at his card, "Mr. Price."

"May I sit down?"

Halfheartedly she nodded and indicated a spot on the other side of the booth.

He removed his trench coat and carefully placed it on the hook outside of the booth. "Sometimes I like to just travel around. It kind of clears my head." Carefully placing his gloves together, he positioned them on the tabletop. "My wife says I do it just to get away from her." He smiled, but Doris did not respond. "Oh, my, this is not going very well, is it?"

"So how does that get to the part where you were following me?"

The waitress came by and he ordered a glass of
iced tea. "It was when you were in that
neighborhood market." Again he smiled, "I often
shop there. Their fresh fruit is the best anywhere,
don't you agree?"

In spite of herself she smiled, "Yes, they have
great produce."

"He was following you everywhere you went. He
would pick up items and then put them back on the
shelves. He was quite clever at it, actually."

"Why was he following me?"

"I really don't know, but being the old fuddy-
duddy I am, I wanted to make sure you got home
alright."

"Why didn't you just tell me about him?" She
found herself believing him and she began to relax.

"Oh, yes. I can see where that had gone. I come
up to you and tell you someone is following you,
and he might not have been noticed. And you think
I am just some old man trying to pick you up." He
rearranged the salt and peppershaker. "I don't
think so."

"So you followed me from the market until I got
home?" She opened her sandwich and added some
red-hots before she closed it. "Why?"

"I was afraid you might be in some sort of
danger."

"You do this often?" She took a large bite out of her sandwich.

He blushed, "Oh, my!" he chuckled, "No. But you see, in my work I sometimes check up on people who take out unusually large policies. They might be untruthful on their application." Conspiratorially, he leaned forward, "I've found people who were sky-divers, or hang-glider enthusiasts: they forgot to mention it."

"Are you checking up on me?"

"No, no. It's just that I was concerned, but it was also why I made no effort to hide from you. When I told Thelma she said, 'The poor girl probably thinks that you are some sort of stalking pervert, Richard.'"

"Was I in danger?" She dabbed the corners of her mouth.

"I really don't know, Miss Mercer. The man walked on past your house after you went inside." What he did know, he was not telling her. He was certain the man had been hired to do the job he had refused to do. "It was probably just my imagination." Suddenly he grabbed his gloves and arranged two dollars on the tabletop. While sliding across the bench seat, he said, "Well, anyway, now I can tell Thelma I talked to you." He slipped into his coat. "She was quite bothered about the whole thing, but she was also concerned you might be in some jeopardy."

For the first time her smile seemed genuine. "Thanks you for looking after me, Mr. Price."

"Richard, please."

"Richard"

"Do keep an eye out, just in case."

"I work at the police department. Maybe I'll mention it to one of the officers."

"That might be a good idea, Miss Mercer."

"Doris."

"Ah, Doris" He reached out a hand and she slipped her hand into his. It felt warm and smooth.

"Do you have any children, Richard?"

For the first time she saw his countenance falter. His eyes seemed to focus on some place at another time in his life, "No, Doris." He managed a pained smile. "We were never blessed in that way." A few fast blinks brought him back to where he was. "We've been married over thirty years. She's a remarkable lady, Doris."

The words just seem to fall out of her mouth, "I'd like to meet her someday, Richard."

Looking at her askance, he said, "Checking up on my story?" His smile showed he really didn't think that. "Tell you what. I'll bring her by for lunch."

Caught up in the exchange, Doris replied, "How about next Friday at TGIF's just down the street."

"Let me call you on that, Doris. May I have a phone number?"

Doris started to write down her number, but she stopped. She placed her chin in her cupped hand and looked up at him.

Chapter thirty-two:

Richard slapped his gloves into his left hand, "Come now, Doris. I'm really not a dirty old man."

She smirked, "I know that, Richard." She hesitated and then began to speak very slowly and deliberately, "Why is it that I think you already have my phone numbers?"

He put both hands on the table and snorted. Softly he said, "Which number would you like me to use? Your cell? Your home? Or maybe the morgue number?"

Laughing she moved her head from side to side and leaned back in the booth, "Yeah, I know. You do this kind of stuff in your business." She looked into his soft, twinkling eyes, "Use my cell."

"Your cell it shall be, my dear." Deftly he slipped on his gloves and turned to walk out of the door.

Turning his head, he rested his chin on his shoulder, "Thelma is going to be delighted." With a spring in his step that would better match a man half his age, Richard Price bounced his way out of the front door.

weird, she thought. *It was as if I had known him all of my life.* Looking around the room she felt a sense of caution. She believed Richard. Was it possible she was being stalked? She would have to talk to Kurt and tell him about the strange man she had met. Maybe she'd invite Kurt to meet Richard and Thelma Price. The thought seemed strange. They had no children, and she had never had any real parents.

The booth seemed lonely since Richard left. Once again her mind began to flit from the ballad of a jilted girl to the image of a body lying on an oversized draining pan.

A brisk wind fluttered the hem of Richard's trench coat and he pulled up his collar and held it tightly in place. His nose was cold and his eyes began to run from the sting of the cold blustery weather, but inside he felt warm and happy he had refused the offer to terminate such a vibrant life. Tomorrow he would begin to find out more about the man who had been following her; by now he was certain the source must be Dr. Bick: he would start there.

Across the street, behind the plate glass window of a video game shop, Richard was being studied. With questioning eyes they sought to take in his regal bearing and confident stride.

Chapter thirty-three:

His feet made a thudding sound as he trotted down the hallway to his downstairs apartment. Sniffling as he held his room key in his fingerless wool gloves, he blinked to clear his eyes while he inserted the key into the battered door lock. Under his arm he held a copy of the morning newspaper.

After kicking off his boots he slipped his cold feet into a pair of fleece lined leather slippers and made his way to a well-worn once blue corduroy couch now covered with an old brown blanket. The paper was dropped on a rectangular coffee table and then The Baker turned on the TV news. Cupping his hands together he blew into the middle and tried to warm his fingers as he watched for the tube to begin delivering a picture.

Settling into one corner of the couch he selected a local news channel and waited for the news concerning his latest prey. After an annoying commercial declaring the amazing powers of the

latest wonder drug, the station switched to film
shot just after sunup that day.

Dressed in a navy blue wool topcoat, the
announcer spoke loudly in order to overcome the
wind which was whirling clouds of snow and bits
of rubble toward the stone bridge behind the
speaker. "This morning, what the police refuse to
say is another murder done by the serial killer
dubbed, The Baker. A fifteen year old boy, on his
way to his aunts, was taking a short-cut through
the city park and down under the Washington
bridge when he spotted the feet of a man sticking
out from under a folded piece of cardboard box
about the size of a refrigerator box. He was going
to walk around the man when he noticed the trace
of what he at first thought was snow and upon
closer examination realized it was flour. Using his
latest birthday present, a cell-phone, he called 911
and reported the scene to the police. The boy said
it took the police twenty minutes to arrive at the
bridge."

With increasing interest, The Baker studied the
screen and chuckled each time the announcer
speculated upon events, motives, and the character
of The Baker. He imagined it would take the police
a little while to find out the man had gone to the
park to feed some stranded pigeons who lived
above the lights in one of the covered picnic spots

on the west side of the park. The Baker had spent
almost fifteen minutes talking to the man and
helping him feed old bread to the lethargic, fat
birds. They had walked as far as the bridge before
The Baker shot the man and slid his body down the
embankment and then dragged him under the
bridge. Seeing the cardboard lying stuck in a
snowdrift, he used it to make sure the body would
not be covered up by drifting snow: it was
important it be discovered.

The coverage was brief and soon the TV set was
placed on mute while he contemplated his next
victim. In the back of his mind was a burning
desire to punish Morton Filman and Betty Powers
for their attempt at framing him for the Ortiz
murder, but he was hoping he might be able to turn
the tables on them and blame them for the murders
he had committed. Perhaps he would then relocate
to another city and lay-low for a while: he was not
yet ready to be caught.

The cantankerous can opener was whirring and
whining and doing anything but opening his can of
chili. In frustration he opened a drawer and pushed
aside a myriad of kitchen utensils until he found
his manual can opener. *Sometime the simplest way
is the best way* he told himself. Turning the knob
on the gas stove he waited until the igniter
managed to produce a flame. From a spotless

looking glass pot he poured a cup of cold coffee from yesterday's brew. He popped it into the microwave and cooked it for one minute.

The wooden kitchen table was encased in a red and white checkered, Italian looking, plastic tablecloth. Seated with his bowl of steaming chili, a box of crackers, and his coffee he began to munch on his chili covered crackers. *So why is that bitch, Betty, following that schoolgirl?* He loaded up another cracker and held it in mid-air as he asked himself *and why is Filman following that lady who works at the police station?* Perhaps there would be an opportunity for some payback. With an almost imperceptible nod, he crunched on his cracker and allowed himself a hopeful smile in honor of his creativity.

Chapter thirty-four:

The receptionist had been her usual abrupt and rude self when Morton Filman had tried to get an appointment for Betty. Snobbery oozed from every bleached white tooth in her head as she informed Morton Dr. Bick was not taking any new patients; of course she was sorry she was unable to accommodate him. Only after he informed her he was a personal friend of Enrico Angelino did she consider relenting. He was well aware Enrico would be furious; if he found out he had used his name.

Placing a serious surgical edge in his voice, Morton told the nurse/ receptionist he must speak with the doctor: **"and now!"** She hesitated, but she complied.

"Yes, this is Dr. Bick. What can I do for you?" It was obvious the good doctor was occupied doing something besides talking to Morton.

A soft frosty voice said, "Doctor, I'm the guy Mr. Angelino recommended. My girlfriend is sick and I want her to see you…**now!**" The last word was spoken in such a tone it was a non-negotiable statement.

The ambient noise ceased as the doctor covered the mouthpiece and checked to see if his secretary was listening: there were no other lights shining on the back of phone lights. In a muffled and tense tone of voice the doctor said, "You know that we should never be seen together." He was hoping to bluff his way out of this perilous situation.

"No sale, doc. One way or the other, you are going to see her now. Or should I come by your house some time tonight."

Unable to think of what to say, the doctor answered with a clearing of his throat.

"I'm in your parking lot, on my cell-phone. She's running a fever, doc." He paused and pursed his tightened lips. "I'm waiting, doc.!"

A mixture of panic and anger painted his words, "Okay, come around the back by the dumpster, I'll let you in the back door."

In a display of confidence, Morton announced, "That's where we are now." He let that fact sink in, "So open the damned door, Hal." The use of the doctor's first name was deliberate; a show of disrespect for anyone who would pay for the murder of another human, much less a doctor who now showed such a disregard of human life.

Dr. Halloway T. Bick, MD, took a deep breath and attempted to calm his speech, it only made his word unstable, "Give me ten minutes to finish up with my patient." With a trembling hand he fumbled the receiver back into its cradle.

More than ten minutes had gone by and Betty was beginning to have trouble breathing. She seemed on the verge of throwing up.

Dr. Bick washed his hands, it was just another way of stalling, but he was not looking forward to being confronted by a contract killer and his sick girlfriend. He welcomed the buzzing of his intercom. "Yes, what is it?" his voice had a decided edge to it.

The surly voice of his secretary, sometime girlfriend, snapped back, "Mrs. Angelino has Martina here, doctor." She lowered her voice, "She doesn't have an appointment, but I think it's something kind of private." Again her voice shifted to that of a judgmental character, "If you know what I mean."

"I have to take care of a problem, so I might be a few minutes, but put them in B-3 and I'll be there as soon as I can." There was a slight tremble in his voice.

Turning her back to the mother and daughter, she asked, "Is everything all right, Hal? You sound really stressed."

"I just need a few minutes to take care of this problem, Nurse." His tone had such a bite in it she immediately turned off her concern.

"Very well, Doctor. They'll be in B-3".

"The doctor will be with you shortly, Mrs. Angelino. He is with a patient, but he will see you in a few minutes." Armed with a patient's chart, she swished in her starched blue uniform that barely dropped ten inches below her waistline. White pantyhose that had the appearance of being spray-painted upon her long legs, caused most people to feel uncomfortable, but Polly Smith enjoyed the attention.

Dutifully, Cortina and Martina followed the nurse to Examination room B-3. It was a well-decorated room that could have passed for a suite at some hotel. Martina marched to an overstuffed chair and dropped her body into the comfortable seat; she folded her arms and made the face of a martyr who had just been lashed to the burning post. Polly read the signs: *this is one troubled girl.*

As Polly reached to close the door she said, "Please make yourselves at home, Dr. Bick will be here shortly." Ceremoniously, she closed the door and then stood outside. It took her less than thirty seconds to hear Cortina tongue lashing Martina.

"I no longer believe you, Martina. You've been lying to us for months. You've been seeing that Ortiz boy!" The words were fast and sharp, leaving no doubt about her anger. "If you're lying to me now, this is your last chance to tell the truth." There was a pause and then the noise of something being knocked over. "Are you pregnant, young lady?"

Words that could have come out of the mouth of some pre-historic evil spirit, sizzled with hate, "Wouldn't you like to know?" Martina's face contorted as she sneered and tightened her eye lids, "Ma-ma!" Her breathing was coming fast and began to frighten Cortina. "You're so old fashioned. You don't know anything, you Sicilian Bitch."

Even through the door the sound was loud as Cortina focused every bit of her one hundred and eighty four pounds into a slap unleashed at the end of her eighteen-inch circumference arms. Martina's head snapped to her right as if it were a ping-pong ball on the end of a string. Her head struck the side of the chair's headrest. "You listen to me, you little brat." Her words were slow and soft-spoken as she leaned close to the red cheeked sixteen-year old. "You ever talk to me like that- again-, and your father won't be able to recognize you mutilated face." So close now that she could smell the garlic on her mother's hot breath, "Do you understand me, little girl?" It was not really a question.

Fear had replaced pain. Almost terrified to move, she cast her eyes downward and gave a silent nod. Cautiously, she raised her hand to feel the hot, crimson brand that covered her left cheek.

Cortina snarled and pulled back, "Good!" She turned and walked toward a window that overlooked a small open courtyard. "Good." She echoed and nodded to herself.

In Martina's mind there was little or no doubt but what her mother meant every word that she had spoken. Rumors had it she had a crippled brother in Sicily: he had dared to cross her.

Polly's white incased knees were shaking as she made her way back to her receptionist's desk. She wanted to tell Hal about the incident, but she knew better than to interrupt him when he was in 'one of his moods'.

*   *   *

With Betty's arm draped over his shoulder, Morton pounded on Dr. Bick's door, immediately a short stocky man wearing a white smock opened it. Quickly the doctor glanced around to see if anyone was observing this clandestine visit. Providing a slight shove to the back of Morton Filman, he quickly forced the door closed and then leaned against it.

After easing Betty into an overstuffed chair, he turned to examine the face of the doctor. To his mind came the picture of The Cowardly Lion from The Wizard of Oz. Dr. Bick was dark complexioned and sported a full, but closely cropped beard. His eyes looked beady and scared. A trembling voice completed the fantasy, "What's wrong with her?" He was standing a good ten feet from her and extending his neck to get a more cautious look.

There was no humor in Morton's tone when he said, "You're supposed to be telling me, Doc."

Both embarrassed and paralyzed, he bobbed his head and tugged at the stethoscope dangling from his neck. After a practiced clearing of his throat, he seemed to be operating on 'automatic pilot'. "Yes, of course. I mean has she been eating?" At this point he was thinking she was reacting to an overdose of drugs. "Did she eat anything that could have been poisonous?" He felt the back of her neck and looked at Morton, "She belongs in a hospital. I'll arrange for her to get the best of care." He reached for the phone, but Morton gripped his wrist tightly and then looked into the doctor's startled eyes. "No hospital, Doc. Just give her a shot of something." He was sporting a grin that did not match the warning in his eyes.

Doctor Bick wanted to argue with the man, but there were forces within his body which would not allow him to challenge Morton. "I can give her an antibiotic and a prescription, but beyond that I can't do much here." Afraid of how he would react, he stepped back and found himself sweating with fear.

Morton seemed genuinely respectful and appreciative as he said, "That will be fine, Doc." He wiped the moist forehead of Betty and asked, "How long 'til she's better?"

Doctor Bick was loading a syringe, "Well, she looks like she has a touch of pneumonia." He gave

Betty the shot and taped a piece of cotton over the intrusion. "If it doesn't turn worse: maybe two weeks or so." The doctor noticed that Morton visibly winced. "If it turns worse, she will have to go to a hospital." Anticipating Morton's wrath, he continued, "I know a number of hospitals where I could put her and no one would ask any questions."

Without comment, Morton stuffed the prescription into his pocket and scooped Betty into his arms, "Thanks, Doc." He walked toward the back door.

Anxiously, the doctor opened the door for Morton. Their eyes met. ."And I'll take care of that problem for you." He grunted, as he turned sideways to take Betty through the door; "Real soon, Doc!"

Seeing no one in sight, the doctor closed the door and gave an audible sigh of relief. *Now I'll see that Italian Cow, go home, and get drunk.* He reached for the phone to tell Polly to meet him in B-3, but his hand was shaking and he felt weak, he would sit down and rest for a while.

Chapter thirty-five:

"You're kidding me, right?"

Doris blushed and responded by tucking her feet under her and giving a Cheshire smile, "No, Carla, I'm not kidding." Her six-foot long couch was a blue-maroon color with pinhead dots of white that could barely be seen. Doris's face blended into its shade. "So who told you about Kurt?" She hesitated only long enough to make her point, "Jolene?"

Between her teeth Carla held a hair band; she was in the act of putting her hair into a ponytail. Nodding her head she removed the hair band and, while gathering her Irish red hair into the band, replied, "Jolene says he is a real catch."

Displaying an appreciative smirk, Doris giggled, "She's right." Not wanting to give the wrong impression she continued, "But that's not what attracted me to him. He's good looking all right, but he's----" She searched for a word, "—comfortable. I could talk with him for hours."

Carla settled into the other end of the couch, her hair clashed with the maroon couch. "Yeah, I know what you mean." Tipping her glass of Wild Turkey and water, she took a large gulp and said, "Aaaah, I needed that." Quickly glancing at her watch Carla asked, "Speaking of Jolene, where is she? She told me to meet her here at seven thirty, it's almost eight and I've got a date at ten;

Quid by the mention of a date, Doris inquired; "When do we get to meet this mystery man of yours?" Doris flicked her eyebrows.

A gray cloud of hurt darted across Carla's freckled face. "I don't know, Dot." Carla put her teeth on her lower lip and then shrugged, "He's married, or at least he says he is." Words flowed like a desert gully washer as she took a deep breath and justified her life, "They got married when they were real young and now their marriage is more like a habit than a romance. He says he is going to leave her, but I wish I could believe that." She tipped her glass and pushed back the sleeve of her daisy white sweater, "My Minnie Mouse says its eight o'clock." Blinking a mist from her eyes she asked, "Have you ever been close to getting married?"

Reflectively, Doris said, "A couple of times, but with medical school and internship, I never really had the time to get too serious."

"I hear those doctors are real sexual animals." Carla literally bounced up and down on the cushions. "That's what I need. I need to catch me a doctor and live like a queen."

Shaking her head, Doris chuckled. "You've been watching too many movies. Most of the time the docs are so pooped or high on pills sex is the last thing on their minds. Sleep and a steak are the big wish, Carla."

"Darn, I guess I'll have to improve my culinary skills." It was evident Carla had no interest in returning to the subject of her boyfriend. She glanced about the room and said, "Jolene told me you had fixed up your place." She bobbed her head and put on a face of approval. "Really appreciate you letting us meet here. Our place is too far to make it back for dinner and a movie." Agitated she looked at her watch, "If she doesn't get here soon we'll have to scratch the movie. I'm not missing dinner."

"How long have you and Jolene been roommates?"

"About three years. We really don't see that much of each other, at least when she works nights."

Doris uncurled and got up. "Want another one?" Tipping her head toward Carla's empty glass, "The cabby's driving." She gave a knowing wink as she passed a ragged bar-cloth over a row of wet circles.

"What the hell…why not? I'm gonna get sick anyway." She handed Doris her empty glass and asked, "Jolene working on anything special? She sure is running late."

Ice chimed as it hit the sides of the whiskey glass, heading for the bottom, "She's just finishing up for me, but sometimes the police or other interested parties drop in and slow us up."

Making a visage of disgust, as if she smelled something worse than a chicken yard or a monkey's cage, "I don't see how you do what you do." Reaching for her filled glass, "I mean doesn't it ever get to you?"

Doris walked back toward her mini-bar. She licked her lips and sighed. "What gets you, are not the bodies. It's what some people do to other people." As she spoke Carla could tell that Doris was picturing some specific murders. "It's just hard to believe anyone could do such things."

"But you help to catch them don't you?"

"I suppose so, but I'd rather be able to <u>stop</u> them in the first place." Normally Doris never thought about her work when she was at home alone. She changed the subject. "So, you like what I've done to the place?"

Before she could answer, the door chimes rang. Carla got up and looked at her watch as she headed toward the door. "I'll get it, and then we'll scoot right out of here. Thanks." At the door, Carla looked through the peephole, "It's a man…you expecting anyone?"

Perplexed, Doris answered, "No!" She tromped to the door and looked through the hole, "It's Kurt." While unlocking the door she said, "Wonder what he's doing here?"

Carla sighed, "Yeah."

The steel reinforced door slid gracefully on its four sets of hinges. Jolene and Kurt both displayed looks that seemed both sheepish and amused.

Carla reached for Jolene and pulled at her arm, "I've been waiting since seven-fifteen, Jo." She glanced at Kurt. "You must be Kurt. Hi, I'm Carla." Without waiting for him to reply she turned back to Jolene, "We're late, let's get going." Jolene shrugged as she turned to walk lockstep with Carla.

"Glad to have met you, Carla." Kurt spoke to the backs of the retreating women. Nervously, Kurt turned to face the confused look on Doris's face. "I was in the morgue checking on the latest Baker job and Jolene told me she was coming here. I, ah, offered her a ride." Kurt smiled and waited for Doris to respond.

She grinned as she pretended to be irritated, "Well, okay. I guess you can come in." She stood aside and gave him an arm wave to usher him in.

"Excuse the mess. It's the maid's night off." She snickered.

Kurt took three steps into the room and turned, "Lucky me." he said as he lookcd around. "I push a mean vacuum, you know. And my dishwashing is in great demand."

Doris walked over next to him and raised herself to her tiptoes. "Well, lucky me." She gave him a soft kiss on his lips. "Got any references?"

Deciding to not pursue that line of questioning, he put his arms around her and looked into her dancing eyes. "You know what I do for a living. I find out things. Tonight I want to find out all about you."

Faking concern, she pinched her eyebrows together and shifted her eyes from side to side. "Okay, but no rubber hoses or glaring lights…deal?"

"Deal"

Chapter thirty-six:

John Miller felt as if he had wasted his entire day, he knew he hadn't, but it still felt that way. After pouring over the visitor logs of the morgue he was still no closer to finding out how anyone knew the Modus Operandi (M.O.) of the serial killer the media called The Baker. His prime killing signature was the three-nine millimeter bullets into the area of the solar plexus, and then the spreading of a pound of white flour over the corpse. None of this information had been leaked to the press, but yet Detective Miller believed the Ortiz killing had been an astonishingly close copycat. The obvious conclusion had caused Captain Won great concern someone had gotten word to a copycat killer.

His toothbrush had worked his mouth into a sea of white, foaming, lather. Pausing to look into the cabinet mirror to his left, he noticed the dark circles were causing him to look old and tired. Somewhere within himself he had sensed he was fighting some sort of illness, but he refused to see a physician or even consider taking a vacation. After surviving two divorces and the successful suicide of his oldest daughter, his work as a police officer was all he cared about. Resisting the feeling of depression, he dipped his head and filled his mouth with water from the sink's spigot. He spit into the sink, ignoring the streaks of blood which laced the mixture as it went down his drain.

The bathroom changed from a room flooded with light to one of utter darkness as he switched off the light and his entire home became as black as his thoughts. Retirement would mean a life full of hours he would just spend alone; at least for now he had his work and a good friend in Kurt Millhouse.

Unable to sleep, he lay between crisp white sheets he had picked up from the laundry earlier that afternoon. The smell reminded him of his first wife, but the pain of the memory caused his mind to skip to the sterile environment of the morgue and the place where he last saw his daughter. That too was a painful memory, but it had been where he had spent a major part of his day. Thoughts, images, and phrases flashed about in his head as he struggled to catch the fleeting logic eluding his foggy brain. *Maybe someone at the morgue is passing on the information? Perhaps a janitor or a deliveryman, certainly not Doris Mercer But if no one in the Crime Unit or the police force was leaking information, then where was it coming from?* His brain seemed impotent.

John rolled over and nestled his head into his starched pillowcase. He could hear the pounding of his heart as if it were an echo from some sort of defective appliance. Quickly he moved onto his back and stared into the black void above him. *I hope Kurt had more luck than I did. The Captain won't be too happy until we can solve the Ortiz riddle.*

Sensing the waves of depression were like an attacking Mongol hoard, he mused out loud, "I'd better check into that K-9 adoption program."

Chapter thirty-seven:

Unaware of the reason for Morton and Betty's hasty departure from their downtown apartment, The Baker made his way across the street and up the well-worn stairs. Although he had passed several people in the stairwell, no one really looked at him. As a matter of fact they seemed to be staring at nothing. The combination of his collar being up and the darkness caused by missing light bulbs assured him he would not really be remembered. With minimal effort he worked the lock on the door and slipped inside. The heady scent of camphor gave a pleasant fragrance to the otherwise mildew stench he had expected.

Looking for nothing in particular, he slipped into a pair of latex gloves and scurried about the room picking up two objects which interested him. Next to the bed stand he read a note: D. Mercer/ Bick 447-8383. Quickly he copied down the presumed phone number. With practiced efficiency he cautiously glided about the room, noting where everything was and how it was arranged. Feeling elated with the information he had obtained he moved toward the door and opened it just enough to assure himself he would not be seen. Swiftly he exited the door, making certain it was locked and there were no tell tale marks on the aged carpet beneath the door.

Having exited the building, he went to the nearest bus stop and took a bus that would go in the opposite direction of his destination. The Baker could not even recall when he had felt this level of euphoria. A new level of excitement coursed through his delirious mind: it was all just too perfect.

After two bus transfers, he found his car and drove to his house. A row of small leafless trees nakedly guarded the median of the tranquil street. A setting sun splashed accents of yellow gold and pinkish red over the west facing side of his house. He waved to several of his neighbors who enthusiastically waved back at him as he pulled into his single car detached garage. He stopped to remove his American flag from its stanchion near the back door: night was approaching. Before he could reach for the doorknob, the door flew open and two smiling faces yelled, "Grandpa, grandpa!"

"Hey, hey, take it easy, you guys." Quickly he stooped down and scooped up the two children.

From the kitchen came the voice of his widowed daughter-in-law, "We about gave up on you, Grandpa: dinner in ten minutes. Your favorite: fried chicken, corn on the cob, and a mess of baked beans." A clanking of plates and glasses interrupted her words. "I'm having salad, if you'd like some."

"That's okay, Carla. I'll settle for real food, none of that rabbit stuff." He laughed as he tussled the hair on the grand kids. "How did your date go last night?"

"Probably better than your babysitting: Andrew and Amy squealed on you." She poked her head around the corner; her red hair fell on her shoulder as if it were the fanning bristles of a paintbrush. "You know I don't like them to be up past eight on school nights. If Andrew doesn't get enough sleep sometimes his asthma act up" She smiled and her green eyes sparkled as she watched him bounce the twins on his knees. "Oh, what the hell, come in here and have a beer." Her voice trailed off as she withdrew to the kitchen, "I swear... you're just as encourageable as Bill was."

Placing the twins on the floor, he walked to the door jam and plucked a beer from her proffered hand, cold sweat was beginning to form on the outside of the bottle. Leaning against the jam he sniffed as he took a refreshing swig from the amber bottle. "I can't stay real long tonight, Carla. I got to work tonight: got a special order that needs to be done by morning."

"No problem." She turned and placed the chicken on a plate covered with a layer of paper towels. She looked at him and smirked, "That way I'll be able to get the kids to bed early, and by the way, Andrew's inhaler in on the counter next to the toaster oven." She paused.

Grandpa nodded and glanced toward the toaster oven.

"Maybe even get some time for myself." Carla raised her eyebrows.

"You guys need anything?" He crossed the room and sat at the eight place oak table covered with a forest green tablecloth.

"We're fine, Grandpa." She whirled and began plucking corn on the cob from a large stainless steel pot. "Oh, before I forget, you got another call from one of those real estate people wanting to know if you're open to sell this house."

He snorted and took a deep gulp of beer. "Not on your life. You guys got this place as long as you want it. It's paid for and I know that's how Billy would have wanted it."

Almost as if she hadn't heard him she yelled, "Kids—get in here." Setting the corn on the table she smiled at the aging veteran and patted him on

the hand, "Yeah, I know, but thanks anyway."
Wiping her eyes with the back of her hand she
mumbled, "God, I miss him."

Six months ago he had not even known about
Carla. He and his son, William, had not spoken to
each other in more than ten years. He hadn't even
known his son was in the military until he received
the death notice. It was almost four months before
he knew he was a grandfather. He wished he had
known earlier, but maybe, after today, it wasn't too
late.

After studying a stripped bone a chicken leg, he
sucked on a piece of meat stuck in a front tooth,
"Jolene working late again?"

"Most of this month she will be on the
graveyard."

"Does she ever talk about her work?" He did his
best to sound as if he were just making small talk.

Carla paused to consider how she should answer
that question. She knew Jolene was not supposed
to talk about her work, but sometime, particularly
when they were up late, she would unload to Carla.
"Not really. She's not supposed to talk about her
work. Police leaks and all that stuff."

Plucking another cob from the platter in front of
him he snorted, "Yeah, I'll bet that's really hard on
her, I mean being a woman and all." He produced

a fake shudder. "She must see some pretty grizzly stuff."

"You can't even imagine, grandpa." She glanced at the kids, but they did not seem to be paying any attention to the adult conversation, "Turns my stomach." She whispered.

He responded with a sympathetic nod. When he thought about it, it seemed strange his daughter-in-law's roommate would be one of the medical team at the morgue who actually examined his victims. He switched the subject, "Billy's insurance holding out?"

"Yeah," She touched his arm, "We're doing fine, but not because of the military insurance, it was his Hartford policy that saved us."

He returned a smile, "Billy always was a smart kid."

Andrew just spilled his glass of milk right into Amy's lap. "Andrew, get a towel and clean up your mess." She turned to Amy, "Honey, go change your cloths.

The stoic Amy shrugged and walked over to her grandfather, "I think he does it on purpose, grandpa." She glanced at the busy Andrew and rolled her eyes, "Guess I better change clothes."

Carla and the grandfather exchanged smiles and shaking heads, "Kids!" he reflected.

* * *

It was well past ten when he finally left the
house; he was beginning to feel he was overstaying
his welcome. Carla was tired and the kids had not
gotten to bed on time. Backing out of the driveway
he saw the beginnings of the predicted snowstorm.
Under the pale yellow glow of the street lamps a
steady stream of amber tinted flakes were dropping
like confetti streamers. On the slick asphalt, his
tires slipped as he placed his car into drive.

Like a layer of white flour, the snow began to pile
up on his windshield. The mesmerizing rhythm of
his windshield wipers caused his mind to drift into
the past: the first time he killed as The Baker.

The news of Bill's death had not only caught him
off guard, it had trapped him with a load of guilt
for all the years he had not talked to his son. It was
not unusual for Billy to have left a message on his
dad's answering machine, but he never returned
the calls. Now he could not even remember why.

It was a stupid death. Billy was a cook in the
Army; he had gone to the mess hall at five a.m.
and discovered it was being robbed. In trying to
apprehend the thieves, he was shot three times in
the solar plexus and left for dead. Sometime during
the struggle a bin of flour was knocked over and
Billy had been covered in it, his life's blood ebbed
in steams and pools of cranberry red. The killers
had never been caught. His son's death had caused

something in him to snap and he reverted to the trained killer he had been when he was in the Special Forces. It wasn't an excuse it was just what happened.

Now the grandkids and Carla had entered his life, he had made several attempts to stop the senseless murders he was committing, but now some strange new thing had a hold on him. He was now looking for a way out!

He blinked as he realized he had almost run into the back of a slow moving car. Billy's murder flashed from his mind, he needed to turn left at the next signal light.

Chapter thirty-eight:

Thelma Price had spent most of the evening before the anticipated luncheon with Doris Mercer, sliding hangers back and forth as she hunted for the perfect outfit. To Richard she seemed as determined to find the elusive ensemble as any hunter on an African safari.

Richard was firmly ensconced in his favorite overstuffed Lazyboy. Feet propped in the air, he was examining his latest Book of the Month on

Actuarial Statistics related to the medical profession. Every few minutes Thelma would emerge from the bedroom and solicit an opinion from the engrossed scholar.

Wearing a very flattering dress of aqua blue cinched with a belt of reddish pink, she held up two different earrings. "Richard?" No response. She glared at him and repeated herself, "Richard?"

He dropped down his book and returned a look of measured patience. "Yes, my dear?" He knew the question, but waited in order to have the satisfaction of having predicted her words.

Holding a sample of each earring next to each earlobe, she asked, "Which one is better? This one?" She wiggled the earring on the right. "Or this one?" She wiggled the other earring."

After pretending to give it the same weighted thought as a man choosing between a Mercedes Benz and a Rolls Royce, he cleared his throat and announced, "I like the one on the right."

"So do I." Grinning, she whirled around and headed back to the bedroom from which he was certain she would soon appear in an entirely different outfit and challenge him to once again guess which jewelry her public would prefer.

By eight the following morning Thelma was at it again, but Richard convinced her they had to leave by nine thirty. After confirming their luncheon date with Doris, they left the house at ten. Having discovered the inadequacies of her wardrobe, Thelma had to do some more shopping.

The parking lot was spotted with large banks of snow. The snowplows had the unique knack of leaving piles in the best parking places. The candy-striped building was emitting billows of grayish vapor who quickly blended with the low-lying clouds.

Richard glanced around as he was removing his gloves. "There she is." He pointed to a table positioned next to what would have been a sunny view of the outside.

Thelma waved and spoke out of the side of her mouth, "Who's that with her?"

Richard indicated to the hostess he had located his party. "That, my dear, is Detective Lieutenant Kurt Millhouse. You recall I mentioned him to you." Firmly he held her elbow as he escorted her toward the table.

With a touch of annoyance in her voice she said, "You might have, Richard." She wasn't irritated with him, but rather with herself for not remembering. "He's quite handsome." She paused her speech and added, "Nice smile."

The usual pleasantries exchanged, and the meals served, Kurt took the lead in addressing Richard Price. "I want to thank you for your concern over

Doris's safety." He patted her hand, "I'm afraid, sometimes, she forgets she is in the big city."

Richard shrugged and displayed a bit of embarrassment. "I'm afraid I gave her a bit of a start." He threw up his hands, "You know, following her and all."

Thelma giggled and her eyes twinkled as she looked at Doris. "I guess Richard isn't very good at stealthing his way about."

Recalling Richard's confession he was making no effort to conceal his presence, she responded, "I think you're underestimating Richard, Thelma. I'll bet he is good at most everything."

"You're right, my dear." A flush of pride bathed her countenance. "Anyway he was quite concerned about you." Kurt and Richard were talking about law and order and then insurance business, Thelma nodded toward Kurt, "Are you two serious?"

Doris's eyes flicked toward the two conversing men. She squiggled her mouth and blinked her eyes. "I'm not sure how to answer that, Thelma." She leaned closer to the older lady and asked, "How do you know this is the person you want to spend the rest of your life with?"

In a hushed voice, Thelma asked, "What did your mother tell you, dear?" In giving advice Thelma had learned it was always prudent to find out how one's family felt about a subject before she opened her opinion.

"I'm an orphan, Mrs. Price." Doris saw the pained look on Thelma's face. "Oh, I wasn't that young when they died, but I've never had a mother or been in any one's home long enough to call it my family."

There was no mistaking Thelma's pain for the young girl. With glistening eyes and quivering lips, she said, "I'm really sorry, dear. I didn't know." She took a deep breath and sighed, "I hope it hasn't been too difficult for you."

Both men had stopped talking and turned their attention to the two ladies. Their concern was evidenced from their facial expressions.

Doris straightened up and said, "We're all right, guys. It's just a girl thing." Her heart had speeded up, but she felt a sense of comfort in conversing with Thelma. She was a sweet lady. The kind of person any woman would have been happy, and proud, to call her, 'Mother'. "You men go back to whatever you're talking about." Dutifully they retreated and revived their discussion.

Having pulled a handkerchief from her purse, Thelma dabbed at her eyes and said, "To answer your question. For me, I just found myself talking with Richard and knew I wanted to talk with him for the rest of my life." She glanced at him and reflected. "He made me feel safe and wanted: valuable. Like, when we were alone or in a crowd, we were the only ones in the world."

Goose bumps and shivers caused Doris to react with a soft shudder, "That's weird, Thelma." Doris's eyes were large and her nostrils flared, "Wow! That's so close to how I feel when I'm with Kurt." She placed her hand just above her breasts and took several deep breaths. From the corner of her eye she could see Kurt was talking but also studying her actions. Undoubtedly, he would quiz her later.

Chapter thirty-nine:

Enrico sat poised in his brass tacked Moroccan Leather chair. His right hand was massaging his stumbled chin as he listened to Cortina's report on Martina's pregnancy. Occasionally he would pinch his nose as if to eliminate the stench of the words she was speaking. His dark eyes narrowed and darted from side to side. When finally he spoke his tone was even, measured and soft. "Where is she?" He nodded toward the upstairs, "In her room?"

Cortina breathed deeply, she had seen his temper and had no desire to have it released at their daughter. "Yes." She smoothed the front of her dress, a gesture stroking the area of her body which had carried Martina for nine months. "She isn't far along, but Doctor Bick is sure." As if reading his thoughts she mumbled, "We can't consider an abortion, Enrico. The Church forbids it."

Without looking at a flood of bad news, he leaned forward and looked at the floor. "Yeah, I know what The Pope says, Cortina." Passing a hand through his thinning, but still wavy hair he said, "But that----" He hesitated because he knew how Cortina felt about cussing in her house, "—that S.O.B should have been killed sooner."

Cortina sat in a matching chair and leaned toward Enrico. Gently she placed a hand on top of his hot and trembling hand, "Enrico, did you have him killed?" Her words were not harsh or accusatory; she could just as easily have been asking him if he had gotten the car serviced that day. She knew he wouldn't answer, but she felt she had to ask.

He raised his head and looked into her eyes, it was the only answer he would give her, but she now knew he had arranged the death of Paulo Ortiz.

"I only bring this up because our daughter thinks she got a look at the two who killed Ortiz ."

In spite of himself he reacted. Suddenly his eyes flashed with a sense of alarm. If she saw them, then maybe some others had seen them. His snitches inside of the police department had told him, for now, they were pinning this murder on The Baker. "She was there?"

Struggling to control her emotions, Cortina said, "Well, she didn't see the killing. She says he didn't open his door, but as she was going into the apartment house she saw two people, a man and a woman, who had just come out. They didn't look as if they belonged there."

"That doesn't count for much. It could have been anyone." Reflecting on the night Ortiz was killed he recalled his virginal princess was confined to her room. He was attempting to control his feelings of betrayal. He waved a hand of dismissal.

"What do you want to do, Enrico?" The way she spoke his name was soft and respectful; why hadn't his daughter turned out like his beloved Cortina. "I could send her to my sister in Sicily."

Enrico smiled, his eyes were already rimmed with red and droplets were slipping down his face, following lines which come with age and responsibility. "You're a good woman, my Cortina." Gathering her hand under his, he raised it to his mouth and rested his lips upon the back of her trembling hand. "We'll see." He patted her hand.

"Do you want to see, Martina?"

"Not yet. I need time to think." He settled back in his chair, exhausted and wretched. "You said the police had been by to see her. Did they ask her if she had seen anything?"

Cortina blinked her eyes and then closed them tightly; it was the technique she often used when she tried to remember. "No. They said they were asking most of her classmates about Ortiz. It seems he was popular with a lot of girls."

"I don't doubt it," he muttered.

In an effort to relieve some of the tension sapping her strength, she allowed her shoulders to sag, "Oh, Enrico. I think they knew more than they were letting on. Her finger prints must have been in the man's apartment."

He closed his eyes and rested his head against the corner of his headrest: his fingers rubbed his eyelids. "If the police have tied her to Ortiz, it is only a matter of time before they believe I arranged for his death."

"But you said they think the Baker fellow is the one they suspect."

"Yeah, I know, but---" He glanced sidewise at her, "---he didn't." He resumed rubbing his closed eyes, "And I don't want Martina to know. She'll hate me."

The confession had caught Cortina by surprise, his words had been the closest to a declaration of guilt she had ever heard her husband or any of the family admit to. "We're back to the same question. What do you want to do?"

"I need to think now, Cortina. My brain is on fire." He responded pleadingly.

"If you don't go to the police they are going to come to you. Is that what you think?"

"Possibly."

Hopefully Cortina suggested; "If Martina didn't get a real good look at the two people, maybe she could look at some mug shots and show we are co-operating." The idea sounded stupid, but it had some merit. "Forget it. It was just an idea."

Slowly he spoke, the words labored as they gave birth, "You might have something there." It was a risk, but uppermost in his mind it would convince Martina he had nothing to do with the death of Ortiz. If she made a positive ID he could have Morton and Betty eliminated and say he did it out of revenge for them having killed his daughter's boyfriend. Either way he would have to kill them before they talked. "It's a bit complicated, but it might throw the police off of the track; if we play it right." He dropped his hand and placed both

152

forearms on the armrests. He settled bolt upright in the leather chair, "As you said, they have her fingerprint from the apartment. I must be at the top of their list." But the real reason he would take the risk was to convince his daughter he was not responsible. She might have been de-flowered, but she was still his little girl.

"So is that what you want to do?"

"It's a possible plan, but I'm not sure it is a safe one. After all, we will be admitting we were involved. I'll really have to think about it." He looked at Cortina and made a feeble effort to smile.

Chapter forty:

Martina was more angry than scared. Her mother had humiliated her, and now her father knew she was pregnant. The anger in her had made her body hot to the point she felt feverish. From one wall to the other she paced, her eyes fixed upon the canopy that signified her purity. She stopped long enough to rip pieces of the covering from the wooden frame that held it in place. *I could have married him if daddy hadn't had him killed.* The thought caught her off guard. It was the first time she really believed it. She stopped shredding the pieces of virginal white canopy and forced her lips into a painfully tight circle. *That's the real problem here. Daddy! He killed the father of my child. Paulo loved me!*

Reflecting on the night she was to meet Paulo Ortiz, she recalled the two figures leaving the apartment house. They were the killers, she was sure of it, *no; they were the ones my father paid to kill Paulo*. Her mind seethed with anger. Miraculously, her guilt had shifted from her, to the killers and then to her father. *I'll make him pay, I'll identify the killers and they will tell the police about my murdering father.*

Her resolution issued in a conflict of fear for her father, but it also satisfied her need for revenge. In her mind it was her father's fault for her situation. It was he who had killed her would-be husband thereby leaving her without the remedy of marriage. Above all, he had caused the death of the man who loved her. To her sixteen year old mind, it all made sense.

Pulling the card left to her by the police she punched up the phone number of Lieutenant Millhouse.

"Police Department: 17th precinct." The officer raised his voice to overcome a sudden burst of noise in the background, "Sergeant Audrey speaking."

Martina hadn't realized how fast she was breathing; she could even hear the sound of her heart where her ear touched the receiver. "I'd like to speak to--" She glanced at the card and read from it, "—a detective Millhouse."

A sound of papers rustling and a nasal tone said, "I don't think he's in, lady, but I'll forward you to his department."

Reacting to a sudden burst of panic, she almost hung up.

"Miller here, what can I do for you?"

The panic was growing, was she doing the right thing? "Ah, I wanted, ah, a detective Millhouse."

Detective Miller listened closely, the voice sounded vaguely familiar: it was a young voice, a girl. "What's it concerning?"

"Oh, that's okay. I'll try him tomorrow." At the news he was not there, she felt a sense of relief. "Thank you." She had already pulled the receiver away from her ear when she heard her name.

"Martina?" Quickly he yelled, "Martina Angelino?" He had recalled where he had heard her voice.

"Yes?"

"I'm Detective Miller; I was at your house the other day. I was with Detective Millhouse."

The panic was returning, "Oh, yes. I remember you. You're the big one."

Miller laughed, "Yes, Martina. I'm the big one." His voice seemed soft and reassuring: a voice she could trust. "And how can we help you?" He could feel her hesitation. "Did you remember something?"

"I believe I can identify the killers, Mr. Miller." She couldn't believe she had said the words. They had come out more like a boast than a statement of fact.

Keeping his voice calm and reassuring, John said, "That's very good, Martina."

"Well, I think I can." She bit down on her lower lip.

Not wanting to frighten her he spoke as matter of factly as he could, "Were you there that night, Martina?" He could hear her hesitancy. Her breath was fast and shallow. "It must have been scary," still no reply. "You won't be in any trouble, Martina. We need your help to catch this guy. You must have been in love with Paulo."

At the mention of Paulo's name she held the remote phone close to her mouth and whispered, "It wasn't a guy." A short pause that seemed to last an eternity. "It was a man and a woman, coming out of the lobby."

"Will you be able to come downtown tomorrow and look at some pictures?"

"I don't think so. I don't want anyone to know I snitched on them." She sounded much more confidant, a sense of her own importance.

Detective Miller's mind was racing. *If we don't get her right away, we'll lose her.* "We could have a police woman come to the school and ask for a few of the students to look at the mug shots. We'll put each of you in separate rooms and rotate the books." He liked the idea, "No one would know if you, or any of you, picked out someone."

Feeling a sense of relief, she smiled, "Yeah... that sounds cool." The thought of all of the individual attention made her feel important. It was even exhilarating!

"We'll arrange everything with your school principal." Mentally he crossed his fingers.

"Yeah, sure;" There was a pause and then she responded with an enthusiastic, "Cool!"

"Tomorrow morning, Martina; and thanks for your co-operation."

"Sure. Goodnight, Detective, ah, ah, Miller. " The line went dead, but Martina had jump- started to life. She felt important. No longer was she an unwed pregnant sixteen year old, she was a star witness. She was going to avenge the death of her 'husband's' killer. And, after all, there was no real assurance it was going to be traced back to her father. He might have had nothing to do with Paulo's death. She rushed to a full-length mirror. She flitted from one pose to another and then asked herself, *I wonder what I should wear tomorrow*? She giggled as she thought about the trial and all of the newspapers and cameras; she would be the envy of everyone at school. It might even be good for the family name. *Oh, my. What will I wear to the trial? I'll need several new outfits, something older looking: sophisticated.* The stain of her status as an unwed teenager vanished like a computer image even when the 'delete' key was pressed.

Chapter forty-one:

Detective Miller made some notes and then picked up the phone. He punched Millhouse's autodial number. The phone started ringing Kurt's cell-phone.

Kurt glanced at his caller ID and responded. He had just opened the door to his car. With one hand he continued opening the door and dropping into the driver's seat. "Okay, who died, John?"

In a voice so fast and yet controlled, John said, "You're not gonna believe who just called me."

Kurt turned on his ignition and prepared to pull out into traffic, "Okay. I'll bite. Who called you?"

"Martina Angelino." There was a giggle of glee.

Kurt slipped the car back into park, "Angelino, the little girl?"

"Yep, and she said she could identify Ortiz's killers."

"Killers: like in plural?" He pictured two unknown faces.

"Sure thing, she says it was a man <u>and</u> a woman. She saw them just as they were coming out of the lobby."

"She's sure?" There was a note of confusion in his words.

"She seems to think so." John waited for a response, but it was apparent Kurt was digesting the information.

"I'm arranging for her to go through the mug books while she is at school. We'll put her and several others in separate rooms so it doesn't look like we know anything new."

"Mmmm." Nervously Kurt ran his hand from side to side on his steering wheel. "That should work okay, but I'm a little edgy about how her father is going to take this."

"He'll never know, Kurt."

"What if it goes to trial?"

John made a face, "Yeah, well, we'll just have to deal with that when, and if, it happens." He didn't really sound that confident about his statement. "You know it could turn out that The Baker is two people. That could explain the two murders on the same night."

"That's great, John, but if she is right they were still at the same apartment house at the same time on the same night."

"Okay, but one of them could have done the couple and then joined the other one at Ortiz's.

"Why…to share the same gun?" There was a bit of humorous sarcasm to his response.

"Remember, Kurt, the ballistics were all messed up. Who knows?

Kurt rolled his eyes and shook his head, "No wonder you're such a good detective, John. To you nothing is impossible." Kurt really meant it as a small token of praise.

John snickered, "I try, Kurt. Got to keep an open mind, buddy."

"The wind is whistling through yours." Kurt slipped his car into drive and began pulling into traffic. "Okay, I'll be into work early and we'll get the mug books all set up. Need any help?"

"Na, I've got it covered." John had a sudden thought; "I think it would be best if we didn't tell anyone about getting help from Martina."

"Good idea!" A car honked at him: it wanted his parking space. "See you in the a.m." He pulled into the traffic; his mind was on automatic as he sorted some of the possibilities. Her dad could be putting her up to this in order to frame someone else. Just why had she had a sudden change of heart? What if it turned out that Angelino had hired the job done? Maybe she did it. Where did The Baker fit into this mix? He smiled at the metaphor. One thing was for sure, it could be dangerous for Martina. If she were able to identify a contract killer, her father would be better able to protect her than the police would. A strange feeling came over him. It took him a few seconds to identify it: he was genuinely concerned about the little teen-ager.

Chapter forty-two:

The last few days had been crammed with excitement and busy work. Doris' relationship with Kurt was going well and she had made some interesting new friends in the Prices. Thelma had called and told her how much they had enjoyed meeting her and Kurt. She had especially enjoyed meeting Doris. They talked for almost an hour and both of them had been reluctant to hang up.

Last night Jolene and Doris had stayed up far too late for Jolene to take the evening buses home. It was not the first time she had stayed over; Doris had suspected it was because Jolene sometimes felt the need to be away from the noise of Andrew and Amy. Not that she didn't like kids, but she was single and sometimes, well, they just got on her nerves.

Doris was awakened by the attracting smell of frying bacon and brewed coffee. Normally she would have slept for several more hours, but she knew this was Jolene's way of getting her up for more girl talk. "You know that that is cheating, girl?"

Sporting a pleased smirk on her face, Jolene held out a cup of coffee. "Bacon will be done in ten minutes, it's baking. We'll have fried eggs, easy over for you, hard over for me." She gestured toward a white four-slice toaster, "And we'll have wheat toast on the side."

Taking the proffered cup, Doris ran her fingers through her tangled hair. A hearty yawn escaped before she could cover it, "Why are you up so early, Jo?" Doris plopped into a vinyl covered kitchen chair. She gestured with her coffee cup, and noted that Jolene was already dressed. "What's the occasion?"

Jolene turned her back to Doris and opened the oven door to attend to the crackling bacon. The movement and smell made Doris' mouth water. "Hey!" Doris raised her voice. "Where're you going?"

"Oh, I thought I'd catch the eight-thirty, and do some shopping at that new store over on 104th." She turned and smiled, "Want to come? It'll be fun."
Her eyes seemed to dance as she leaned her head forward and begged with her nodding head.

Doris sipped her coffee and said, "Gee, I'd love to, Jo, but I promised Kurt I would go with him to see his boat." She winced, "It's just a small speed boat, but he's proud of it. He wants a kind of picnic. We're not going out on the water or anything."

"Well, we could go shopping and be back here in time for you to go with him." Her voice was hopeful and almost pleading. "Come on, it's not very often we are off at the same time." She raised her eyebrows and smiled, "We could take your car."

Her face showed she was considering it, but she knew she would never make it back in time. "Na,

I'd just be a drag. I'd spend most of my time looking at my watch."

Jolene crinkled her nose and bobbed her head, "Yeah, you're probably right. You'd be a real drag."

Doris liked the way Jolene was always so perky and fun to be with. Vivacious is what most people called her. Even when they were doing autopsies, she sometimes pulled weird jokes. Like pulling out plastic wrapped ham sandwiches from the inside of a corpse "Look what he had for dinner she would quip." Doris never knew what Jolene would come up with next time.

Doris pointed to a small key rack on the wall of the kitchen, "Take my car. I won't need it. I have the day off and you won't be going into work until ten."

Jolene hesitated, "Go ahead…spend the day here. We'll be gone most of the day."

Jolene did one of her perky dances and gushed, "Thanks, Dot" She started pulling the bacon from the foil lined glass cooking-dish, "You know I was angling for that offer. Don't 'cha?" She looked over her shoulder and winked.

Doris ignored the mini-confession and said, "Just take the darn thing." In a faked stern voice, she growled, "And, bring me my breakfast!"

The meal was quickly consumed and then they settled into girl talk mainly about Kurt and how Jolene hoped she would find 'Mr. Right' someday.

"I can't say that our jobs make it easy to meet anyone but stiffs, Dot, but maybe I can find a good cop, lawyer, or someone who wanders into our dungeon."

Doris was watching a different Jolene. She was serious and she kept playing with her fork, a sure sign she was annoyed. "Maybe when we rotate back to days your luck will improve." Doris put a smile in her voice and said, "You'll be a fine catch for anyone, Jo."

Jolene wrinkled her forehead and asked, "You really mean that, Dot?"

"Yeah, sure I do. You're pretty. You're smart. And, lady, you are fun to be with!" Jolene gave her the response she wanted, she was grinning and seemed infused with a new surge of hope.

"Yeah, you're right." She jumped up and rushed over to Doris. Bending over she gave her a firm hug, sniffled and said, "I'd better get going."

"Wow. And I'd better get ready. Kurt could be here any minute." Doris gave Jolene a hug and said, "Have fun, and make sure you lock the car." Quickly her thoughts turned to finding an appropriate outfit to go 'boating' in cold weather.

"No problem." She went bounding for the hallway to put on one of Doris' warm coats. She pulled on one of Doris' wool caps and turned up her coat collar before she made her way to the outside entrance to the garage. It was situated just below Doris' bedroom.

Jolene held onto the railing as she waddled down the snow-covered stairs to the garage door. It had to be opened manually and it was heavy. Considering last night's snow it opened quite easily. Jolene whistled when she saw the white Toyota Camry. It wasn't the first time she had seen it, but she always admired it. The snowplows had not yet arrived so the few inches of fresh snow was not going to a problem to a girl who had grown up in Spokane, Washington. "Nice wheels!"

Traffic was light, and she quickly maneuvered the Toyota into it. The snowplow was just coming in her direction on the opposite side of the street. She glanced up at the morning sky and wiped away a thin layer of mist on the window. *Hope that mess the snowplow leaves melts before I get back.* She spotted some sun making its way through the eastern clouds.

At the next traffic light she turned on the radio and punched her way through Doris' preset buttons, none of them suited her: they were all to slow or too newsy. By the next traffic light she had found a station that fit her euphoric mood. Sun was out; she was driving a nice car: had a great friend. Life was good. No...life was great!

Thirty feet past the last light was the beginning of a steep hill often referred to as 'the run' because it reminded people of the bobsled runs at The Olympics. It was four and one half long blocks of snow covered steep city streets. Sometimes kids would rush at the street in order to become airborne and experience the thrills of a ride at Six Flags.

Jolene crossed the street toward 'the run'. At first the street seemed to disappear as the front of the car started down the hill. Just as she could see the street she began to smell a strong acidic odor: *Hydrofluoric Acid?* Her experienced nose kept sniffing in disbelief. She wrinkled her nose and her vision was beginning to blur from the pain. *It can't be!* She tried to look around in the car and still steer down the treacherous hill. Her body began to shake, as she was flooded with a mass of adrenalin. *I've got to pull over!*

Knowing she was on a steep hill which still had a thin layer of snow, she tried to keep her wits about her. Gently she applied her foot to the floor brake. Her heart seemed to stop and move up into her throat. Again she tried the brake; it went all of the way to the floor. Frantically she tried again and again. She had been so concerned about the brake she had not realized the car was now racing out of control. Faster and faster it was shooting down the hill as if it were an Olympic toboggan. Fighting for control, she tried the hand brake, but still nothing happened.

Ahead of her there were still three more blocks of snow-covered hill and then a small dock marking the end of a short section of Flat Street. The next block had a stoplight green. A tsunami of nausea crashed through her body as she saw the light change to yellow. There were three cars in front of her, no way to stop and their taillights just changed to red. Desperately she turned into the lanes on her left: the uphill lanes. She slid sidewise smacking the left rear end of the car in front of her. The maneuver allowed her to continue downhill, but it almost caused her to tip over and roll down the hill.

At the intersection, the runoff from the hill had helped the cars to be able to stop, but the crossroad cars were having trouble getting traction. She managed to get through the light but was tagged just as she crossed back into the correct lanes for going down the hill. Jolene recovered from the skid and bounced off of a parked car and careened back into a downhill lane. By now she was traveling so fast she did not dare even look at the speedometer. With some relief she realized she had passed the last stoplight, the other streets had stop signs. *God... don't let anyone run one of those signs!*

A strange feeling came over her as she began to watch everything as if it were in slow motion. Ahead of her she could see the end of the hill, but beyond it was the wooden dock and a solid beam of wood marking the end of the dock and the beginning of ice-cold water. No longer was she afraid of the icy hill as much as she was afraid of striking the end of the pier and, if she survived, plunging into the icy cold salt water: probably unconscious. She had seen bodies dragged from the sea. She had seen bodies dragged from car wrecks. She could not tell which she would prefer.

With a sudden jolt she reached the bottom of the hill, she fought for control. At this speed any attempt to turn would result in a quick crushing death as the car would roll over and possibly catch on fire. Jolene closed her eyes, as the car was moving at incredible speed.

She was surprised she felt nothing when the car stopped.

Chapter forty-three:

It was a habit developed over years of police work and being a third generation police officer. At first the noise of the sirens sounded like another routine fire or traffic emergency, but as he got closer Kurt realized the fire and smoke were coming from the pier just a block away. As he got closer he slowed down to see what was going on. His vision was partially blocked by a large fire truck and an emergency vehicle. A gust of wind pushed aside the smoke and he reacted with a sudden pain in his stomach. The white vehicle had evidently collided with the back end of a double tractor-trailer rig.

Fearing the worst, he put his portable dome light on the roof of his car and zigzagged through the traffic until he was close enough to stop and walk to the accident.   While he kept telling himself it couldn't be Doris' car because she was waiting for him to pick her up, some force seemed to be drawing him closer to the smudged white vehicle.

As he approached, he could hear the familiar sound of the 'jaws of life' hydraulics as two firemen were huddled together on the driver's side of the car. The car was pinned between the back end of a double trailer's second trailer and the

four-foot high wooden beam to the left of the one
on the seaside. The Camry was almost in the shape
of a capital letter 'L'.

Kurt coughed as he drew near the car, the thick
black smoke was whipping along at ground level,
but no flames could be seen. Flashing his badge,
he asked, "What 'cha got here?" The license plate
was dirty, but he was pretty sure it was Doris'. He
fought to remain calm, but his insides had turned
to a hard ball of twisted organs.

"Girl trapped inside. The smoke is coming from
a tire on the rear trailer."

Kurt hesitated. He was afraid to ask the crucial
question, "Is she alive?"

The fireman shook his head: Kurt's stomach
jumped. And then he said, "Yeah. You wouldn't
believe it." He stopped rolling the hose and
pointed at the trailer. "Talk about luck. They said
the car came screaming down the hill. Evidently
the brakes weren't working." Kurt barely heard
him as he had looked at the car and the men
working to get 'Doris' out of the car. "She hits the
beginning of the dock, headed straight for that
beam over there, when this rig backs up and she
hits it just enough to slow her down and push her
into the side rail instead of going for a cold swim.
As if ignoring the story Kurt asked, "But you said
she's alive." His eyes registered his concern.

Realization dawned on the face of the fireman, "Yeah." He hesitated and in a more compassionate tone asked, "She somebody to you?"

Kurt swallowed and fought back tears. He looked at the smoke as if to blame the black stuff for causing his eyes to water. "I think so. My girlfriend lives up there and drives a white Toyota Camry just like this one. "The fireman, attempting to make him feel better said, "Well, it's a pretty popular car, officer." He smiled, "Maybe it's not her." He went back to rolling the hose.

"Hey, Officer!"

Kurt kept his eyes on the car and spoke out of the side of his mouth. "What?"

"Try calling her!"

Chapter forty-four

The thought was so simple he wondered why it had escaped him. His cell-phone was inches away, but his hand would not move toward it. He wanted to know and yet he didn't. If it were good news then he would be happy, but what if she didn't answer, then he would be panicked. He had almost decided to use his phone when he saw the men withdraw a woman from the vehicle. He held up his badge as he moved closer to the gurney upon which they were placing the unconscious woman. He took in staggered breaths as he recognized the blood stained hat and coat.

Roughly, the Emergency Technicians pushed him aside as they maneuvered the gurney toward their truck. "Hey, Mack, get out of the way, will ya?" He grumbled some other words as they wheeled by.

Kurt looked down as they went by, he could not tell if it was Doris or not, but it must be he told himself. The hat, the car: the coat. "Sorry, guys, but I'd like to ride with you to the hospital."

"Yeah, sure." was the surly response.

"She's my girlfriend." He showed his badge.

The driver stepped in front of him, "Look, officer. They're going to have to work on her from here to the hospital." He jumped up into the truck, "The best thing you can do is to let them do their job."

Reluctantly he backed off, "I'm parked over there."

"Follow us." The driver heard the back doors close, "Got a red light?"

Kurt just nodded and turned toward his car.

Questions and something to watch had held back his anxiety, but now he was inundated with fears and doubts. *What did he mean they would have to work on her from here to the hospital? Did they think she wasn't going to make it?* By the time he reached his car, the ambulance was already well on its way through the traffic. Kurt fired up his dome light and pulled away from the curb. Even with his red light flashing, he was going to have a tough time keeping up. He looked at his hands; they were trembling and his knuckles were white from his rigid grip on the wheel. He was somewhere between tears and despair.

Between concentrating on his driving and the frantic thoughts flitting through his mind, he was confused when he felt his cell-phone vibrate against his chest. He was in no mood to answer the irritating instrument, but by habit he reached into his inside pocket and pressed 'select', "Yeah?" His voice was distant and it was obvious he was annoyed at the intrusion into his life at this time of crisis.

Caught off guard the voice asked, "Catch you at a bad time?"

Kurt pulled the phone from his ear and looked at it. His senses refused to believe he had just heard Doris' voice. He wanted to be happy, but his mind fought against the possibilities. "Doris?" His tone was slow and bewildered.

Not knowing why Kurt sounded the way he did, she responded in kind, "Yeah?" She hesitated and took time to blink and register a face of confusion. "What's wrong? Are you on a case?"

Kurt slowed down and headed for a parking spot. His nerves were firing so hard they overpowered the frantic pounding of his heart. "Oh! Thank God. Thank God."

"Kurt, what's wrong?" Now there was alarm in her voice. She repeated, "What's wrong!"

He was struggling to control his body and his emotions. Slowly he spoke in measured words, "I was at a car accident. I thought it was you." He took a deep breath to try and calm his speech.

Her tone was loaded with compassion as she assured him, "Well, it wasn't. I'm here, at home: waiting." It now occurred to her why he had sounded so strange. He loved her. "It must have been awful for you."

He wasn't sure what words to say so he just said, "I love you, Doris. I don't know what I'd do if anything happened to you."

Even though she liked hearing the words, she would rather he were there in person so she could hold him and savor the moment. "I love you too, Kurt, and I'm right here, safe and sound."

"Thank God" he repeated. "It's just that there were so many similarities. The car was a white

Toyota Camry and the woman driving had on a coat and hat just like yours."

She smiled as she pretended to chide him, "Really, Kurt, you of all people should know there are thousands of cars just like mine and my hat and coat are quite stylish." She laughed at his silliness. Her eyes moved to her coat rack and abruptly she stopped laughing. Audibly she sucked in a shallow gulp of air. Her hand flew to her mouth, "Oh, my God!"

"What?" He thought she was being attacked or something.

"Jolene!" Her eyes searched around the room as if hoping it were not true. Again she looked at the coat rack by the door. Maybe she had put her hat and coat someplace else. "Jolene borrowed my car."

"When?" he waited.

"Ah, ah, about forty or forty-five minutes ago." She sounded addled.

"Would she have gone down 'The Run'?" He closed his eyes knowing what the answer would be.

"Yes. Why?"

He tried to turn the thoughts, "Well, she's alive: if it's her." He paused and then explained, "I was following the ambulance when you called me." Again he tried to calm her down. "You know,

Doris, it might not be her. After all, I thought it was you and it wasn't." He knew it was a weak argument, but it was the best he could do.

"What are we going to do?" His tone was a blend of fear and confusion.

He thought about the wise words given to him by the fireman, "Does she have a cell?"

"No, she doesn't believe in them."

"Okay, I'll call emergency services and get her name and the license plate on the car."

A thought suddenly occurred to her. "She asked me to go with her. Maybe if I had been driving, it wouldn't have happened, or maybe I should have let her take the bus."

All Kurt could hear was her sobbing and more self-incriminations. He waited until she calmed down and then he said, "I'll be right there, Doris."

Morton Filman was somewhat disappointed as he watched the white Toyota plunged into the truck and jack-knife. His plan had been for him to tail the car until, as it started to go down the hill, electronically detonate a small charge that would shatter a glass container of hydrofluoric acid. It would eat through the fluid line to the master brake cylinder and release all of the brake fluid. As a backup he had also placed a small charge that stopped the car's hand brake from working. There was absolutely no reason why the car should not have been mangled by the beam at the end of the dock. Then the car should have gone into the bay and destroyed most of the evidence that it had been messed with.

Filman was being jostled about in the crowd as he attempted to see if Doris Mercer was dead or just seriously injured. It was hard for him to control his rage when he saw the gurney was carrying a lady who was not in a body bag. He watched as Kurt was talking to the fireman and the ambulance driver, but he was unable to elbow his way through the crowd to his car and follow the ambulance.

He closed the door to his car and slammed both hands on the steering wheel. He still could not believe that, at the last second, that truck had backed up right in front of the Toyota. "It's not possible!" he screamed. He started the car and pulled out in front of one that had to brake and slide to keep from hitting him. Flipping on the radio, he searched for news of the accident and where she might have been taken. He felt cheated. He had done everything right, she should be dead. He had earned his money, only a freaky thing had happened to rob him of his earnings.

Driving in the same direction the ambulance had traveled, he listened to the heater as it forced hot air into the car. The windshield wipers labored to move the snow off of the windshield, but it was

piling up on each side of the window. If she lived
he would have to come up with a plan to
complicate her recovery.

Believing it was most likely thcy took her to the
Good Samaritan Hospital located downtown, he
turned and headed south at the next block. Almost
unaware he was even driving, his rage began to
assuage. Morton was within sight of the hospital
when a strange, but not unfamiliar, feeling began
to nag at his mind. *If they examine the car, and
they probably will, they will be able to tell that the
car's breaks had been tampered with.* The thought
caused him to look into his rear-view mirrors as if
they were already hunting for him. Impulsively he
changed directions and began to drive away from
the hospital. *I better go check on Betty; she might
have heard something on the radio or TV.*

Chapter forty-five:

While driving toward Doris' house, Kurt called
into headquarters and asked for his partner, John
Miller. It took only a few moments for a jovial
voice to come on the line.

Kurt heard the sound of the phone as John picked it up and began lecturing him, "Hey, Kurt, thought you were out showing off that excuse for a boat of yours."

"Something came up. You hear about the crash at 'The Run'?"

"Sure, everyone has." John's voice turned serious, "Someone you know?" he asked gingerly.

"We think it was Doris's friend, Jolene Talbot. You know the one who works in the lab with Doris."

"That cute little thing who always smells like formaldehyde?" It was not a joke: he was seeking clarification.

Kurt powered his car through the mound of snow left by the snowplow and pulled into the driveway in front of Doris' house. He could barely see the car tracks made by the Toyota. Looking out of the windshield, up to his left, he could see Doris looking down at him from her living room. Even from that distance he could tell she was crying. He was still talking as he opened his car door, "Yeah, that's her: Jolene. See what you can find out about her condition and call me, I'll be at Doris'."

"Sure thing," Kurt could hear John making notes. "Tell Doris I'm sorry about her friend."

"Yeah, will do," He snapped his cell-phone closed and reached for the doorbell.

Doris pulled open the door before his finger could push the bell. Still in her slippers she stepped into the snow and rushed into Kurt's consoling arms. "Oh, Kurt, I feel so bad. So guilty! I never should have let her use my car."

Her words were muffled into the thickness of his wool overcoat.

With her arms still around him he held her tightly and lifted her enough to take her out of the snow, across the threshold and into the house. With his foot he closed the door. Slowly he pulled his head back from her and smiled, "You'll catch you death out there, Dot." He used his knuckle to dab at a tear forming at the corner of her eye. "Dot, these things happen. She must have lost control on the snow, or hit an icy spot. Those things happen." He kissed her forehead, "It's not your fault."

She was shaking her head, "I should have gone with her."

He dropped his grip and removed his overcoat. With his arm around her shoulder he guided her toward the couch. They sat down. "It wouldn't have made any difference. You can't torture yourself this way."

She blew her nose and stared at her knees. "I don't expect you to fix it, Kurt." She turned her head and looked into his sympathetic eyes. "I just need to talk about it. Okay?"

He returned a small smile of understanding as he remembered his mother telling his dad the same thing. "Sure. I understand."

It was well into the afternoon and Doris and Kurt were at the kitchen table nursing cups of coffee when they were stopped mid-sentence when Doris' phone rang.

At first Doris registered a questioning look, and then she said, "I'll bet it's the lab. I should have told them about Jolene's accident." She got up from the table and crossed to the kitchen wall to the left of the sink.

Kurt replied, "I told John to call me here. He's checking on Jolene."

Nodding her understanding, she picked up the cordless phone, "Hello." With a pained expression on her face she extended the phone toward Kurt, "It's for you. It's John." She put her teeth into her lower lip.

"What cha got?" His eyes wandered about as he listened. Then he locked eyes with Doris and whispered, "It's her. She's banged up, but they think she'll pull through." He returned his attention to the phone, "Okay, that's great. Thanks. Keep me posted." Pause, "Yeah."

Doris took the phone from his hand and studied his expression. "What's wrong?" Cautiously she asked, "Is there something you're not telling me?"

Kurt took a deep breath and sighed, "I don't know." He looked at her. She saw his expression change so that his forehead was wrinkled and his eyelids were flickering. They locked eyes, "John said she's not really gained consciousness, but she had kept muttering something about the brakes not working." He stared blankly as if expecting an answer from her.

Putting her hand over her mouth she muttered, "That doesn't make sense. It's practically a new car, Kurt."

"Maybe the brakes got wet." He proffered.

"On a Toyota, I don't think so, Kurt. The car has been in my garage all night and it's not that wet out there." She grabbed her coffee cup from the table and held it as if it would warm her hands and give her some comfort.

Kurt asked, "When was it last serviced?"

She started to feel as if he were accusing her of vehicular neglect, but calmed herself as she replied, " Month ago, maybe six weeks. Certainly not long enough for there to be a problem."

He shrugged and tossed his head as if to shake off the confusion, "Anyway, the police lab team will go over the car to check it out." He gave her a look of assurance, "If there's anything funny, they'll find it." Again he shrugged and smiled, "At least they think she's going to be okay. Let's go by later and see if she is conscious."

Doris sank into her kitchen chair and closed her eyes. Sighing with relief, gently she rocked back and forth while her eyes began to mist over. "I guess I had better call the morgue and tell them she won't be in for a while." Her words had a double meaning. She would not be into work and they would not be working on her corpse.

Chapter forty-six:

After parking in the hospital's underground parking lot, Kurt and Doris walked to the nearest elevator; their footsteps echoing against the gray concrete walls, the smell of wet concrete casually invaded their nostrils. Even on the elevator they were quiet, each occupied with their own thoughts about Jolene's accident. The doors parted and the odor changed to the smell of food from the nearby cafeteria. Standing next to the reception desk was John Miller; he raised his hand in order to attract their attention.

Kurt looked around at the swarms of people, "Anything new, John?"

John hesitated and looked at Doris, "Let's talk." He grabbed Kurt by the shoulder and led him toward a small alcove, "The crime boys don't think it was an accident. The brakes had been tampered with. Some kind of chemical was used to eat through the brake system. It was almost immediate."

Pressing his lips together, Kurt nodded and said, "I'm not really surprised. Well, maybe not really surprised is a little bit too strong, but we had a guy tell us someone was following Doris. I guess it was more serious than we had thought."

John looked puzzled, "You had a guy tell you someone was tracking Doris? Who was he?"

"An elderly guy who works as an investigating actuary: he's a freelance agent named Richard Price." Kurt told him the rest of the story about how Richard happened to notice the man shadowing Doris.

Noticing Doris was getting annoyed, John nodded toward Doris, "I think she's getting a bit irritated, Kurt."

Doris watched as Kurt and John approached her; she was looking for clues about their hush-hush conversation. "Anything I should know about?" she tensed, prepared for bad news.

Kurt looked at John and then turned to Doris, "It appears your friend was right. Remember Mr. Price was concerned someone was following you?"

She nodded, but was wondering where the conversation was going.

"The brakes were tampered with. Since they could not have known Jolene was going to be driving the car, we have to assume the 'accident' was meant to harm you." Kurt watched to see how she would take the news.

"So Jolene was just an innocent victim?" Her words were tainted with guilt.

John answered, "It looks that way, Doris, but the Crime Unit isn't through with their analysis."

Kurt put his arms around her, "It wasn't your fault, Doris. It was the people who did this are to blame. You've got to get that straight in your head or it will eat you alive."

"I know what you're saying is true, Kurt, but if I hadn't loaned her the car she would be safe at home." All pretenses at holding back her tears ended and she began sobbing out loud. Strangely no one seemed to pay any attention to her crying, after all she was in a hospital and it was a common sound.

Eager to distract her from her self-inflicted guilt, Kurt suggested, "Let's get upstairs and check on Jolene."

During the ascent to the third floor, everyone in the elevator avoided eye contact or any form of communication. The familiar sounds of the doors opening and closing: the whirring of the cables moving the car up and down, even the dinging announcing a new floor had been reached, all went unnoticed. Minds were focused upon the condition of their loved ones and the consequences to their own lives.

The parting of the doors brought in new sounds and smells. A medical odor dominated by isopropyl alcohol and cleaning agents, alerted their senses to where they were. The floor seemed almost deserted as they made their way to Jolene's room. Outside of her room was a patrolman who was sitting and drinking a cup of coffee from a paper cup; a rumpled magazine was in his lap.

John spoke out of the side of his mouth as he explained, "I had a cruiser drop off an officer to keep watch on the room. I could be wrong, you know. They might have been after Jolene, or still think it is Doris in there." John walked over to converse with the guard.

The door to Jolene's room opened and a man dressed in doctor's clothes came out, "May I help you?" He shifted his eyes as if he were suspicious of them. "I'm sorry, but no one from the press is permitted on this floor."

Kurt flashed his badge, "I'm Lieutenant Millhouse, and that big gentleman over there is Lieutenant Miller. We are investigating the accident as a possible attempted murder. This is Dr. Mercer, our M.E., and a friend of Jolene Talbot."

Bobbing his head in understanding, he turned to address Dr. Mercer. "Her injuries are mostly internal, but she did suffer a broken leg. At the moment we have her stabilized, but as soon as we can get her strength back, we need to do more extensive testing."

Carefully, Doris lifted the chart from the Doctor's hands. "So you expect her to live?"

"Oh, most certainly, but we will know better when she becomes conscious." Politely, the Doctor retrieved his clipboard. "I'm sorry, Doctor, but it is against hospital policy to allow non-staff persons to examine medical records. I'm sure you understand." The doctor shifted his eyes to see if the officer was going to cause any problems.

"Here's my card, doc. Let me know the minute she can be interviewed by us." He looked around the hallway. "Has anyone else been here to see her or call about her condition?"

Shaking his head he said, "No one has been to see her, but someone, a man I believe, called to ask about the lady who was in the accident at the wharf. I thought he was a reporter. I only told him she was in critical but stable condition."

"Did he give a name?"

"No...not that I recall."

"Okay, but if anyone else calls get a name and don't give out her condition. She may have been the victim of foul play." Kurt waited for the doctor to respond. "Understand?"

"Yeah...sure;" The doctor looked around the hallway and whispered, "Are we in some kind of danger here?" He furrowed his forehead.

"Not really. Just do as we ask and everything will be fine." Kurt turned on his heels and tugged Doris with him. "I guess we'll have to wait to talk to Jolene, but my guess is she won't be able to tell us much." He stopped and turned to face Doris, "Now, my dear, the question is—why would someone want you either injured or dead?"

Doris struggled to laugh; "You don't really think someone wants me dead, do you?" Her countenance indicated she wanted a 'no' answer.

"Sorry, but it looks that way." Attempting to turn from a familiar to a professional attitude, he asked, "Are you working on any sensitive cases?"

She made a face, "The Baker." Of course he knew that.

"But have you or Jolene got any information you haven't passed on to us?" Quickly he recalled Captain Won's question, 'Who is leaking information?' "Have either of you discussed The Baker case with anyone other than us?"

"No…of course not;" She was feeling irritated and her tone showed it.

Ignoring her hurt feelings, Kurt asked, "Okay, how about Jolene?"

"I wouldn't know, but I don't think so."

Making a mental note he said, "Okay, we'll look into that." He was about to hold off on the questioning when he asked, "Owe any money?"

"No!"

"Any enemies you know of?"

"No, just a few irate people who didn't want their friends or family members cut up." She rolled her eyes, "No, no one." The edge in her voice was unmistakably defensive.

Kurt was going through his usual list of questions, "How about insurance? Anybody profit from your death?"

"No!" She tipped her head to the side, "Only the Key Man policies that all of us doctors at the clinic have."

Kurt acted mildly interested, "How much and who is the beneficiary?"

Casually she said, "Five million and the clinic gets the dough."

"Huh." He considered asking a few more questions, but John was headed their way so he leaned close and kissed her, "You be careful. Do you hear? I think this may be more serious than either of us think, so trust me."

Chapter forty-seven:

Morton Filman crept into the room. He could see her breathing was fast, but regular: she was asleep. Slowly he approached the bed and bent over to study her face, she was pale and her forehead was moist. He felt the back of her neck: it was like ice. He was surprised when a rush of fear shot through his body. The shot Dr. Bick had given her had seemed to help, but now, for the first time he began to fear his Betty was going to die.

Retreating to his stained and lumpy overstuffed chair, he sat and looked at her. There was no doubt but what he had not been a good 'husband' to Betty. He should not have sent her out to the phone booth the other night: it had been cold and windy.

For years she had tried to get him to quit their life of crime and settle down and raise a family. He had refused for the most pitiful of reasons, changing his excuses to fit any argument she could give. He had cheated on her, lied to her, and made her live in some of the most poverty infested places in the city. Now she was seriously ill, he was weighted down with unbearable guilt. He leaned forward and placed his face into his shaking palms. Startled by the vibration of his cell-phone, he bolted from his chair and rushed into the bathroom. After fumbling to get his phone from his shirt pocket, he pressed 'select' and softly said, "Yes?"

The voice on the other end was muffled. It spoke in a staccato fashion as it said, "The Angelino girl identified you, Morton."

"When?"

"At her school;" There was a pause, "This morning."

"Are you sure she said it was me?" Morton was hoping for a negative answer.

"Actually she picked out three pictures, but you were one of them." The voice said. "I think it is only a matter of time now. They'll be wanting to talk to you."

His heart was racing. How many things could go wrong in one day? He furrowed his brow as he asked, "How do you know this?"

There was a brief silence and the sound of crying. "I came down to the police station to check on Jolene. She was in a serious car accident. They don't think it was an accident and they wondered if I knew anyone who wanted her hurt."

Brushing aside her words, he said, "And?"

"I was talking to Detective Miller, he works with Detective Millhouse, Dr. Mercer's friend. You know the one who is going out----"

"What makes you think the Angelino girl picked me out?" His tone was edgy and irritated. He was getting angry, "How?"

"I was sitting beside his desk when the three pictures were given to him. I saw your picture along with the other two. The officer who handed him the pictures said, 'The Angelino girl picked these three. She's not sure which one, but she thinks it was one of these three that did Ortiz.'" Her tone changed to one of disappointment, "You never told me you had trouble with the police."

Ignoring her disappointment, he said, "It was nothing. Where are you now?"

"I'm at home. Amy and Andrew should be home pretty soon. They're out with grandpa."

"Okay. We need to talk. Can you get out tonight?" Morton opened the bathroom door just enough to check on Betty. She was still in the bed; her back was to him.

"Sure. I want to see Jolene at the hospital. I can meet you there." There was a touch of suspicion in her speech. "Did you get the money yet?"

"Yeah, I got the money." His words were flat and unfeeling.

"You said we could leave for Florida if you did this favor for that man." Meekly she asked, "Was that Mr. Ortiz really that bad?"

Nervously he replied, "Yeah. He was that bad. He raped young girls."

"Oh!"

"I told you that last time, Carla."

"I guess I forgot."

"Look I got to go now. I better not meet you at the hospital; it's too public for now. There's a Denny's about a block west of there."

"Oh, yes, I know the place. I often go there for their pies. They're really good."

Mentally he flinched, "Okay. Ten?"

"If I can't be there I'll call you."

With a hint of a threat he said, "Be there."

"I'm sure grandpa will be glad to take care of the kids. I'll ask him when he gets back."

194

"Ten." He terminated the call and peeked out the door. Betty was still asleep. He walked to the kitchen and poured himself a drink of whiskey, but changed his mind. *I need to keep my head clear. What am I going to do about this ditz?* Something she had said began to force itself into his thoughts. *'Jolene was in a car accident.'* His mind began to struggle with the possibility.

 "There is no way that could have been anyone but that Doc in the car." He spoke out loud. He downed his drink with one swallow. Nothing was going right. The Angelino girl had fingered him. That meant Mr. Angelino would be after him so he couldn't implicate him. His wife was sick and possibly dying. He might have got the wrong woman and lost out on his fifty thousand dollar fee. And now he had this dumb widow after him. She knew too much, but he really didn't want to kill her. He poured himself another drink and turned to watch the flashing of the neon sign: it's pink and green invaded the room like flashing lights from a UFO. For the first time in his life he began to feel the impact of fear: his hand trembled as he moistened his lips with the amber liquid.

 While it was possible Angelino would lose interest in him if he left the country, it was unlikely. The fact he could tell his daughter her father paid for the hit was not a risk he would probably take. As long as the police had thought The Baker had killed Ortiz, Morton was no real threat, but now the police would be looking for him. He couldn't run and leave his wife Betty alive: she would talk. Glancing in her direction his body seemed to move of its own accord: he walked to the edge of her bed and looked down at her. His cold hand touched her forehead and she moaned and attempted to roll her head away from the freezing object. She had stopped sweating, but her head was still feverish.

Options! Options! There must be something I can do.

Morton began pacing and sipping his drink. From one end of the room to the other he walked and sipped, even after his glass was empty. Almost in mid- stride, he halted and nodded to himself. He knew what he was going to do. Placing his empty glass on the rubber pad covering the draining board of the sink, he began to collect a few personal items and place them in a bag. Quickly he searched through Betty's purse and removed her phone book and cell-phone.

As he closed the door to his apartment, he pulled his collar tightly against his face and buttoned his old navy pee-coat. The door opened at the bottom of the stairs and a cold breeze slipped inside as if to warm itself in the radiator- heated hallway. The

odor of alcohol and stale cigarettes, stirred by the
cold air, offended his nostrils and started his nose
to run. Morton eyed the man who was standing at
the bottom of the stairs; he was a drunk who often
slept under the stairwell of the hotel.

"Cold out there, Harvey?"

The old man wiped his red and swollen eyes and
blinked, "Yeah, but it's that damned wind that's
really nasty." Betty had said the man had
evidently had a good education; she wondered
what happened to him. It was hard to take him
seriously when one looked at his swollen face and
missing teeth.

"Going for a bottle, Betty needs a hot toddy."
Again Morton looked at him, but then he shook his
head and opened the door. Amidst the sound of
rustling newspaper and the old man's coughing,
Morton ducked his head into the wind and closed
the door. Using one hand to hold his collar
together, he looked up and down the snow covered
street. In some spots the manhole covers had
melted the snow and wisps of vapor floated up
until they were caught by the marauder wind.

Across the street he spied what he was looking
for. With no traffic moving up and down the street,
he easily made his way to the empty building
covered with large pieces of age-grayed plywood.
Around the back he could smell the remaining

embers from a fire that had been burning in a fifty-gallon drum. Pushing aside a four by eight-foot piece of plywood he made his way into the darkness. Carefully he walked around the puddles and objects strewn about the concrete floor. In one corner he saw a candle burning: it was close to going out.

"Percy…you in there?" Morton asked as he kicked the edge of a large triangular piece of cardboard. "Percy?"

"Who's asking?" Came the slurred reply.

"It's me, Perc."

Chapter forty-eight:

"Who the hell is 'me'?" A bearded face squinted up at him.

"Bob. From across the street," he whispered.

"Oh…oh, yeah." The man started to wiggle out of his water-stained cardboard cocoon "Got a drink?"

"Sure, but I need a favor, Percy."

The young man shrugged, and then narrowed his eyes suspiciously. He sniffed and wiped his nose on the sleeve of his khaki parka. "Jesus, Bob, I just got settled for the night. Man, it's cold out there."

"I got some heavy things I need to move around in my room. It won't take five minutes, Percy."

The drunk waved him off and said, "I ain't doing no house work. 'Specially when it's so damned cold out." He started back into his box.

"Okay. Okay! I just thought I'd like to move some things around and I thought of you 'cuz I just opened a bottle of Jack." Morton turned and started to walk away. Behind him he heard a cough.

"Ah, well, I guess I could help for a few minutes." He was grunting as he slid out of the box and got to his feet, "I don't want to seem un-friendly there." He moved over next to Morton, "But just for a few minutes. I got to get my beauty sleep, ya know." He laughed and his stale breath caused Morton to make a face and turn his head.

Together the men made their way over to the hotel. Morton opened the door and quickly the two men charged inside. Morton held up his finger indicating they needed to be quiet. He listened and watched to make sure no one had seen them enter the building.

"Nice place you got here." Percy whispered as he looked around the room. Morton closed the door behind them. "Warm, too."

Morton indicated that Percy should sit in his overstuffed chair. "I'll get us some drinks before we go to work."

"Yeah, sure;" Percy settled back into the chair and said, "No water, Bob. It's a horrible thing to do to good liquor."

Morton poured two drinks. His he put in a dark amber glass: his drink was mostly water. Percy's drink was almost a water glass full of straight whiskey. "Here ya go, Perc." Morton gestured a toast. After two more filled glasses, Percy was fast asleep in the big chair.

Working as quickly and silently as he could, he stripped the clothes from the drunk. With some effort he put his bathrobe on the slumbering man and added his slippers. Placing the bottle next to Percy, he put a spilled glass on the floor. By now his heart was beating fast, his palms were moist with sweat and his breathing was shallow and audible.

Betty was still asleep when he picked up his bag and dropped it beside the door. Placing his hot plate on the radiator, just below the yellowed curtains, he put on a pan that contained a dash of cinnamon and an inch of water. He placed the hot plate on 'high' and retreated toward the door. After one final glance around the room, he closed the door and sighed.

After the fire they'll think Betty and I died in a fire, then I'll make my way to Mexico. Angelino and the police won't waste time looking for a dead man.

With catlike stealth, Morton made his way down the hall. His heart was pounding with fear that someone would recognize him and blow the whole thing. Working his way down the stairs, he tiptoed his way to the door. 'Homeless' was sleeping under the stairs; he hoped the man would remember he said he was going out for a bottle. Swiftly he opened the door and closed it before the cold wind would wake him up.

From a set of blurry eyes, the homeless man peeked over the comic section of the newspapers. Trying to clear his eyes he squeezed them together and peered at the man who fluttered his papers. *I thought he already got his bottle.*
Using the sports section, he patched an open spot and closed his eyes.

Upstairs, the water was boiling, sending a sweet smell of cinnamon into the damp air. Abruptly, the water disappeared and the pot began to turn a peculiar shade of gray and then black. In seconds the glowing surface of the hot plate turned the pot into a combustible liquid that responded with a miniature explosion. Almost instantly the flames ate their way up the curtains and began to flow across the ceiling.

The man in the chair stirred. His eyes fluttered but he seemed powerless to understand the strange sight above him. He closed his eyes and snorted as the smoke began to burn his lungs.

In the corner, Betty coughed and threw back the covers, the room was becoming hot. "Morton, open the window. It's too hot." She thought she heard him answer, but it was the rapid choking of Percy Maxoff.

Chapter forty-nine:

Harold Zane glanced at his watch: it was one-thirty. He was seated behind a glass display case that sporadically displayed various dust-covered models of handguns, knives, and Ninja weapons. A vintage silver cash register rested on the top of the glass case. He stretched his neck in an effort to look toward the door. "Late again," he mumbled. Tossing aside a dog-eared issue of <u>Guns,</u> he stood up and stretched. Again he looked at his watch, "Carla is really going to be p.o.ed". In an effort to relieve the tension he began to pace about the

Military Surplus store, mindlessly his eyes glanced about the various displays of clothing, weapons, and military equipment. Faintly, in the background, he could hear the police scanner chattering; they were talking about a fire at a hotel located in the run-down part of the city center. It was the address that caused him to quickly move toward the shelf where the scanner was always kept.

Two bells that hung over the front door served as an alert someone was entering or leaving the shop. The bells sent out a non-musical announcement someone had just entered. "Sorry about being so long, Zane, but I was--"

Harold Zane held up his hand indicating that Pete Corbin should stop talking. Pete listened to the scanner.

"That's what I was going to tell you. I think that's Filman's place, isn't it?"

With tight lips and narrowed eyes, Harold shot a look of disapproval. Mumbling some choice words, Pete shrugged and made his way behind the cloth curtain separating the store from 'the office'.

Finally satisfied, Harold nodded and spoke to Pete, "Yeah, that's what I was thinking. Where did you hear about it?"

"On the car radio: they talked about the fire. I guess it's a doosie." Pete set down a small grease-stained brown bag. "They think it got started in one of the upstairs apartments. Probably a couple…dead."

"What side of the building?"

"Huh?'

"On what side of the building did the fire start?" Harold realized he was speaking too loudly. "Sorry, I'm a little short; I promised Carla I'd watch the kids." He glanced at his watch, "Which side?" he asked more calmly.

Making an exaggerated smiley face, Pete said, "Don't know, Buddy." Patting Harold on the back he continued, "Sorry I was so late. You better get going."

Without comment, Harold grunted and grabbed up his coat. The bells rang as he opened the door. Pete shouted, "Say 'hello' to Andy and Amy!"

Harold grunted and dashed out to the snow packed sidewalk. *That damned fire might have really messed up my stuff. Why couldn't it have waited for a few more days? Maybe it didn't get to Morton's apartment.*

When he reached his car he brushed the snow from the windows and dropped inside. *I'm gonna be late, but I've got to check this thing out.* His tires had trouble getting traction, but he managed to pull a U-Turn and head for the hotel. Ten minutes later he was struggling to find a parking

place because of the fire trucks, emergency
vehicles and TV news trucks. Sloshing his way up
the opposite side of the street, he elbowed his way
through the huddled crowd.

"What happened?" he asked one of the strangers
who was next to him.

"Bad fire!" She pointed to the upper level, "They
think it started in that place there." Gesturing with
her finger she asked, "See that place there: where
all of the black is above the window?"

"Yeah."

"That's it." She turned her head and looked up at
Harold, "A couple burned to death. They took
them away just a few minutes ago."

As casually as he could he asked, "So who were
they?"

This time the girl looked up at him as if she were
studying him, "You know someone in there?"

"No, just curious."

"You're not from around here." As if hoping to
be interviewed she asked,   "Are you a reporter or
something?"

"No just passing by."

She smiled and teased, "You want to buy me a
drink?" Receiving no answer she said, "It's really
cold out here."

It was a familiar feeling. A hot flow seemed to
surge through his body and abruptly he was

looking at her in a different way. Like a giant eraser, his mind began to rub away all sense of reason and rational. Swiftly his thoughts processed his options. He had placed his murder weapon in Morton's apartment along with several sacks of his brand of flour. He would have tipped off the police, but then maybe they would find those things when they investigated the fire. They should have deduced that Morton was The Baker, and then he would be free to live a 'normal life', but now he was faced with the urge to help this urchin to get rid of her miserable life.

"I don't think I have enough time. Maybe some other time." he answered.

"Hey, I live just around the corner." She snuggled up and pressed her body against him. "I'll buy you a drink." She winked and said, "I can be real hospitable."

"Maybe just for a short one." Again the fire within surged.

As they slipped their way through the crowd, he glanced over his shoulder as if to be able to predict what the police would find. Inside himself he made one decision: The Baker was dead.

She led him down the darkening street. While they passed a lot of people eager to gawk at the fire, no one seemed to pay any attention to them. Around the corner was a small apartment house that once was a private home. The front door was set at the top of a flight of ten concrete steps worn down to the point where they had been patched so many times it was difficult to tell which concrete was the original.

Pausing at the base of the stairs, she pointed up to the top left side of the building. "That's my place." She tightened her grip on his arm, "I live alone."

He nodded, but said nothing.

"My Mom told me I shouldn't pick up strangers, but, you know, I have really met some of the nicest people I know that way." She slipped her key into the weathered brass lock and cocked her head to one side. Looking up at him she asked, "You are a nice guy, aren't you?"

Behind his generous smile he could feel surges of anxiousness pulsing through his tense body, "Can't you tell?" He winked at her.

She laughed.

***

"What I can't understand is why anyone would want to kill you." Kurt accepted the cup of hot coffee. "Most of the time these things boil down to jealousy or money." He paused before he asked, "Is there someone that might feel jealous about you?"

Doris Mercer made a face displaying disgust with the question, "Don't be silly. I haven't had time to become romantically involved, and I'm not after anyone's husband." Squirming deeper into the large overstuffed chair, she looked across at him and continued, "You're the closest thing I've come to, if we're talking about being romantically involved." She tilted her head down and sipped at her heavily creamed coffee. Her eyes floated up as she looked at him, "I suppose I should be asking you. Got any jealous girlfriends?"

Kurt smirked, "None I can speak of," he chided.

"Hey, I'm serious here." She growled

"So am I." He shrugged, "Who's got the time?"

Doris studied the man sitting across from her. Did she really know him? Maybe he was just some kind of flirt who jumped from one woman to another. Perhaps she had overestimated her value to him. "I thought we were making the time."

Kurt wanted to kick himself; he had forgotten how sensitive women could be. "Now don't go all paranoid on me, Doris. I feel badly enough because I'm glad it was Jolene and not you in your car. I will never be able to tell you how panicked I was when I thought I had lost you." He set down his coffee cup and stood up. The movement was obvious; he was going to come over to her chair.

The sound of the front door chimes stopped Kurt;
he looked down at Doris, "Expecting anyone?"
 She shook her head, but got up to join him in
going to the front door. When they got close to the
door she looked at him. Her expression asked,
"What shall I do?"

Holding her back he pulled his weapon from the
black leather shoulder holster. Carefully he moved
to the peephole and instantly started to put away
his nine-millimeter Glock. "It's John." As if to
make sure she understood him, he repeated, "You
know. John Miller, my partner."

Thinking about the apology she was about to get
she put on a tolerant grin and nodded, "Yes, Kurt. I
know who he is."

As the door swung open, both Kurt and Doris
were startled to see a large German Sheppard
sitting on the stoop. In spite of the cold, he was
panting. His long tongue flopped to one side, and
his mouth seemed set in a perpetual smile. His
white teeth, set against a jet-black coat, sparkled
like miniature elephant tusks. They both looked up
at John: they weren't sure they should move.

John displayed his obvious pleasure with their
discomfort, "Hi. Meet Max." Gripping the dog's
leash, he barged past the two 'statues', "Actually
he prefers his full name, Max-a-million. We stole
the name from a credit union, but we doubt that

they'll mind." He gave Max a hand gesture and the dog sat next to the couch, "Coffee smells good. Got an extra cup?"

Doris folded her arms and narrowed her eyes. Kurt closed the door and asked, "Is it okay for us to move?"

Nonchalantly, John glanced at the attentive dog. "Oh, you mean Max."

"We don't mean you." Doris answered as she headed for the kitchen.

"He's harmless! He just looks scary!" John shouted after her.

Kurt walked over to the dog and offered his hand. The dog sniffed it and covered it with an affectionate coating of dog saliva. Kurt responded by gently rubbing the tips of the dog's ears. "He's a department dog, isn't he?"

"Used to be, but he got shot and almost died. Look there, just in front of his left hindquarter. Ugly scar."

Kurt moved his hand toward the scar. Max responded by turning his head and fixing his eyes on Kurt. "I think I'll take your word for it."

Doris brought out a cup of coffee and offered it to John. "Black?"

"Is there any other kind?"

Doris studied the dog, "You say he used to be a department dog. What is he now?"

John gave the dog another hand motion and Max stretched out on the floor. "Well, he's undergone----rehabilitation."

"Why, so he won't chew up little children or household furniture?"

"Nope." John glanced from Kurt to Doris, "He was in drug rehab."

Doris knelt next to the dog and patted him on the head, "He was a sniffer."

"Yep." With his coffee cup he gestured toward the dog, "Damned shame how they turn them into junkies just so they'll sniff out drugs."

Chapter fifty:

Kurt gave John a sidewise look, "Are you trying to tell us Max was never an attack dog?" Max rolled his eyes upward and stared at John.

A sheepish smirk crossed John's face as he shrugged, "Okay, so he worked the streets for a few years. He's a cop!"

Max nuzzled Doris's inattentive hand. She resumed petting him.

"Bad habit for a trained dog, John." Kurt plopped down on the couch next to John. "So how did you come by him and what is he doing here?"

"Easy, Buddy. I've been working with him for about six months now. This is only the second time I've taken him out with me." John glanced an affectionate look at the dog. "He's great company."

"So why didn't you tell me?"

"Hey, it might not have worked out. I didn't want you feeling sorry for me."

"Okay, but why is he here?"

"For Doris."

"For me?" She stopped petting and stood up, Max groaned. "What am I supposed to do with a dog?"

"For protection, Doris; Kurt and I have got to go and check out some leads and I was thinking Max would enjoy being with you. His partner on the force was a woman."

As if putting in a pitch for more attention, Max raised his head and fixed his pleading eyes on Doris.

"I don't have any food for a dog and I certainly don't know any of those hand signals." She spoke the words of objection, but she was not very convincing. She just wanted to be sold.

"No problem." John stood up and Max looked for instructions. "I've got food, a leash, water bowl, chew toy and his 'blankie'; I threw in a sheet on hand instructions." John held his hand for 'stay' and Max relaxed. "I'll get them from the car."

Without further comment John disappeared out the door, leaving Kurt and Doris staring at Max.

"He looks at home, Doris." Kurt furrowed his brow, "I could get jealous though." He put his arm around her shoulder. They looked like a set of proud parents admiring their first-born.

John burst through the door and spotted the scene, "Shall I get a camera? Kodak moment and all that, you know." Everyone laughed as they set about making room for 'Max-a-Million'. While Doris was in the kitchen getting Max's water and food bowl set up, Kurt took John aside and started to fill him in on his time with Martina Angelino.

"I got to hand it to her, Kurt, she picked out three real possibilities, but I like this Morton Filman the best. He's been picked up for contract murder at least six times, but never even one indictment." For emphases he pounded his hand, "Not even once."

"And the others?"

"You know, Kurt, I think she just threw them in. She didn't have the same look on her face when she talked about the other two."

"What about the other person? Was that a woman?"

"Yeah, that's what she said, but we didn't have anyone she liked."

Kurt glanced toward the kitchen and watched Doris throwing Max's chew toy, a black rubber handgun. "Dog's a good idea, John, thanks."

"Hey, Buddy, don't get too attached. He's my company, you know."

Kurt made a face of disbelief, "Get a life, Partner;" Changing his tone he talked as he approached the kitchen; "You two having fun?"

"Yeppers, you bet, Mr. Policeman." She rubbed the scruff of the dog's neck. "I suppose you two have to do some police work, eh?"

"We're going to check out a guy who might have done the Ortiz job."

"Thought you guys liked The Baker for that job." She got excited, "Are you guys going to nail him?"

Calmly Kurt replied, "We don't know, but the Angelino girl fingered him as a possible for the Ortiz killing so we're going to check it out."

She tossed the chew toy, but Max just stayed and demanded some more neck rubbing.

"Looks like you two will be just fine." Kurt bent over and gave her a quick but tender kiss. It was the one he was going to give her before Max and Friend had arrived. "Don't take any chances, hon. Wait until we get back before you even think about opening that door."

"Don't worry, Max and I will be just fine."

Kurt winked, "Well, don't get too attached to him." He nodded toward the sitting dog. In response Max tilted his head as if to better understand the man's words, "He's just on loan." As if he had understood the words, Max twisted his head and looked up at Doris.

"Awe, now you've hurt his feelings." She giggled.

Mumbling something about being replaced by a dog, Kurt went into the living room and gestured to John to get up from the couch, "First thing we had better do is to swing by the hospital and check on Jolene. It's on the way to that Filman's place anyway."

As they went out the door, Kurt flipped the latch on the door bolt, "Don't forget to lock up everything. And don't open the door **for anyone**." Turning his attention to John he said, "Whoa, it's cold out here. Doris keeps her place so hot I guess I forgot." Inside he felt unsettled as he glanced about the neighborhood. What if he was missing some eminent danger?

The snow crunched under the tires of the big police sedan. John's expert handling of the car made it seem as if there weren't a flake of snow on the road. For a short time they talked about Jolene's luck at bouncing off of the delivery truck, but when they considered how close she had come to being killed, she didn't really seem that lucky after all. "So what theory are you chasing? Think someone really was after Doris?"

"It looks that way, but I suppose it could have just been a lousy coincidence, but you know I don't believe in coincidences." Kurt shifted his gaze out the side window, "I think it was meant for Doris."

"Maybe it was meant for both of you. Hell, Kurt, you've got a lot more enemies than she does."

"She thinks it could be some nut who got mad at her for cutting up a friend or relative."

"She's got a point, Kurt, those things happen, you know." John pulled into the hospital entrance and stuck the 'Police Business' sign in the window. "Better than a 'Handicap Sticker'." John patted the sign as he wedged it into place.

"If Jolene is up to it, I'd like to ask her some questions. She might know something." Kurt's attitude was off hand, but his voice seemed distant.

"I thought she already gave the boys her version of the accident."

"She did, but I think we might be able to point her in a more specific direction." Kurt paused, "At least I hope to."

Jolene was just finishing a hospital protein drink. She managed a painful nod as the two officers entered her room, "God that stuff is awful." It was evident her jaw was swollen and it pained her to talk. "They must give you this crap just to get you out of here sooner." The more she talked, the more difficult it was to understand her.

"Hurts, huh?" John took her empty cup and dropped it into the trash, it hit with a dull thud.

Jolene managed a weak smile and a stiff nod.

"We'd like to ask a few questions, if you don't mind?" Kurt took out his tattered notebook and began to search for a pen. John handed him his pen.

After rolling her eyes and giving a reluctant shrug, Jolene waited.

"We know the brakes were tampered with. Can you think of any reason why someone would mean you harm?"

She blinked as she stared at Kurt and then looked at John as if to ask him 'what's with him?' "It wasn't my car."

"So you think the brake failure was meant for Doris?" John's tone was flat and factual.

Jolene wrinkled her forehead and peered at him, "Of course." Her attitude seemed to question his intelligence.

"Just needed to get that straight, Jolene. I didn't want to lead you into a statement." John was still scribbling in his notebook, "Can you think of anyone who would want to harm Doris?"

Jolene winched from a spasm of pain, then, closing her eyes she shook her head. "Everyone likes her."

"Whose idea was it you take the car?"

With a look of suspicion, Jolene answered, "Doris'."

Casting Jolene a look of compassion, Kurt said, "Well, I guess that's all for now." He looked at John, "Anything else?"

John shook his head and Kurt returned John's pen. "Just—get better."

"Need anything?"

Jolene was beginning to look sleepy. "Drugs: they make me sleepy." She liked her lips and pointed at her water pitcher. "Have Doris give me a call."

"Will do; But, for now, she is restricted to her house until we can get this thing straightened out." They turned to leave and Kurt spoke over his shoulder, "I'll ask the officer outside to keep an outlook for any suspicious characters."

He didn't see her 'whatever' shrug.

Chapter fifty-one:

Before they rounded the corner they could detect
the distinctive lingering odor that always
accompanies the burning of an old building. The
car's air intake seemed impervious to the pungent
stench.

"I think that's the address, John." Kurt checked
the writing on a crumpled piece of paper, "Yep,
this is where Filman was supposed to be living;
Looks pretty bad."

John responded with a drawn out 'yeah'. He
pulled the car in front of a fire hydrant and parked
behind a Jeep marked, 'Fire Department
Investigations'. Reluctantly they got out of the
warm car and shuffled as they walked over the
frozen strips of water that had been left from the
water drainage. At the bottom of a charred set of
stairs, they spotted a man dressed in civilian
clothes but wearing a set of Fire Department issue
boots. In the background they could hear the
chatter from a police scanner.

"It started upstairs: probably from a pot on a hot
plate. The place was so old and dry she went up
like a piece of cellophane." Using a large
flashlight, he pointed to the places as he spoke
about them. "You guys from the insurance

company?" He spoke without looking at either Kurt or John.

Feeling relieved they had not stumbled upon some fire nut, John shouted, "Nope. We're cops."

The investigator moved his flashlight and examined the two intruders. "Oh!" was all of the response they got.

"What happened here?" Kurt asked.

"Fire. There was a fire." They could hear a soft chuckle in his voice as he resumed his flashlight activities.

Since they were trying to get information from the man, they decided to play along. "Really, we thought this is where they planned to have the next fireman's ball."

The Fireman turned to face them. He had a wide grin and soft red-rimmed twinkly eyes. His nose was large, red, and sported a decisive drip. Wiping his nose on the sleeve of his red flannel shirt, he said, "Damned nose. Runs like a broken hydrant." With the flashlight still on, he let his arm drop toward the floor. "I suppose you're here about that couple who got fried upstairs."

Kurt and John exchanged looks, "Could be. I guess." Kurt responded, "What were their names?"

After using his sleeve on his nose, he opened a small three-ring binder, "Man-Filman and woman-

Powers." He closed the book and then added, "We think."

"What?" John cocked his head.

"Well, that's what the neighbors and the super said, but I think the final ID is up to you boys."

"Sure. So you said the fire started upstairs? Whose place?" Kurt was taking notes.

"Filman and Power's place; she was on the bed and he was sitting in an easy chair. They were really grilled, boys. I don't imagine they felt a thing, because they made no effort to get up or get away from the searing flames."

Realizing they hadn't given their names they said, "I'm Millhouse. And this aged looking gentleman is Miller."

"Really? Miller and Mill-house, how strange;" He poked out a dry and craggy hand and said, "I'm Deville, like the Cadillac." He continued, "What's your interest here?"

"We wanted to question Filman about an investigation we're following."

"I turned over a gun and some partially burned stuff that looked like it could have been narcotics. At least one feller thought it was, but it was in a store bought bag. I think it was just plain flour." He brushed his hands together as if he were shaking the flour from his hands.

"Think it was set?"

"Don't know. It could have been set, or they were just plain stupid." He shook his head and wiped his nose, "I mean how dumb do you have to be to put a pot of cinnamon-water—some people do that for the smell. My mom used to do it all the time. The water boils out and the pan gets so hot it flashes." He dropped his head and looked like he was looking over a set of eyeglasses. "The pot is under the curtains, and swooshes, up she goes."

"So, you think it was set on purpose?" Kurt coaxed.

"Like I said, I don't know…yet." He shrugged and smacked his lips. "Sure you boys aren't insurance" They gave him a disgusted look, "Could have been either way."

Kurt put out his hand and shook the dried limb, "Thanks Deville. Mind if we keep in touch?"

"My pleasure," he said as he turned his flashlight toward the ceiling and mumbled, "Wish those insurance guys would get here. It's too damned cold."

Carefully making their way back to the car the two officers said nothing. After the doors were closed, the car heater on, Kurt asked, "What's your hunch?"

"If he knew we were after him, he could have faked his death, but how would he know?"

"Yeah…and what about the gun and the narcotics."

"Or flour" John corrected.

"Yeah, or flour. If he did the Ortiz hit he used flour."

Kurt wrinkled up his mouth. "I don't see this guy as The Baker."

"I'll buy that, but then how did he know The Baker's mo?" He paused, "And for that matter, who might have tipped him off he had been fingered?"

"That's a lot of questions, John. Got any answers?"

"It's got to be someone who works at the department or spends time with someone who works at the department."

Kurt and John both stopped and stared out the front window, softly Kurt said, "Jolene?"

John gave a thoughtful nod, "Jolene." He echoed.

Kurt sensed something in motion and turned to his left, "That inspector is headed our way." "Maybe he wants to get warm." John quipped as he rolled down the window.

The cold air seemed to be struggling to get into the car, but the heater was a good match for its efforts. Kurt leaned across John and looked up at the old man. In the light of fading day, it was easy to see he had been severely burned on the left side of his face. He did a partial squat in front of the car door and wiped his nose.

"I thought I'd ask you guys if you were working the case just around the corner." He paused to take a deep breath, "It's not a fire, but a truck and medical team just pulled up to the place and reported it was a homicide." Evaluating the blank looks on the faces of the officers he asked, "I guess you didn't get the call, huh?"

John picked up his car mike and pressed the key, "Dispatch this is Miller and Millhouse we're at 56th and Belmont."

"Miller, this is dispatch. Can you respond to a possible homicide at 3244 Belmont?"

"Ten-four, dispatch. We will be there in ten minutes." John put down the mike and looked at the smiling Fireman, "Guess that answers your question, Deville. Thanks."

The wind made a moaning howl as John rolled up the window and started to pull away from the curb. He looked around as he edged out into the snowy traffic, "I know I should have asked you, Kurt, but I got some kind of hunch this is more than a coincidence."

"Yeah, I know what you mean, but our case load is getting a little bit out of hand so I hope this might be a lead for one of our existing cases."

They rounded the corner and saw the emergency vehicles double-parked to the right side of the road. Their flashing lights sent out beams bouncing off of the windshields of the parked cars; the effect was that of a carnival and not one of emergency or death. The fire team was remounting their truck and beginning to pull away as they slowly took its parking place. Hopping out of their car, the officers flashed their badges to the Emergency Medical Team milling about.

"Jesus, you guys got here fast." He gave a suspicious glance at the men, "This some kind of hot case?"

Ignoring the inference, John and Kurt responded with condescending smiles. "Where's the scene?"

"First floor back left, Officer." The medic gestured with his head. "You'll see some of our boys keeping out the gawkers."

Returning a nod of thanks, the officers stopped and looked at their surroundings. They were typical, lower income walk-ups that used to be single-family homes. Once the envy of middle income America, they were now converted into small apartments. The effect on John and Kurt was the same as it was with most people: it reminded them of their own mortality.

"Must have been a beautiful place about the turn of the century."

"Yeah, you can almost hear the sound of muffled hooves on these old brick streets." John took one last look and nudged Kurt, "Let's see what's inside. The CU team will be here any minute now."

Hustling up the patched concrete steps, they were surprised by the various smells of food being prepared. Tenants had their door open as if they were standing in line waiting for the next movie to start. The familiar scent of Italian sauces mixed with baked bread all blended with several other international dishes that were strange to their nostrils. Further down the hallway they could smell the distinct aroma of Hindu spices.

They again repeated the routine of flashing their badges and nodding to the Medical Team. "The CSU team will be here shortly, anybody been in here?"

"Just Fire, sir: they took one look and stopped us. That lady across the hall called in the fire." The nervous EMT nodded toward the closed door about four feet down the hall.

"But there was no fire?"

Chapter fifty-two:

"No, sir: she has a grandson who is a fireman; he had told her if she was in trouble to call the fire department first because they would respond faster than the police." He added an apologetic grin.

"He's probably right." Kurt mumbled. "John, will you interview her while I walk the scene?"

"No problem." He winked, "I like old ladies." With a slight chuckle he turned and headed for the old lady's door.

Kurt shook his head and squatted to study the door: he could feel a draft of cold air coming from inside of the apartment. *No forced entry.* He made a note in his book. He had only taken several steps when he noticed the strong stench of cheap dusty-bottled cologne: the kind that run-down drug stores set out on the counter at Christmas time. He made a note and continued down the short hallway far enough to use his pen to turn on the hall light. The walls were covered with metallic-red wallpaper which had been stuck over what once was yellow paper: edges were loose and some spots were torn as if by a salad fork.

He was halfway through his next step when he realized the aged carpet beneath his feet was sopping wet. He halted and used his pen to slowly open the door to the adjoining bathroom: the light was off so he used his pen to carefully flip the switch. He was rewarded with blinding sparks and a jolt that sent him staggering backwards against the papered wall of the hallway. His body responded with a strange throbbing sensation that made it hard for him to breathe. His mouth worked like a goldfish who had been spilled from his bowl and onto a tiled floor.

Seeing the sparks and the way Kurt fell against the wall, an EMT shouted, "Hey! You okay?"

Kurt took a deep breath and considered the question, "Yeah, I think so, but I sure got the hell scared out of me!" He could feel his heart pounding against his rapidly expanding chest. "Just a slight shock; I should have used a plastic pen." In the dim light of the hallway he looked at the scorched line which was now etched deeply into his Cross Pen. In the midst of his panic he had noticed the bathroom light had remained on. Guardedly, he peered into the room, by habit his eyes swept over the room before settling on the nude body of a middle-aged woman. Knowing he was going to get his leather shoes wet, he tried to walk on his heels as he made his way over to the tub.

"You have any idea how silly you look?" Kurt heard the snap of latex gloves.

The voice was unmistakable, "How did you catch this one, Bruce?" He gave the man a polite smile, "You bucking for a promotion out of CSU?"

"Hey, don't knock it. I'm working harder because they told me they were going to demote me from Crime Scene Unit to your job." Bruce pointed to his knee high boots. "Some of us come to work prepared."

"Don't give me that, buddy. You stole those boots from the fire truck."

"Borrowed is the word, Lieutenant: borrowed." Bruce put down the lid and seat on the toilet bowl and set down a large black tool kit. "Was that radio floating in the tub when you came in?"

"Haven't touched a thing, Bruce."

"That's not what the EMT at the door says."

"Just triggered a faulty light switch." He showed him his pen and jabbed it toward the light switch.

Sporting a small grin, Bruce said, "So why is Homicide here?"

"I told you I didn't touch anything."
Kurt gave him a sidewise look and said, "Fire Department called it in as a possible homicide." Kurt leaned forward to watch Bruce go through his routine. "How long ago?"

"The cold weather; no heat in here. She was in a tub of cold water." He made a gesture of wetting his finger and sticking it into the wind, "Let's say—eight thirty last night—or this morning."

"Where'd you get that from?"

"Clock on the radio, my good man." He feigned a Sherlock Holmes attitude. "But it's probably been played with."

"Okay, but you do think it was last night?"

"What was last night?" John stood back from the pool of water and looked down at Kurt standing on his heels.

"Bruce says the 'accident' happened about eight-thirty last night."

John nodded as he pulled out his notebook; "Super says he had to reset one of the breakers at a quarter to nine." Again he nodded as he said, "Fits!" Waving his arms he added, "Each apartment pays its own electricity."

"Let me guess. This one was reset." Kurt raised his eyebrows, "So how did he know it was this apartment?"

"Easy. Her neighbor has been behind in his bill so she let him run an extension cord over to his apartment. The power went off in the middle of the Lakers playing the Timber wolves." John looked toward the tub. She looked peaceful, as if she were just ducking her head to rinse her hair. Her

230

complexion was tinted to a faint blue and parts of her body displayed singe marks.

"Maybe she died of shock. The Lakers won that game."

Several more men of the CSU team squeezed past the bathroom. John and Bruce called out to them, "So far it could be an accident." Bruce looked up at the makeshift shelf attached to the wall above an electrical outlet. It stood only four inches from being directly over the water in the tub. "Check the bed. Chances are she was a workingwoman, at least part-time!"

"I vote for murder, Bruce." Kurt crossed his arms.

"Yeah, I know, but there could be another explanation." Bruce paused and then turned to John, "You know any reason why a woman who goes into a tub would have the toilet seat and lid both in the up position?"

"Sure, she could have just entertained and then the gentleman left and she went straight into the tub." John paused, "She reached to pull back the curtain and somehow grabbed the curtain and the cord to the radio."

"Sounds good, boys, but I'll bet you there is no water in her lungs. See where the marks on her throat are starting to show?"

"Someone strangled her?" John asked.

"Well, not exactly. It appears that someone choked her to death by shoving something large into her throat and cut off her breathing." Bruce wrinkled up his face, "Some sick SOB wanted to watch her flail and gasp for breath." His head seemed to move spasmodically, "You better catch this guy quick. He likes what he does."

"Bruce, we found some clothes in the bedroom. They smell like smoke." The man took a sniff of the articles and wrinkled his nose.

"You mean cigarette smoke?"

"No…like fire smoke. You know…from a fire."

John looked at Kurt, "How about from the fire yesterday, it was just around the corner. Would that do it?"

"No way, guys. This stuff is strong. I'll bet she was at a fire someplace. Could have been the one around the corner. Talk about jammed. Everyone was there."

Kurt thought about the old fireman and what he said about it being deliberate. "John, find out if they had a TV crew there yesterday."

The EMT in the hallway said, "You bet they did. Channel 5…they were blocking the street until the cops chased their truck out of the way."

"Check on it, John and see if we can get a copy of the footage. All of it."

"Bruce, you mind if I grab a picture of this lady?"
Kurt's speech was cropped and commanding.

"Hey, as long as you log it –I don't care."

Kurt turned to go, but Bruce shouted to him, "I'll
give you the finals after the M.E. is done, but my
guess is her throat is clogged with some kind of
bread."

Kurt nodded and quickly chased after John
Miller. In the car Kurt began rubbing his face: a
sure sign of frustration. "Drop me off at the
precinct, I need to pick up a car and head for
Enrico Angelino's place. If this is the Filman guy,
I want to talk to Martina. You get the footage of
the fire and look for Filman and the lady in the
tub." A pang of guilt rushed through him as he
realized he didn't even care enough to find out her
name.

John sensed his guilt, "Marylyn Thornton, age 53,
single, and a sister died two years ago. Everyone
seemed to like her, but no one knew how she made
her living. Super said she always seemed to have
plenty of money though."

"Marylyn Thornton, uh?"

Chapter fifty-three:

Kurt was surprised when it was Martina who answered the door. She was a beautiful child. He wished he didn't know so much about her sordid swim in life's cesspool. "Martina, you're just the one I would like to see. Are your folks home?"

She smiled and flounced her hair, "They're in the living room." She flashed a seductive smile and said, "I think they were expecting you."

In order to keep his mind clear, Kurt avoided looking at the wealth displayed on every wall or pedestal. Almost any item sold for more money than he made in a year, many of them sold for more money than he would make in a lifetime.

"Officer Millhouse, isn't it?" Enrico displayed a set of cigar stained teeth. "We have heard about the fire. Now we hope you have good news for us."

Kurt could not resist the irony of the Angelinos all wearing expectant faces like a family waiting for the reading of a will going to bring them untold wealth. Mindful of the people with whom he was dealing; he put on his most professional face. "Well, the preliminary thought is Morton Filman and Betty Powers both perished in the fire." He paused to drink in their joy over the death

of two people. Three unemployed store clerks
could not have been happier over news they had
just won the state lottery.

"That man was a horrible murderer," decried
Enrico Angelino.

Kurt could not help but think, ' *he ought to know* '.
"Of course there are a number of tests that must be
done before we know, but we believe the fire
might have been set on purpose." They now had
the look--*you mean we didn't have the winning
numbers?* "It is even possible Filman found out
Martina picked him out and decided to ditch his
partner and fake his death." Kurt thought *of course
there is always the possibility that you had
someone set the fire.*

Enrico put his arm around Martina, "You mean
there is a chance that that----
He looked at his wife and daughter, "——that killer
is still on the loose?" His obvious concern for
Martina was evident. Enrico knew a man like
Filman was fully capable of hunting down Martina
and killing her. "How did he find out that she
identified him?" Enrico's face was a brownish red.
He was struggling to control his temper, but the
anger was bursting from his narrowed brown eyes.
He tightened his grip on a frightened, pale-faced,
Martina.

Kurt shifted his look to Cortina Angelino, hoping to find a more understanding face, but her nostrils were flared and her lips were so tight they should have caused her pain. Desperately Kurt tried to play down the speculations of The Department. "Nobody said he was alive, Mr. Angelino. We still have several things that need to be checked to verify who really died in that fire" He shrugged and said, "I just thought it was best to keep you up to date." Kurt shrugged, "And there is no reason to believe he knew Martina picked him out." He smiled.

"You're lying, young man. You think he's alive!" Cortina challenged. Her lips had changed to a sneering curve. Her lower lip quivered with anger. "Because someone in your department can't keep his big mouth shut, our daughter might--" She struggled for the right words. "—might be in danger."

Tears were already streaking down the face of Martina. Her skin looked so pale it almost looked yellow. Her eyes seemed to be darting about as if she were looking for some place to disappear.

It seemed out of place to feel compassion for a man who had murdered so many people just because they did not do as he wished, but nevertheless Enrico's concern for the safety of his daughter found a soft spot in Kurt's heart. "Look,

Mr. Angelino, I told you what I did because I suspect you have some resources to keep your daughter safe until we can verify Filman is dead." Kurt glanced at Martina; "I know that you would not want me to withhold information that might put Martina at risk."

Enrico stroked the hair of his daughter and looked at Kurt, "You're right, officer." With a swift glance of his eyes, he looked at Cortina and then back at Kurt. The emotion in his voice seemed out of place for a man with his reputation. "You know about my business. I make lots of enemies, but I also make some friends. I would appreciate anything you can do to help keep my daughter safe." He finished his words by tipping his head and giving Kurt a look that could only be interpreted, as 'you know what I mean'.

"I have to get back to the precinct, but I'll keep you informed." Not knowing how to end the conversation, Kurt gave a silent nod and turned to leave.

Enrico Angelino reached out his hand accompanied by a wan smile, "Thank you for your concern, officer Millhouse. I won't forget it."

Kurt didn't know how to read his own feelings. On one side there was this gangster and on the other a concerned father; for now he decided to go with the concerned father. "I'd keep her at home for a few days." Kurt paused, "At least until we know what we're dealing with." Kurt smiled and walked to the front door. In the background he could hear Martina saying, "Daddy, I can't stay home. It's boring. What about my friends?"

It was Cortina who answered her, but by then the door was closing and the cold evening air swept away any chance to hear the retort. He suspected it would be more stern than the words of her father.

Chapter fifty-four:

For a few minutes after the fire, Morton Filman thought about his wife, Betty Powers, but the thoughts were shallow and short. Right now his main concern was to get a place to hide and to pick up some extra money. He had bungled the Doris Mercer job but he had no intentions of letting that money slip through his fingers. If people thought he was dead it would be easier for him to grab the Mercer babe and force Doctor Bick to pay up. The only other thing which stuck in his craw was the Angelino girl had caused him to kill his wife and start running. It was her fault and since he was dead, her daddy wouldn't know it was him who snuffed her. It could just as well have been one of his criminal friends. He drummed his fingers on the steering wheel while he listened to the purring of the car's engine. *I'll take them to Pete Corbin's place out back of the store. If I give him some cash he'll look the other way. All I need is a couple of days. I could rent a boat and make my way to Mexico. Maybe drop off some baggage on the way. I hear that there are a lot of hungry sharks in The Gulf.* The thought made him giddy and filled him with a strange tingling sensation as his mind began to drift into a world of lustful fantasies.

Above his car, a soft pile of snow slipped from the branches of a snow-laden evergreen, the thud of the snow as it dropped on the hood of his car brought him back to the present. He was not on a boat out in the middle of the warm Gulf of Mexico listening to the guttural hum of a diesel motor. He was in a car listening to the whirr of the fan from the car's heater and snow was dropping on his car as if it were guano from some giant bat. Pinching his eyes tightly, he concentrated on his situation. *I'll get Mercer and the money, and then the brat; she'll make a choice cabin boy.*

A city bus passed by and splashed slush against his parked car, but he paid little attention to the incident as he reached into his glove box and plucked a piece of paper from it. Unfolding the paper he studied the symbols and words. At the top of the page was one word, 'Mercer'.

*   *   *

Some six blocks away, Jolene gave a soft moan as she began to wake up. She recognized the sensation in her right hand: someone was holding her hand: the hand was small and cold. She opened her eyes and blinked a soft smile, "Carla." Jolene moistened her lips, followed by a dry swallow, "Wondered—when – you'd come by." She could tell there was a look of concern on Carla's face, but she wasn't sure whether it was for her, or some other problem. "I'm gonna be okay."

"Yeah that's what they say." There were unspoken words in her statement.

"What's wrong?" Jolene had all the problems she could handle, but she knew her friend had expected her to ask. "Are the kids okay?"

"They're okay." She spoke softly. "But it's my boyfr--, the guy I have been seeing. I think he's in some sort of trouble." She paused to reach for a facial tissue and blow her nose, a few tears escaped from her misty eyes. "I've got to meet him tonight and I just know I shouldn't."

"Then don't go!" it was a muted shout, but given with worry in her tone.

Carla gripped Jolene's hand so tightly she almost cried out, "I can't help it, Jolene. He just sounded so desperate. He needs me."

Jolene winced from the pain in her hand, "I don't know what to say, Carla. I don't know him…hell; I don't even know his name."

"I know it's because of his wife, Betty, she's real jealous. He's going to leave her just as soon as he can get enough money together." Her eyes pleaded for understanding, her lips began a slight quiver. "I know how it sounds, but if you met him you'd see how sincere he was."

"What's he do?"

"Huh?"

"How does he make a living?" In spite of her pain she struggled to focus on her friend.

"I'm not real sure, Jo. I think Morton has something to do with sales." Carla cast her eyes to the floor, unable to meet the probing eyes of her friend. "Oh, Jo, I think I've gotten myself into a mess."

Jolene managed to get her hand free and pat Carla's hand. "Why do you say that?"

As if she were experiencing a sudden gas pain, Carla contorted her face and spoke softly, "He asks a lot of questions about your work at the morgue. I mean like he's a reporter or something." She shifted her eyes to observe a nurse who was just entering the room, "Lots of questions about The Baker murders."

The nurse was almost to her bedside when Jolene smiled and said, "Maybe he's an undercover reporter." Her smile faded as she realized it would mean he was just using her to get information. "I doubt that, Carla. He's probably just showing interest in what we do. A lot of people are just curious, you know." She steadied her head as the phantom nurse stuck an electronic thermometer in her ear and began to take her blood pressure.

With a suddenness that startled Jolene, Carla looked at her watch and said, "Hey, I got to go. It was good seeing you. You look great. I'll call you later." After giving Jolene a quick peck on the cheek.

Carla fled for the door so swiftly she didn't seem to hear Jolene's words of caution. "Be careful!"

Chapter fifty-five:

She sat in her car. Not able to force herself to go into the restaurant and meet with Morton Filman, she sat as if she were a mental patient in a catatonic state. There had been something rather sinister about the way he had asked her to meet him. A million times she told herself she was just being stupid and silly, but there was another part of her that wanted to believe a dream where all he wanted was for them to take the twins and live happily ever after. She knew she might be wrong, but she wanted so desperately for the dream to become a reality: it meant she would have to take a chance. Some would call it a risk, but it was her life and right now she felt she was entitled to have a dream come true.

The diner was a converted railroad car, or at least it looked like one. It was silver and had the large windows which would afford the passengers a fine view as the train shot through the open countryside or the dark woods of the Pacific Northwest. Wearily she walked up the six steps taking her to the windowless door. Hopefully she opened the large door, anxious for it to usher her into the presence of a man she was not now sure she could trust: he was at the back of the car, the corner was dimly lighted. At first sight of her he beamed as if she were an angel shimmering with divine beauty, clothed in garments of glistening gold, wrapped in clouds of virtue. Her fears, doubts, and sense of foreboding were rubbed away like charcoal tracings from an artist's pad.

"Carla" He rose from the table, desperate to embrace her and smell the sweet fragrance of her soft hair, to drink in the warmth of her eager and sensuous body. He shut his eyes just enough to watch the looks of the envious waitress who had been 'checking him out' for several minutes. "Cara Mia, I have been in agony waiting for you." He held her at length and closed his eyes as he took in her scent, "How can I be anything but a subdued man? You are worth waiting a lifetime just to behold you." He gestured for her to sit down. While she was sitting, he looked up at the waitress and politely motioned for her to come to their table.

The waitress was disappointed with the size of their order, but she smiled at Morton and gave Carla less attention than a needy saltshaker. "Thanks!" was all she managed as she turned to slink as if she were a high fashion model working her way down the fashion-ramp of some swanky hotel.

Morton's mind was racing with possibilities. Carla was a loose end. The only question was how to best dispose of her, but then he already had that figured out.

* * *

Having given up on the dull and repetitive news, Doris went into the kitchen and began searching through the leftovers and some possibilities for dinner if Kurt showed up in time. With one hand on top of the open door she bobbed her body up and down and from side to side. Just behind her, to her left, Max was studying her movements. At the Academy they often stored some of the dog's meat in the refrigerators. Confirming the famous study by Dr. Pavlov, his long tongue slid from one side of his jaw to the other anticipating some juicy pieces of meat. Like some little schoolboy hoping for a generous helping of cookies, Max sat tall: ears up and nose level.

When Doris closed the door to the refrigerator without retrieving anything, Max looked up at her and tilted his head from side to side, "What's wrong, boy? Expected some goodies, uh?" She re-opened the door and snatched two hot dogs and was just closing the door when the front doorbell rang. Ignoring the food, Max went on alert.

"Easy boy, I mean, Max." Softly she patted him on the head. "We'll check it out."

It was obvious he was not only well trained, but experienced. The dog went to the backside of the door and sat, his eyes trained on Doris, waiting for a command.

Matching the dog's stealth, she moved to a side window and looked out; she did not recognize the car blocking her driveway. A strange empty

feeling leapt into her stomach and her limbs began
to tremble. Kurt had said, "Don't let anyone in."
Moving slowly to the peephole she closed her left
eye as she looked through the hole. What she
viewed was a circus version of Richard and
Thelma Price. Caught between Kurt's orders and
her desire for company, she reached for the
doorknob. Max tightened his hind legs as she
began to open the door.

"Hi!" Doris knew her voice sounded nervous.

Richard and Thelma were all bundled up in dark
wool clothing accented with matching maroon
scarves. Sensing her uneasiness, Richard asked, "Is
this a bad time to visit?"

"We don't want to intrude, dear, but we heard
about your friend and Richard's contacts with the
police said …it was not an accident and that you
might have been the one for whom it was
intended." A stout wind rushed by stirring up
fallen snow and dropping snow from the branches
above, Thelma clutched her coat about her, "We
were quite concerned for you. Especially since
Richard had seen that person following you."

Doris felt like some kind of a fool keeping the
elderly couple standing in the cold, "Oh! Please
come in. I wanted to ask Richard about the man
following me." She closed the door behind them.

Richard, sensing something behind him, swiveled his head to his left, "I didn't know that you had a dog. He looks trained."

Shyly she said, "That's Max. He's a retired police dog. Kurt thought it would be a good idea to have him here."

Doris struggled to remember the hand signals John had taught her. She remembered Max had been special training. The first hand signal told him what to do, and then a hand pat told him to execute the command. Instead she said, "It's alright, Max. Come here." Reluctantly the dog sauntered over by her. For a few seconds he studied both of the intruders: then he began to walk by both of them. With obvious intent, he sniffed at each of the guests, but stopped when he reached Richard. Max tilted his head so that he could look into the eyes of Richard, then he produced a soft growl. Richard froze.

Doris was both confused and shocked, "Oh, please forgive him, Richard. I guess it's just that he doesn't know you."

"Not so, my dear. That dog is indeed well trained. He smells the gun powder or gun oil on my pistol." Richard held eye contact with the dog while he said, "The problem is... I'm not sure what he wants me to do."

Thelma clucked her tongue, "Well for Pet's sake, Richard take out the gun."

Looking at Max, Richard talked out of the corner of his mouth, "I don't think that would be a good idea, dear." Pleadingly he looked at Doris, "Would you please remove it. It's under my left armpit."

With great interest Max watched as she removed the weapon from his holster. After a few more sniffs, Max relaxed and stepped to Doris' side.

"That's some dog you got there, Doris. He's a good one." Richard slowly moved over to the couch to join Thelma. "You say they retired him?"

"John Miller said he used to be a street dog, and then they had him doing narcotics. They had to de-tux him. I guess he works best with women because his handler was a woman who got shot up too badly to continue as a police officer." Her facial gestures indicated she was trying to recall something, "I think they called him 'a sniffer'".

Quickly changing the subject, Thelma asked, "How are you doing? Can we do anything to help?" Without waiting for an answer she said, "We went by the hospital to visit your friend, Jolene. She looks pretty bad .A lady, I think her name was Clara, had just left. At first she thought that I was she. "

"I guess she should have been dead, but a freak movement of a truck saved her life." Doris looked at Richard.

Addressing Thelma he said, "Her name was Carla, Dear" Then he turned to Doris, "The answer is-- I know that man's name, he goes by Morton Filman, but I doubt it's his real name. Apparently the police were looking for him on a murder charge: Paulo Ortiz." Richard paused to reach for a cigarette, Max stiffened. "May I smoke?"

Doris smirked and nodded toward Max, "I don't mind if he doesn't." The laugh lightened the tension.

Richard continued, "It seems he might have perished in a fire that happened at his apartment. Supposedly, he and his wife both died."

"Two questions, Richard. Was this before or after Jolene's accident and why are you saying 'might' and 'supposedly'?"

Richard lit his cigarette and exhaled the smoke toward the ceiling, "It might have been some sort of ruse, intended to throw the police off of his scent." He glanced at Thelma who was beaming with pride; she loved to listen to her husband try to make sense out of it. "Most definitely, the fire was after the accident." Without warning he leaned forward, Max jumped to all fours but did not lunge. "Who would want you dead? And why?"

The question was academic considering the job of
killing her was first offered to him.

Flustered, Doris' eyes widened and she shook her
head, "I don't know. Kurt asked the same
questions, but all I could tell him was… sometimes
the families don't like for us to cut up their loved
ones. I've had several threats concerning that, but I
think it was just temporary emotion." She
furrowed her brow, "Don't you?"

Richard shrugged and dropped some ashes into
his hand, "It's certainly not a common motive.
Most people kill for jealousy or profit. Any
disgruntled suitors?"

Doris looked at Thelma as if she would have the
answer, "No…no one. I haven't dated in years; my
work keeps me too busy." She registered
embarrassment.

Thelma gripped Richard's arm, "A girl--." She
stopped herself and looked at Doris, "---Pardon
me; a woman knows when she's got somebody
bothering her, Dear."

Richard patted her hand and continued, "Okay,
let's say you're all clear on the romance." He
narrowed his eyes and asked, "How about
money?"

Doris squinted and closed her eyes, "Kurt asked
that question, but I live alone and have no
relatives. I only have a small burial policy and

actually I don't need that because my job covers all my insurance needs."

Puffing out his lips he seemed in deep thought, "How about medical insurance? Liability? 'Key-Man'? Retirement?"

"Of course she has that, Richard!" Thelma declared.

"We have Liability, Retirement, and a Key man policy to cover the medical group with whom I am associated. I am subcontracted to the morgue." Raising her shoulders she added, "But nobody would kill me for that? They wouldn't get a dime if they were found out."

"You'd be surprised what people would do for money", he responded. "How much is it?" Having already checked he knew the policy on her was for five million dollars.

She thought for a second, "I think it's five hundred thousand on each of us partners." Tilting her head she asked, "Is that a lot?"

Thelma and Richard exchanged looks, "Yes, my dear, it is a lot. Not unheard of, or even enormous, but it certainly could be a motive." Slowly he reached across and held Doris' hand. "Are any of your partners known for having money problems?"

Doris shifted her eyes back and forth. Should she tell this man about professional gossip? Doris took a deep breath and said, "Hal, that is, Dr. Bick, has been known to 'spend too much'." Hastily she continued, "At least that's the talk in the office. He gambles and plays the field: lots of girlfriends." Neither Thelma nor Richard said a word. A mask of concern seemed to wash her face. Her breathing became short and audible. Shaking her head she asked, "You don't think he tried to kill me just so he could get a share of the Key man policy, do you?"

"Obviously I don't know, Doris. But it's a possibility. I also believe you will find out the amount of the policy on you is for five <u>million</u> dollars" He patted her hand, while she stared at him. "Don't be surprised, Doris, after all I am in the insurance business. It was easy for me to find out." He paused to grant her a reassuring smile. "I am certain that **he** didn't try to kill you, but it might be why Filman was following you." Richard looked at Thelma and then back at Doris, "Filman had been questioned for several killings, but was never indicted, much less convicted."

Thelma got up and crossed over to Doris, "Richard told me of his suspicions so I insisted we come over here and make sure you were safe and informed." Thelma sat on the edge of the overstuffed chair and pulled Doris to her, "I hope you don't mind, but we rather think of you as a daughter. I was worried." The gentleness in

Thelma's voice began to penetrate the veil of fear in which Doris now found herself.

As Richard removed his hand from hers, Doris began to wring them. She squeezed until the knuckles looked paper white. "What should I do?" Looking up at Thelma, her voice muffled by Thelma's ample bosoms, she sobbed, "Am I safe here?"

Chapter fifty-six:

Richard thought for a few seconds and then answered, "Well, you seem to be well protected against an intruder, do you have a gun?"

She nodded.

"The problem is they know where you live. There could be a gas explosion or something like that. They really would not even need to enter your home. Things like that are quite common." He sounded like a lecturing professor. "That's why they tried the car. It has to look like an accident." He nodded to himself, "Yes. If we are right, then they will want it to look like a common crime or an accident." He looked up at Thelma, "And we don't know if Filman is really dead. Do we?"

The cordless phone lying on the coffee table began producing an electronic ring. Every set of eyes, including Max's, shifted to look at the phone. For a brief second everything seemed to be on hold.

"Expecting a call?" Thelma inquired. Her voice seemed tense almost to the point of cracking.

Reaching for the phone Doris said, "It's probably Kurt checking up on me." She looked at the caller ID slot, "I don't recognize that number, but he uses lots of different phones."

Richard shifted nervously as he said; "Perhaps it is best if you answer it."

Without hesitation she plucked the phone from the coffee table, "Hello?" she asked.

Kurt signed, "What took you so long to answer. You had me worried. Is everything all right?" He was talking so fast she couldn't answer.

As he talked she studied the faces of Thelma and Richard, "We weren't sure if I should answer."

Concern was in his voice as he asked, "We?"

"Yes, Thelma and Richard are here. They were at the hospital visiting Jolene. They were concerned for me."

"Oh! Yeah, I remember them. That nice old couple we had lunch with." Kurt stopped and his tone changed, "Say... isn't he the one who said someone was following you?" His voice registered a mysterious strain.

"That's right. A mister Filman, he says." To make sure she had given the right information she looked at Richard. He nodded.

Everywhere he turned the same name kept cropping up: Filman. Not wanting to worry her, he said, "Filman, uh?" He paused, "Yeah, I've heard that name before. I'll check into it." He also had another thought; *I think I also should check a little further into Mr. Price.* "Tell him thanks for the info."

"You sound a bit stressed. Is everything okay with you?" She looked embarrassed to ask the question.

He laid "Just the usual garbage stuff to deal with." He paused and thought, "I think I'll be another four hours or so, so keep buttoned up. All right?"

Not wanting to disconnect even with his voice she asked, "How's the Morgue doing?"

After a brief humorous snort he said, "They brought in some hot shots from the 32nd. They needed to deal with some fire victims and a tub electrocution."

Doris shook her head, "You'd think that people would learn, wouldn't you?"

"It might have been murder this time. Not just some idiot with a radio in the bathroom." He put his hand over the speaker and then said, "Look, I got to go. See you in four hours. Love you."

"Love you too." She sighed and set the phone back on the coffee table.

While she was daydreaming Richard asked, "Did he say anything about Filman?"

"Only that he was familiar with the name."

Richard nodded, but he was quite concerned Kurt would wonder why he had not told him sooner. Those kinds of questions could trigger an investigator like Kurt to start checking up on Morton. He had kept his police record clean, but a good investigator could have tied some of his travel with the deaths of some rather high profile low-lifers. Shaking off his concerns, he looked at Thelma, "Suppose you could brew us some coffee? I don't think Max wants me to move." He laughed.

***

Feeling he was still safe from discovery, Morton Filman relaxed in the booth at the diner. Sliding his back toward the window, he put his legs up on the bench seat and sighed as he looked at Carla. "What's bugging you, dear?"

0h…nothing really;It's just that my friend, Jolene, you remember her."

He nodded. "Sure she's the one who works at the Morgue; Right?"

"Yeah." She leaned forward, "She's the one who gave me the info on The Baker killings when you wanted to do that favor for some big shot."

"Oh, she was the one, huh?" He acted as if he hardly remembered the event.

"Yeah, well she was in a bad car accident: almost killed her."

"Gee, that's too bad." He put on a mask of concern, "You know... the way people drive around here…" He did not finish the sentence, but just shook his head in disgust. "Is she going to be okay?"

"The docs think so."

He reached out for her hand, "Hey, not to change the subject, but when we're done here I'd like to introduce you to a friend of mine." He acted a bit embarrassed, "You know I talk about you all the time, and I'd like him to see the gal I plan to marry."

The proposal was not all that new, they had talked about it when he was doing the job for 'the big shot'. After the favor, he was supposed to get enough money for them to sneak off and get married. She blushed and produced a coy smile, "Okay, but I have to get home soon. Grandpa has been babysitting most of the day."

"Oh, yeah? How is the old coot?"

"He's fine, but he gets grumpy if I make him late for work. Sometimes he has taken the kids with him. They enjoy it, but they get in the way sometimes."

Filman snorted and then swung his feet to the floor as he saw their food being ushered in their direction. *That gal really has the hots for me. I'll have to remember that.* Behaving himself, he politely thanked the waitress and then turned his full attention on Carla. Outside, the sun was just beginning a slow settling behind a hill which was concealed by the adjacent buildings. Amber street lights glowed like old-fashioned gas lamps turning the black of night into some mixture resembling dirty brass. Several blocks away, Morton Filman had stashed a stolen black Honda; he would need the car to transport Carla's body to a reed-infested lake nicknamed Lover's Marsh.

"Eat up, Dear; we don't want to stir up the grump." He gave her an adoring smile and muffled chuckle. *Next thing I need to do is take care of that doctor and collect my five percent. Maybe I'll demand more. What can he do? With that money I can take the Wop girl to Mexico.* He allowed himself a self-satisfied grin.

Flirtatiously Carla looked at him. She moved her fork about in her food, picking at items but not lifting them. "Soooo? What are you grinning about?"

"Nothing…absolutely nothing, my love;" He winked, "I'm just happy. That's all." He sipped at his coffee.

For almost an hour they joked and talked about the future. If he should ever be questioned there would be no doubt in anyone's mind but what they were very much in love. When it was time to leave, he helped her on with her coat and silently they made their way out the door and into the brassy night.

"I felt like walking so I parked a ways down the street." He offered her his arm and she slipped her arm through his and then slightly turned to place her other arm on top of his and leaned against him. They small- talked their way for the twenty minutes it took them to reach the Honda. For a few moments he leaned against a lamppost and engaged in romantic chatter while he studied the car: just to make sure it was not being watched.

Giving her a joking pull he said, "There's the car. We got here fast, huh?"

They were almost to the car when he looked about to make sure no one was watching. "I've got a present for you. I left it in the trunk." He swung his arm around her, "Didn't want anyone to steal it now, did I?"

Leaning her head against his shoulder she murmured, "You really didn't need to."

"Of course I did." Gently he held her by her shoulders and purred; "Now I don't want you to peek." He turned her so that her back was to the trunk of the car. Quickly he again checked his surroundings: still on one watching. He opened the trunk.

Carla started to giggle, "I feel like I'm on my first prom date."

No sooner was the trunk open when he grabbed the 'L' shaped tire iron and struck her on the back of the head. She had barely begun to slump when he scooped her up in his arms and quickly dropped her into the plastic lined trunk. Deftly he taped her mouth, hands and feet. For a few seconds he studied her as if he couldn't remember why he was doing this, but then he slipped a black plastic bag over her head and securely tapped it about her neck. By now he had begun to sweat: one reason was from the exertion, another from the adrenalin rush of being discovered. Wanting it to look like a robbery, roughly he slipped off her rings and then he tugged at a gold heart shaped necklace: he had to pull twice before the chain would break. *Huh, probably close to a grand in jewelry! Not bad! Might come in handy.*

For several minutes he sat in the car and shivered, not from the cold but from the excitement. *It went easier than I thought.* It seemed it was not he who was thinking, but someone else telling him how smoothly it had gone. He turned on the ignition and the little black car responded with the sound all too familiar to people who live in cold country: it whined. He looked up and saw his headlights cast pale yellow beams of light upon a small mound of curbside snow left by the snowplows. Angrily he tightened his grip on the steering wheel. Since he had not pulled the lights on, he must have left them on when he had tested them earlier, or maybe it was just an old battery. He wanted to bang his fist against the steering wheel. There should be some way to punish the car, but there wasn't.

I'll just leave the car here. I'll leave the keys in the car: someone might steal it. Maybe it's just as good as driving it into the lake. It'll be found sooner, but right now it can't be helped. "I knew everything was going too good. Damn it," He shook his head, "Those damned lights."

After reviewing his movements to see if he had covered his trail, he exited the car and crossed the street. He had planned to steal a car at the lake so now he was on foot, but he would just have to make his way to Pete Corbin's gun shop and get his supplies for the Doris Mercer job. Morton was not afraid of Corbin telling anyone he was really alive. Corbin was a man who knew how to keep his mouth shut.

His words turned to vapor as he softly laughed out loud, "Bet Grandpa will be mad when she doesn't come home so he can get to work." He chuckled to himself as he picked up his pace and headed west toward Pete Corbin's war surplus outlet. Glumly he recalled he had usually sent his wife, Betty, on such trips: he hated having to associate with criminals like Pete Corbin and his helpers. He pulled up his collar against the evening's chill; it was times like this he missed Betty.

Avoiding public transportation, Morton finally arrived at his destination. Across the street was a twenty-four foot long sign that read, 'WAR SURPLUS: CLOTHES AND STUFF'. Under the top line were the words, 'Pete Corbin, Prop'. Over ten years ago the sign had been painted on three quarter inch thick by eight feet long pieces of marine plywood. The red white and blue sign now had cracked, pealed, and splintered, sort of likc the owner; Morton thought it was kind of funny…the sign was aging just like its owner.

A northern wind had begun to pick up, so Morton stepped into the entryway of a deserted shop across the street. The shop looked as empty as usual, only one man and two kids who were playing tag among the clothes racks.

The alley to Pete's back door was desolate except for several scattered dumpsters. Hastily he dashed across the street and found the olive drab metal door at the back of the shop. To protect his hand against the cold metal door, he slipped his hand into his coat sleeve and balled his fist. Only once did he have to bang on the door before Pete looked out of the oversized peephole. The door opened so rapidly it almost knocked Morton toward a nearby dumpster.

Morton scowled at Pete as he barked, "Jesus, Pete, you almost killed me."

The grinning Pete chuckled as he said, "Word is—that's already been done, Mort."

Brushing past Pete he mumbled, "I told you not to call me Mort, my name is Morton, not Mort."

"You're pretty touchy for a dead man, Mort-ton." Pete pushed aside a World War II army blanket separating his office from the backroom storage area and helped to keep out the cold. "I was just leaving for the night." He dropped into his creaky wooden swivel-chair, "What 'cha need?" Pete looked up at Morton and studied him: he didn't like what he saw: Morton seemed too nervous. "You got any cash? I can't give credit to a dead man."

With a sneer of disgust, Morton narrowed his eyes and said, "Cash...about one hundred bucks."

Pete's senses went on alert. Here was a man who was supposed to be dead, seemed desperate, and was a known killer. "Okay, but that depends on what you want, doesn't it?" As he slid open a desk drawer containing his nine-millimeter Lugar, he wrinkled his forehead and asked, "So, what will it be?"

Angered by Pete's actions, Morton spoke with an edge to his words, "Look, Pete, we have been doing business for a long time. Trust me."

Pete just looked at him and plucked a package of cigarettes from the pocket of his olive-green wool shirt. He shook the pack until one of the cigarettes popped up; then he used his mouth to pluck one from the package and tossed the pack on the desk. "What you want?"

"Nine-mil and a box of ammo;" He acted as if he were ordering a burger with fries. "I got a job." He grinned and explained, "It's a lady M.E. of all things. I could pay you later." Normally he would never have talked about a job, but he was desperate, at least that is how he rationalized it to himself.

After running his tongue over his nicotine-stained dentures, Pete smacked his lips and said, "Five hundred—CASH!" He watched Morton tense, "Hey, man, it's not likely that I'll see you any time soon." Pete shrugged and tilted his head, "Five hundred. Take it, or leave it." He moved his mouth and his cigarette pointed at the ceiling and smoke escaped trailing up his cheek and stinging his eye. "Well?"

Morton shifted his eyes from side to side, he was certain Pete would at least wound him if he tried to rob him.

Morton reached for the pocket of his jacket and the Lugar in Pete's desk drawer seemed to leap into his hand,

"Easy, Pete, I got some really valuable jewelry in this pocket." He pointed with his thumb.

"Okay, but if anything else comes out of that pocket you'll have an extra eye in your forehead, Mr. Deadman."

Chapter fifty-seven:

With extreme caution, Morton pulled out Carla's rings and her necklace. "Worth about a grand, Pete." He offered a smile to show how non-threatening he was.

Using the Lugar as a pointer, Pete said, "Put the stuff on the desk and turn around." As soon as Morton turned he added, "And keep your hands where I can see them." Being mindful to watch Morton, Pete slid the jeweler's lens from the corner of his desk and brought it up to his eye "Not bad stuff, Mort. I'm not going to ask where you got this, but there is blood on the chain of this necklace."

Without a retort Morton Filman asked, "Will that cover it?"

"Yeah, along with your hundred cash."

Morton winced, "So what do you have?"

"Just a second, Mort."

Morton turned around and watched as Pete slapped an automatic and a box of bullets on the desk.

"This here has no serial number." Pulling back the slide and looking down the barrel he said, "It's a nine-mill, Hungarian PJK. A bit old fashioned and a bit heavy, but it will do the job." He pushed the gun to the corner of his desk; "I'll give you the bullets and the clip when you leave."

With clenched fists and a sneer on his face Morton was a picture of smoldering anger, "You know that gun's not worth more than a hundred bucks."

Pete grinned, "It is to you."

Without another word, Morton threw down the money and grabbed the gun. He thought about grabbing the clip and the bullets, but the risk was too great. *I'll come back here and even this score, you ugly scumbag!* Could easily be read in his eyes.

"Don't even think about coming back here, Mort." He pointed his Lugar at Morton's knee, "First I'll kneecap you and then I'll skin you alive, boy." He stood up, "I ain't no week-kneed girl. Now ---GET!"

When the door slammed, Pete shouted toward the front of the store, "Harold, lock the store! We're closed!"

"Okay, Pete!" After a few minutes Harold Zane came into the back of the store, "I thought you went home, Pete."

"Yeah I was on my way out when that Filman guy showed up." He paused and pointed to the money and jewelry on his desk, "Wanted a gun."

Harold made a face, "I thought he was supposed to be dead." He hesitated, "Died in a fire they said." He recalled when he was on the street across from the fire. For a split second he could still picture the woman who invited him up to her apartment. He could not recall why he had killed her, "You say he was here."

"Mad as hell when I sold him that PJK I've been trying to move." He snorted and said, "Hell, he didn't have but 'hundred bucks." Pointing at his desktop he said, "Bastard gave me jewelry. He probably stole it."

Harold Zane, The Baker, alias Grandpa, stared at the rings and locket on the desk. His face contorted into a mixture of confusion and unbridled hate. "He gave you this stuff?" Noting the smear of blood on the chain, he picked up the locket and opened it. Inside were two pictures, his granddaughter, Amy and grandson, Andrew. Pete watched as tears began to form in the old man's eyes. Harold's hands were trembling both from the loss he suspected and the rage he felt. It was like losing his son, Billy, all over again.

Pete was shocked by Harold's reaction; he moved over to see what was in the locket, "Hey, Hal that looks like your grandkids." Pete acted as if he had not put the facts together. Morton Filman was a ruthless killer; why else would he have his daughter-in-law's jewelry?

Sniffling, Harold held back the next flood of tears, "That's them all right, Pete." Mindlessly he began to mutter, "She was so happy, Pete. She was going out to meet her fiancé." He looked into Pete's confused eyes, "I think she's dead, Pete."

Attempting to comfort his friend, Pete put his hand on Harold's shoulder, "Now, Pete, you don't know that for sure. She might be alive, you know." He knew he sounded like a muttering fool while inside, in his gut; Pete knew it was unlikely.

Abruptly, Harold stopped his weeping and his eyes took on an unearthly appearance. His nostrils flared, and his mouth tensed, "Where did he go, Pete?"

"Now, Harold, you don't want to mess with this guy. Let the police earn their money. He's dangerous!"

Scarcely had Pete managed to get out the words, when Harold replied, "So am I. Now where did he go?" His body was shaking with rage. "WHERE?"

At hearing their grandfather yelling, the twins rushed in to see what the matter was. Andrew was the first to arrive, "What's wrong, grandpa?" Amy pulled up beside him, "We weren't doing anything wrong, we were just playing hide and seek, grandpa."

Harold Zane, grandpa, kneeled down and hugged his two grandchildren. Looking up at Pete he said, "Pete, I'm losing time. Where did he go?"

"Who, grandpa?" the twins asked in unison.

"Just a mean man, kids; I need to talk to him." His eyes were pleading with Pete.

As if he were confessing under duress, he said, "I really don't know." He paused, "He said he had a job. An M.E. I believe he said."

Recognition registered in his eyes. Harold kissed the twins and said, "Uncle Pete will watch you while I go run an errand." He reached on the desk and took the Lugar and a box of cartridges. "A man left his stuff here and I have to deliver it to him." He messed up their heads, "I'll be right back." As he headed out the back door he shouted, "Mind Uncle Pete now, you hear." He didn't hear their responses.

Outside Harold headed for his car. He knew who the ME was because he had followed Filman after Filman had killed Ortiz and tried to make it look like it was Harold's Baker work. Doris Mercer was his 'job'. *I'll meet him there and he had better be able to tell me where Carla is. And she had better be alive and well.* He glanced at his watch; *it will take me about a half hour to get there. Can't go too fast, the cops might stop me* Once he was seated in the car, he placed the gun and bullets under his seat, started the car and headed for the house of Doris Mercer.

Earlier, Harold Zane had driven his pickup truck to Carla's, but because she was late getting home and his truck did not have enough seat belts, he used Carla's car to transport himself, Amy and Andrew to work. Almost as soon as he settled into the driver's seat, the radio warned drivers of two serious accidents on the expressway: he would have to take several roads in order to bypass the tied-up traffic. Having already lost his son, he was experiencing a mixture of emotions which would have sent most psychiatrists to their reference books. His fear that his grandchildren could now be deprived of their mother was sending him into a murderous rage so strong his imagination was being stretched to boundaries previously untouched even by The Baker. As a result of his anger, his blood pressure caused his face to turn to reddish purple. His breathing was reduced to short, fast snorts of air. The combination of heat in the car and his rapid breathing was making him light headed. He rolled down the window and allowed the cold night air to blow over his hot face. Even as the cold air kept him from passing out; his anger and fear had sent floods of rancid acid into his stomach. Harold wanted to crunch up into a fetal position, but not possible.

He glanced at the built-in dash clock; it had already taken him thirty minutes to get to the street where Doris Mercer lived. He would be there any minute now. Harold eased off on the gas pedal and began looking for her house. It would be important to catch Morton by surprise: he wanted him alive for several reasons. First he would tell Harold where to find Carla, and then he would make him pay for whatever he had done to her. His fury had changed from the windy rage of a hurricane to the back side of the storm. The worst half, the second half, was yet to come.

Chapter fifty-eight:

Since Kurt and John left Doris's house, Kurt had been calling every twenty minutes to check on her. After the last call, Doris had decided she needed to talk to Jolene.

"I know it sounds unreasonable, but I simply must go and see her." She shrugged and frowned, "I don't know why. I'm just going whether Kurt likes it or not."

Thelma pushed an elbow into Richard's ribs. He responded by giving her a disgruntled look. "Richard! Go with her. Max and I will be fine, and if Kurt calls while she is out, well, I'll just tell him what happened. He could call her at the hospital, you know." She flashed him a look of mock disgust, "Someone has to stay here in case Kurt calls." With a jerk of her head she gestured toward the door.

Richard considered her statement and said, "Okay, I can do that, but are you sure you will be okay by yourself?"

Thelma winked at Richard and called Max to her. "Here boy." Max got up and obediently responded. His tongue drooped from his mouth as if he were expecting some sort of sweet treat. "See, it's just like John said, he likes women." She looked up at Richard and smiled, "I'll be fine…really."

"Doris, can we make it a quick trip?"

"Of, course, Richard, but I've just got a nagging thought that's really bothering me."

"Why not just use the phone?"

"Sorry, but this needs to be a face to face thing." Doris looked at Thelma, "It's okay. I can go by myself. I'll be right back."

"Richard!" Thelma had a distinct edge to her voice." She narrowed her eyes as if to threaten to beat him up.

Richard shook his head and laughed, "She really thinks she's tough." He bent over and grabbed Thelma's small hand. In the tradition of the old

European style he kissed the back of her hand, "Your wish is my desire, your Highness."

Tugging her hand from his, she provided the appropriate sag of distain," Get out of here."

Max watched as Richard put his pistol back into its holster, but he did little more that offer a feeble growl. Thelma was petting him and massaging his ears, "Dog's love to have their ears rubbed." Thelma remarked.

"So do I, but it doesn't do me any good. See, he likes me already," referring to the Max's token growl. Richard nodded toward the steady-eyed Max.

Richard and Doris clutched the metal railing as they made their way down her slippery stairs and out to the street where Richard had parked his Cadillac. When they reached the car, Richard held up the car keys, "If you feel like driving I think it best for me to act as your bodyguard. That means I can't drive and protect you at the same time."

Joyfully, she snatched the keys from his hand, "I'd love to drive your Caddy. I once dated a doctor who had one. They're fun to drive."

Thelma watched as the vertical slits of the red taillights disappeared down the automobile lined street. "Well, Max, I guess it's just you and me, boy." Releasing her grip on the curtains, they fell back into place. "Max? Where is that chew toy of yours?"

As if reading her mind, he dashed into the kitchen and reappeared in the doorway. In his mouth was a simulated nine-millimeter pistol. Pieces of black rubber were missing, but it didn't bother Max. He held the chewed up toy as if he were a Golden Retriever holding the afternoon's prize pheasant between his wetted jowls.

"OH, MY!" She laughed, "That thing has seen better days."

Head held high he pranced over to Thelma and laid his prized and slobber soaked possession at her feet. Then he sat back on his haunches and smiled. His enormous pink tongue dangled from one corner of his mouth. His eyes were glistening with the anticipation of the hunt and kill.

Thelma picked up the drool-covered toy. She used her index finger and thumb and tossed the toy-gun into the kitchen. She almost fell over with laughter as she watched the eighty-five pound dog slide on the kitchen tile and bang into the cupboard doors: his feet frantically flailing for traction.

* * *

Morton Filman had been careful to not arouse the attention of the neighbors. The clothes he was wearing were not those of a workman, but they were in line with the neighborhood. To determine

275

which way to enter the house, he studied the layout. He wanted to go in the back way but there was no pathway to the back of the house: everything was covered in snow at least calf deep to knee deep. There were no cars in front of her house, and if she had a rent-a-car, it must have been in the basement. Someone was at home because he had seen the street side curtain pull back and then drop in place.

A car was coming down the street so he crossed the street and moved closer to a covered bus stop and waited until the car passed by. He stomped his cold feet and blew into his cupped hands: amber-white vapor drifting out of his mouth as if it were cigarette smoke. *I could rig the house for a gas blow, but I better check and make sure that she is in the house.* In the back of his mind he wondered how the insurance companies, and the police, would take the coincidence of two accidents in a row. Desperate to leave town: he would have to disappear for quite a while. It pained him to think he might even have to stay away from the money he had stashed in the Bahamas, at least until the case had gone cold.

In the distance he could hear the sound of the transit bus as it made a wide swing to enter the street where he was loitering. It was decision time and he was not yet ready. Furtively his eyes sought for an option, the best one he could find was the driveway of the house next to Doris'. From where he was it appeared they had shoveled a path around to their back door. Counting on the phenomenon that people do not usually concern themselves with other people who seem to know where they are going, he crossed the street and boldly proceeded around to the back of the house. A thick hedge line in the back had given him the break he had hoped for: the side opposite Doris' house had only a trace of snow on the ground. Quickly he dashed for the row of hedges.

Inside the house, Thelma and Max were playing a game that she nicknamed, 'throw and slobber'. She threw underhanded and Max slobbered all over the play gun. Several times Max stopped and pricked up his ears, but Thelma encouraged him to stick to the game.

Morton could not tell what was going on in the house, only that there was a woman who was doing a lot of bending and using her arm as if she were moving some things as she was pushing a vacuum cleaner. Glancing at the utilities at the back of the house he was excited when he located a gas meter. With a little luck he could put out the pilot light and then rig it to look as if the vacuum had a defective cord or that the wall circuit sparked and caused an explosion. Sneaking in the back door of one of these older houses would be easy. Knocking out Dr. Mercer would be a piece of cake. *It's spur of the moment, but it should work,* he told himself.

With the cold beginning to penetrate his clothing, and body heat melting snow which had worked its way into his shoes, he was getting cold and desperate to get into a warm place.

Following the shrub line as closely as he could, he crept toward the back stairs which would take him up to the back door. Using a broom standing against the stairs, he carefully removed the snow from the three stairs. A short half-curtain covered the bottom of the window built into the door. Using his very sharp pocketknife, he cut around the putty holding the window in place: the explosion would explain the absence of the pane. With a little prying the small window easily popped into his hand. His heart was beginning to beat faster, no so much in fear but in the doing of the act: he found it stimulating. After reaching through the opening, he undid the lock and carefully pulled open the door: he was now on the back porch. Something was not right. He closed the door and looked at the door to the kitchen, the vacuum was not running. *She must have finished.*

Thelma had had enough of throw and slobber and headed for the bathroom. Like a mother looking at her child's diaper, she made a face of mock disgust, "Max you've got a smelly mouth. You need your teeth brushed." She ruffled his head and he trotted along behind his playmate: toy firmly at the ready.

The water running in the bathroom sink worked to Morton's advantage as he slowly opened the kitchen door. Somewhere in the house he could hear water running and someone either singing or talking. He stepped inside and moved toward the stove, it was an older model perfect for his plan. He lifted the lid and extinguished the pilot lights. He was about to turn on the gas when the hackles on the back of his neck shot him a signal of alert.

Aware of some noise, Max had left the bathroom and crept toward the source of the sound. Trained to freeze his prey before he attacked, he curled back his upper lip exposing a set of teeth able to crush human bones. From somewhere down in the primitive past of all dogs, he brought up a bone-chilling growl. Instantly, Max could smell a wave of fear coming from the man standing at the stove. He was waiting for either a command or an imprudent move by his quarry.

"Max, what are you growing at?" Thelma had come from the bathroom and now she could see half of Max's body as he was standing half way in the kitchen and halfway in the dinette area. As she approached him, she repeated her question, only this time there was concern in her voice, "Max, what are you growling at?" Max did not flinch but rather tensed his muscles: ready for any action.

Morton could not recall ever being so filled with fear. The dog looked like some kind of giant prehistoric predator. His mouth refused to move. His tongue acted like a piece of dried out felt. His body was tense but he managed to slowly turn so he was facing Max. Morton's eyes danced about the room looking for a weapon. He had a pistol in his waistband, but he was sure he would never make it. "Nice doggy. Nice doggy." He repeated over and over.

"And just what are you doing here?" demanded Thelma. Her hands on her hips and her eyes narrowed in a bold challenge. "Well?"

He knew the lady was not Doris Mercer. What kind of a story might he be able to sell? "I—I'm the neighbor who lives next door. I—thought I saw someone lurking about in our back yard." He gestured toward the back of the house. "When I got here I was going to knock on the back door." Again he moved to gesture, but Max took another step toward him. "I saw that the back door was open so I came in to talk to Doris." Pleadingly he looked at Thelma, "Will you call this dog off of me?" He paused, waiting for his story to sell, he could tell she was considering, "Please?"

Thelma considered what she saw and what he said, "What's your name and phone number. I'll call your house and see if your story checks out."

"Sure my name is Charles Aldrich, 555-8327." Morton managed a smile.

Thelma squinted at him and said, "Poppycock!" She patted Max on the head. "Good boy," she assured him. "Guard him, or whatever you do." Thelma went to her cell-phone and Morton's hopes soared as he thought he might have a chance to reach for his pistol. "I'm calling my husband. He and Doris can be here in a few minutes. If she says you're Charlie Whatever, then I'll call off the dog. So, mister, if you know what's good for you, you'll just stand there and don't move." She gave him a gremlin smirk and announced, "He is a trained and experienced police dog, mister. If you're not the neighbor, you're in trouble."

Thelma was punching in the last digit when the front door opened and Richard and Doris walked in.

"Wow! It's cold out there." Richard was saying as he started to remove his overcoat.

Doris was doing the same, but her eyes went to Max then to Thelma, "What's wrong, Thelma?

Richard looked over his left shoulder and spotted Max and the look on Thelma's face, "What's happened?" He started to reach inside his jacket and pull out his gun.

Max was confused; he turned his head to see a man reaching for a gun. Behind him he had a man standing at a stove, Max turned to go for the gun and immediately, Morton reached for his own gun. Max heard the movement and looked back to see Morton pointing the gun at him. The tile on the kitchen floor made it difficult for Max to change directions. Morton fired at Max and Max yelped in pain.

Doris hit the floor and Thelma just froze in confusion. Morton's second shot was at Richard: the impact caused him to lose his balance and stumble back against the front door. As Morton rushed out of the back door, he fired a parting shot at Thelma: she crumpled to the floor next to Max.

Morton lost his footing when he rushed out the back door; he slammed his head against the doorjamb and then reeled forward into the snow. Because he had been sweating with fear, the snow felt like he had just fallen into ice water. As he struggled to get to his feet, his only thought was to get away from there: everything was going wrong. When he reached the street, he spotted an older model F150 Ford pickup truck. His back hurt from the fall off of the steps and he was having trouble getting traction on the sidewalk, but he made his way to the passenger side of the truck and used his coat sleeve to muffle the sound as he used the butt of his pistol to break out the window. Crawling over the glass he quickly hotwired the truck and put it into drive.

This whole night has been a disaster.

The phone was ringing, someone was saying, "Get the phone." Doris was stunned, but her medical training had prepared her for just such an emergency. Grabbing the phone, she didn't wait to exchange pleasantries, she said, "Get me an ambulance...NOW!"

Kurt's voice was an explosion of anxiety. Turning his head, he keyed his mike and shouted into his car radio, "Send an ambulance to Doris Mercer's home: you have the address...do it NOW!" Trying to control his trembling voice he fired off a string of questions, "What happened? Are you all right? Who's hurt?"

Like the experienced physician she was, she said, "Later!" She paused and said, "I'm okay. I got work to do." She hung up the phone.

Kurt's insides turned to slush; his lungs ached as he reached up to put the dome light on the top of his car. Instinctively he called for backup. Scenarios of blood, bodies, and mayhem forced their way into his mind. *I can't lose her. I can't lose her!* He tightened his grip on the steering wheel as he pushed the accelerator to the floor rapidly closing the distance between his demons of fear and the reality of what had really happened.

Chapter fifty-nine:

Detective John Miller was already on his eighth cup of somebody's excuse for coffee. It was so bad he was forced to resort to using white sugar and a powdery substance supposed to dissolve and give coffee a creamy flavor. He had placed the VCR on pause while he forced the lumps of creamer against the side of his cup and attempted to crush the elusive substance that managed to squirt to either side of his spoon.

Three TV stations had given him their unedited tapes they had shot while at the fire. Kurt and John had hoped one of the camera men managed to get a shot of the crowd, and if they were lucky, they might get a shot of the girl with the smoky clothes talking to the perpetrator or at least someone who saw her last. John had just finished tapes from two stations; he had no reason to assume he would have better luck on the last tape.

Using a white plastic spoon, into the sink he flipped the chunks that refused to be crushed or dissolved. He rubbed his eyes and pressed 'play'. The unedited tape was expected to run for ninety minutes. Editors would snip out about fifteen seconds worth for use at the five o'clock news. Understanding the way most things work, John zipped through the first half of the tape, if he didn't find the woman in the second half he would go back. Fighting a massive attack of boredom and general fatigue, John struggled as he was reaching the last six minutes of the tape, but suddenly, there she was. Across the street, he saw her dressed in the smoky smelling coat they had found in her apartment. He was so surprised he couldn't remember what to do. His body came alive, as he felt rewarded for their hunch. He stopped the tape and ran it back to where she was first seen. He leaned forward, squinting in order to get a better look. In the videotape, at one point, she turned and said something to a man who was standing next to her. He froze the frame and attempted to zoom in on the face of the man. The face was blurry, but he spooled it off to be printed. Then he resumed the tape. The man was talking to her and seemed to be turning to follow her; it would have been in the direction of her apartment. John could not believe their luck: and then the cameraman flipped back to the other side of the street where they were doing street interviews. Fadeaways and close-ups of the reporter filled out the final five minutes.

As if he had just awakened from a peaceful night's sleep of eight hours, he grabbed the photo and headed for the lab to see if they could make it even clearer before he went to the computer mug file. He slugged down the last dregs of the concoction in his cup. Without making a face, he set the cup in a nearby sink and informed an incoming officer the coffee was great.

One kid, who had drawn the short straw, occupied the photo lab. He was stuck on the night shift because of the backlog of verifying photos, documents, processing crime scene shots, and doing photo enhancements. Six months ago John had served on the back shift: it was a favor for a friend. During that time he had become buddies with the Photo Lab's retiring photographer, so when John walked in the kid greeted him. "Hey, John what you doing here? You doing another favor?"

John headed for the photo scanner, "Na, this time, Sammy, I got the fun of looking at three hours of TV video tapes." Sitting down in front of the computer he continued, "I got a picture of a suspect. He was on the video tapes." He worked as he explained, "I need to clean up this picture."

Sammy responded with a snort and the noise of moving some equipment around, "You can do it yourself. Right?" He wagged his head and waved at the stack of papers and packages strewn about his workbench, "Dude, I'm really suffering here."

John was in a good mood; he chuckled and went to work, "No problemo, **Doode**."

Sammy sighed and grabbed another packet of photos.

It took John a little longer than he would have liked, but at last he had a clean picture. After dumping the picture to disc he took fast strides toward the door, "Thanks, Sammy." He wasn't really sure Sammy was still sitting at his desk.

Disc in hand he headed for the department computers primarily used to make matches. He ran the disc and asked the computer to try for a match. It took the computer fifteen minutes to find the most probable match. The file was pegged to a military file of a Harold Montgomery Zane. Current address: unknown. Known associates: none.

Next he used Zane's name and checked the national telephone directory and the United States Postal Service. Zane was in town. He printed out the address and phone number and headed for his car.

While in the corridor, he pulled out his cell-phone and punched up Kurt's number. *He's got to be impressed with this*. No answer. The operator said the phone was not operating at this time, but he could leave a message: he did. Out loud he murmured, "This is no time for goofing off, buddy."

Next he tried Doris' home, but again there was no answer. He stopped and shouted over to the desk, "Randall, you got anything on Millhouse?"

In order to quiet down a number of people clambering for his attention, Randall held up his hand and then said, "He's at the Good Samaritan, John." He paused and added, "Had quite a ruckus at---" he paused and looked at his duty pad, "—a Miss Mercer's place. We sent an ambulance and a CSU team over to her house."

John blanched. It was obvious from the expression on his face he knew nothing about the 'ruckus'.

"Something bothering you, Lieutenant?"

Holding up his hand, John said, "I'm okay, Sergeant." As he headed for the door John shouted over his shoulder, "Log me out for Good Sam."

John's head was spinning. Why hadn't Kurt called him? Was he hurt? Maybe he should have

asked the sargeant to be more specific. He turned
the key in the ignition and suddenly realized he
had entirely forgotten about the murdered woman
and Mr. Zane. They would have to wait until he
found out more about what happened. From the
underground garage, he drove his car up the
concrete ramp and turned toward the hospital. The
night was getting colder and the slush was now
hardening into mini-peaks of ice. Cars were
banging into one another and traffic was moving
slowly. John found himself surprised with the
feeling he was experiencing. It wasn't a flood of
fear, but almost a grieving at the possible loss of a
good friend. There was guilt too: he should have
been there to help his friend.

The hospital entrances were so packed he
declined to use his police privileges to park
wherever he wanted, instead he squeezed into a
slot between an SUV and a station wagon. He
slipped and slid as he crunched over the snow and
stepped into drifts that filled his shoes with pieces
of crusted snow: his only focus was to get inside of
that hospital and find out what had happened.

Bursting through the second set of doors, he was
met by a wall of hot air. People were milling
about, reading wall plaques, magazines, buying
items from the gift shop, but there was a barrier of
people between him and the reception desk. At

first he thought he could tame his impulses and wait for his turn, but he found he did not have the internal discipline to hang around and wait.

Pushing his way into the crowd, he held up his badge and asked, "What room is Millhouse in?"

The receptionist responded with a perturbed look. She shrugged at the others who were waiting and said, "One moment please, officer." She consulted her computer and announced in her most officious tone, "We do not have a Millhouse, officer." Dismissively, she returned to the others waiting in line.

John turned and looked for the entrance to the emergency reception area. He chided himself for not going there first. Pushing his way past nurses, orderlies, maintenance people and doctors, swiftly he moved down the hallways. He became irritated as he began to feel as if he were in an Alice in Wonderland maze filled with Mad-Hatters.

Bursting through the doors that took him into the receiving area of the emergency ward, he stopped cold in his tracks. The scene before him looked like something depicted in Dante' Inferno. He had seen these scenes before, but this time it had meaning. The cries of pain, the pleas for help, the tears of the worried ones, the red stains of life's fluid, the gashes, broken limbs, and others who were unconscious all flooded into his eye gate and shot arrows of pain into his troubled soul.

John struggled to control his emotions long enough to ask about Millhouse, or Mercer.

One of the Emergency Medical Technicians overheard John asking about his friends, "Officer."

He turned and recognized the EMT. Looking at the man's badge, John said, "OH! Brubaker." John thought he was just saying 'hello'.

"Your partner was in here about forty minutes ago." He pointed toward a set of doors; "He went up to surgery on the third floor."

John gulped, "Was he hurt badly?"

The EMT looked taken back, he frowned, "What do you mean? He was here to see some people."

Gratefully, he reached out and grabbed the arm of the messenger, "Thanks, Brubaker." He leaned into his walk as he headed for the set of green doors. After charging through the doors the tempo changed to a subdued roar and he began to feel his body lose some of the nervousness that had been attacking every one of his senses. Again he found himself searching for a direct path that would lead him to the Intensive Care Ward, but the signs above each corridor just never seemed to make sense.

The way to the ICU ward was supposed to be directly under the arrows above the causeway: he charged in that direction. After two wrong turns, he finally burst through two large green doors equipped with scarred plastic windows at the top. No more than fifteen feet away he spotted Doris and Kurt pacing in the hallway.

As a habit of reacting to sudden noises, Kurt looked up and saw his anxious faced partner trotting toward him. Kurt raised his arm and waved, but even in his wave he could see that Kurt was definitely not enthusiastic

John was still dressed for the cold outside and the hospital was geared at keeping its patients convinced they were living somewhere in northern Africa. With sweat leaching from his forehead and saturating his clothing, John, gasping for air, panted his way to Kurt's side, "So what's happened--?"

Under any other circumstances the sight of someone as big as John Miller half bent over struggling to catch his breath could have been considered comical, but in an ICU ward, the staff was eyeing him with considerable concern.

Doris' medical background alerted her to check John's pulse, "John, you look absolutely awful." She had placed her fingers on the side of his neck.

John swallowed and struggled to take several deep breaths, "What happened?" His voice was stronger and he managed to straighten up and look less like a heart attack victim.

Kurt hesitated, his voice cracked a little as he said, "I'm sorry about Max."

John's eyes seemed to double in size. "What do you mean, 'sorry'?"

"Filman shot him. Max is at a vet's, just around the corner." Doris paused to take a breath.

"Shot?" John's eyes darted around the room, "Shot? How?" He looked at Kurt, "Filman shot him?"

Kurt put a comforting arm on John's shoulder, "The vet expects him to pull through, but since he's not a young dog and he has suffered several injuries, he can't say for sure."

After taking a second to digest the news, John looked around the ward and said, "Then what are we doing here?"

Doris said, "Filman came to the house and Thelma and Max were holding him at bay. Richard and I came in the door and that's when Filman managed to shoot both Richard and Thelma."

Kurt jumped in, "Richard had on a Kevlar undershirt. It slowed the bullet, but bruised the hell out of his chest."

Doris interjected, "The shock waves didn't do his heart any good either."

"Thelma?" John asked. "Is this Thelma and Richard Price?" he stared at Kurt, "The guy you were checking out?"

Kurt nodded, "Yeah." He tried to act contrite.

Cutting into the lull, Doris continued, "Max was the real hero, John. If he hadn't keep Filman stuck in the kitchen, he would have killed Thelma and then killed Richard and me as we came in the door."

Acknowledging her comments he bobbed his head. "Then what about Richard's wife?"

"Thelma took a round clipped her left lung and barely missed her heart. She is in surgery now." Kurt spoke softly as if she were already dead.

"Medically speaking, if she can make it through surgery, she stands a good chance of a full recovery. It really depends on how healthy she is." Doris' voice seemed to trail off, as if she were a balloon leaking out confidence.

John seemed to be nodding his whole upper body, "Okay, if you guys are alright, I'm gonna find that vet and check on Max." He searched Kurt's face, "Where did you say he was?"

Using hand signals, Kurt said, "Out the front entrance. Two blocks north: 'Friends of Pets'. You can't miss the lighted sign; it's white with green lettering." John had already turned to go when Kurt added, "The Vet's one of the best."

Pursing her lips together so tightly that they looked bloodless, Doris said, "He really loves that dog. Doesn't he?" Her eyes misted with compassion.

"Yeaaah. He hasn't had much luck with friends or family, that dog is kind of a second chance for him to care about someone." Softly, Kurt pulled her into his arms and held her. He stroked her hair and smelled the scent of it. The thought that she might have been killed caused him to take several shuddering breaths.

* * *

The clinic had been just as easy to find as Kurt had said, but no one would answer the front door. John considered breaking the glass on the front door, but settled for trudging his way up the driveway which lead to the back of the building. He balled up his fist and banged on the back door. Almost immediately he could see a sliver of light enter the darkened room: someone had opened a door into the room.

An angry voice asked, "What do you want? We're closed." From the tone of the speaker he was certain he did not expect a reply.

Trying to sound as officious as he could, John said, "I'm a police officer." He fumbled at his belt and held up his badge for the silhouette to inspect. "You have my dog in there." Realizing that the

man probably had more than one dog, he said,
"Max! He's a black German Sheppard."

With no further response, the locks on the door
began to click and the man opened the door. As if
not really convinced, the man peered at John's
badge and spoke, "Max. Yes, I have him. Come
this way." The man turned and began to make his
way toward the open door and a lighted hallway.
"He seems to be a strong one, your Max." He let
out a little chuckle, "Can't say that he took too
well to me putting a needle in him. Thought I was
a goner when he rolled his head toward me and
flashed those two inch fangs."

John's eyes flooded with tears, "Then he's going
to be alright?"

The old vet laughed, "Alright? Alright?"
Realizing that John was crying he tenderly added,
"Boy, it would take a lot more than a nine-
millimeter bullet to put that dog down." He made
a turn and opened the first door on his left, "He's
in here."

The sight of Max covered in bandages and
suspended in a sling caused a renewal of anxiety.
"I thought you said he was okay."

This time the vet looked at John as if he were
some sort of alien. "Son, he's been shot. How
would you be doing if you had a bullet graze your
spine?" He gave a Walter Brenan chuckle and said,

"The sling and the bandages are mainly to keep him still while he is healing; otherwise, he might be chasing me all over the place." He patted the hindquarter of the unconscious German Sheppard. "He'll be good as new in six weeks. The bullet didn't hit anything vital, but it came close enough to his spine that it caused him to lose control of his legs, but just for a few minutes. "Want to sit with him for a spell?"

Without another word, John sat down and laid his head against the dog's head. He listened to his breathing and said a short prayer of thanks. "I won't be long, Doc." Without looking up he said, "Thanks, Doc."

Shuffling toward the door he said, "I love 'um too, son. That's why I've been doing this for over thirty-three years." He closed the door. John could hear the old man coughing as he disappeared down the hallway.

Chapter sixty:

Harold Zane turned into the street where Doris Mercer lived. About two blocks down he could see the flashing lights from two police cars. Driving slowly past the cars he stopped. A young officer approached his car and bluntly said, you can't stop here. Zane smiled, "Sorry, just curious." He bobbed his head in order to see around the officer. "What happened?"

The patrolman looked to make sure the car was not blocking traffic, "There was a shooting. We're looking for the suspect now."

Looking concerned, Harold whispered, "Is he in the neighborhood? Is he on foot?"

Assuming Harold lived in the neighborhood, he said, "Oh, no, sir. He stole a Ford pickup truck. He should be quite a ways from here by now."

Harold nodded as if considering what the officer had said, "Well…thank you, officer."

The officer started to ask Harold where he lived, but at that moment another car pulled up behind him. Harold drove off wondering if Doris Mercer had been killed and where would Morton Filman go now. Time was running out, suppose Carla needed medical attention. Absentmindedly he maneuvered the car down the dark, snow-covered

street. *Where would he go? Where would he go?*
Over and over he asked himself the same question.
Having spent some time following him, he could
only think of two places: Doctor Bick or Enrico
Angelino's. If the police wanted him, then
Angelino would have the contacts Filman would
need in order to disappear. He would go there first.

Harold felt a sensation of cold creeping up his
back. Tonight his life would change no matter
what happened next. If Clara were dead he would
have to see to the children, but even if she were
alive, his life would be altered because he
suspected the police were closing in on him. The
Baker would have to be caught, killed, or
disappear. Like black birds diving at him in order
to protect their nest, thoughts kept attacking him.
Where was Carla? Would he be too late? Would
the police catch him before he could rescue Carla?
The thoughts would not go away. He was still
driving her car, and every breath he took seemed to
have her smell.

Up ahead he could see a roadblock, *it's probably
for Filman*, he thought. Slipping down the next
exit ramp he came to an unfinished dirt road that
paralleled the freeway. Because the road was
seldom used, it had not been recently plowed.
Harold Zane hesitated, there were no streetlights,
and the snow was a good two inches deep. With

conflicted feelings, he moved to where the dirt road started: he could not believe his luck. Ahead of him was one set of tire tracks. It could be Filman's tracks. He would be trying to avoid the roadblocks. Taking his foot off of the break, he put his tires into the tracks in front of him.

* * *

For several miles Morton Filman had been glancing at his fuel indicator and hoping it was faulty. *Of all the rotten luck, I had to pick a truck on 'E'.* The red light at the bottom of the E was like a giant stoplight or a laser beam piercing his stomach. Beach breaker waves of anxiety were making him feel frightened and weak. It would be just his luck to run out of gas out here in the middle of nowhere. The truck bounced up and down as it dropped into potholes and then hit a large boulder protruding from the dirt. His headlights were weak, giving him only limited vision.

The large, snow-topped, yellow caution sign seemed to pop up out of thin air, frantically he looked to see if the road dead ended or had a quick dog-leg to the right or left. Morton slowed down, he moved closer to the windshield, but he could not tell until he came to a dead stop just a few feet from the caution sign. With no moon light and no streetlights, all he could do was open his car door and look around: there was a turn to the left, toward the freeway. Maybe he had enough gas to reach the lights in the direction of the road. Putting the car in drive, he turned left, and as he did he caught a glimpse of a set of headlights behind him, his lips curled in contempt, "Cops! Only cops would be out here. They're following my tracks." He pushed hard on the accelerator and the truck responded by fishtailing: a lump of panic appeared in his throat and he backed off of the gas pedal. "Running low on gas, out in the middle of nowhere with the cops on my tail." He grinned, "This could have gone a little better." Laughing out loud, Morton Filman eased down on the gas pedal and headed for the lights. He was now putting distance between himself and the car behind him, but if it were a police car, they might have radioed ahead. He placed his gun on the passenger seat and kept driving.

Martina Angelino will make all of this go away, just the two of us sailing on the blue waters of the Caribbean. His mind drifted, floated, even surged from one fantasy to another even while his eyes scanned from the road, to his rear view mirror, to his flashing red gas gauge. "I shouldn't have wasted so much time in the roadblock line." He mumbled to himself.

Harold followed the red taillights as they moved from side to side: *that could be a pickup truck.* He was struggling to reassure himself. Without warning the brake lights had seemed to shoot beams of red light in every direction: Harold stiffened as he considered he would surely be noticed; after all, there was no one else on this road except the car in front of him and himself. He wondered why the police had not blocked that exit ramp he used, but if the police got a hold of either himself or Filman, Carla could be lost.

When the truck made a sharp left turn, Harold knew why the brakes had been applied. Glancing to his left he could see the road would lead back toward the freeway. Turning over and over in his mind was the question, "Where is Carla? Oh, God, I hope she is all right. Don't make her pay for the bad things I've done." His plea left him with a feeling of hypocrisy and guilt.

Chapter sixty-one:

Dressed in hospital pajamas, and sitting in a wheelchair, Richard sat next to Thelma's bed. The wires and tubes gave the illusion she was some sort of alien creature needing to be kept alive by a myriad of artificial means. The steady beat of the heart monitor was the dominant sound in the room. Richard could not help but think it seemed like some sort of echo announcing that Thelma was alive for one beat more. He gripped her hand, endeavoring to pass some of his strength into her body, and yet aching to reassure her he loved her and sought to encourage her to fight for life. Existence without her was unthinkable.

Instinctively, he found himself praying and repenting for the lives he had taken in his role as 'The Actuary'. He knew they had been bad people, even evil, but yet there were others who loved them and felt as he did now.

In one corner of the room a nurse sat at a small desk. She was monitoring Thelma's vital signs and scanning several documents which were in a pile of manila folders. Next to her desk were two padded chairs separated by a small coffee table. Kurt sat in one of the chairs, Doris in the other.

Kurt leaned over the table that separated them and whispered, "I've got to get to work and catch this Filman guy." He produced a forced smile and continued, "John has a lead on the guy who killed a woman who was living around the corner from where Filman lived. There might be some connection, maybe it was Filman."

Unable to speak, Doris nodded and closed her eyes.

"Look, Hon., you can't feel guilty about this. He almost killed all of you. If Max had not panicked him he probably would have."

Doris nodded and sniffed. While grabbing a facial tissue for her running nose and dripping eyes, she said, "I know you need to catch this guy." She paused, "He might shoot someone else who won't be so lucky."

Kurt stood up. The nurse gave him a monitoring look and went back to her work. "I'll stay in touch, and you be careful. It's possible we have not seen the last of this Filman guy." Kurt shot a look in the direction of Richard and Thelma. "Even though the operation didn't go as well as they expected, she still has a better than even chance."

An involuntary nod was all Doris could manage, "Go get that guy, Kurt." Her face contorted in anger, "I hope to be working on Filman when I get back to work." She looked away as if she were ashamed at what she had just said.

Kurt bent over and gave her a kiss on her wet cheek, "If you need me, call." He tiptoed as he made his way across the room to the utilitarian looking green metal and chicken-wired glass door. In the hallway he found a phone and called John Miller.

After the first ring John answered the phone, "Yeah?"

"John? Kurt." He paused, suspecting bad news, "How's Max?"

A throat-choked voice said, "He's wonderful." There was a pause and John cleared his throat, "He's going to be okay, partner."

Kurt was overwhelmed with the sobbing his partner suddenly released. By now John's emotions were on overload. Kurt took a deep breath and closed his eyes as he asked, "Are you ready to get the s.o.b. that shot him?"

The words seemed to be like a bucket of ice water dumped over John's head, "You damned right I am!" He slid back his chair and stood up, "Where are you?"

Crisply Kurt responded, "I'm here; at the vet hospital."

He was about to ask John what he wanted to do when John shot back, "Pick me up." Before leaving he stroked the slumbering dog. It seemed strange to him, but he understood the innocence sleeping before him. Dogs were peculiar. What is it that they say about dogs: 'they will even lick the hand of a master who kills them.' Tenderly he kissed Max on the snout and exited the room.

Kurt spotted John waiting by the curb; he slowed down so he wouldn't splash him; "Great news about Max, huh?"

John smiled, "I know it seems stupid worrying about a dog, but he's gotten to me, partner." As they pulled into traffic he asked, "So how is Doris taking all of this?"

Kurt raised his eyebrows, "She feels guilty. She thinks it's her fault."

"That's stupid." John turned his head to ask, "Where does she get that?"

"Darned if I know; she seems to think, if she had been there, Filman would have just shot her and no one else would have gotten hurt."

"Women!" John snorted, "Reminds me of my mother. She was the same way...never heard a guilt she didn't like"

"Mine too."

Shifting his voice, John asked, "So where are we going?"

"Doctor Bick is probably behind this. I think we should check him out first."

"They got a dragnet out for Filman?"

"Yeah, but nothing so far;"   Kurt glanced at John, "So what about this Zane guy. You like him for the bathtub lady?" He paused, "Or could it be Filman?"

"Well, Zane seems the logical guy, you know. He was with her just before she was killed. At least he's a lead." Nervously, John started tracing lines on the passenger car window.

"What's bothering you?" They passed under a streetlight and for a second Kurt could see the concerned look on the face of his partner.

John looked up at the headliner in the car, "Several things, Partner." He turned toward Kurt. "You ever just have a kind of a hunch, a speaking: something just nagging at your gut?"

"Sure." Kurt glanced at John, "So what's nagging?"

John held up his hand and pointed to his index finger, "Number one: we should have talked to Jolene about the departmental leaks concerning The Baker killings." He touched his middle finger, "Next, the bathtub lady. I know it's a reach, but what does a baker make?"

Kurt shot him a confused look, "Bread, cookies, cakes, donuts, rolls, ---"

John interrupted him, "Yeah, partner, BREAD." He waited to see if Kurt got the connection, but

Kurt's mind was still working on the threat to his girlfriend, Doris.

"Bread! So what's so special about bread?"

John shot Kurt a look of disappointment, "Jesus, Kurt, the bathtub lady had BREAD shoved down her throat." He tilted his head and gave a hangdog look, "Don't you get it?"

Kurt shrugged and nodded, "So you're saying the bathtub lady was killed by The Baker, only he's using a different signature?" For a brief second Kurt thought he understood how Watson must have felt when lectured by Sherlock Holmes.

"Bingo!" John paused and then said, "With all of the excitement, we never got around to asking Jolene if she ever talked to anyone about the case."

Kurt saw the roadblock up ahead and nudged John, "Put the light up." Steering to the emergency lane, he was keeping an eye out for any Ford trucks, "Okay, we have some dead time, call Jolene---" Kurt looked confused, "What's her last name?"

"I don't know."

"Call Carla and ask her and then we can go though reception." Kurt was pulling up to the roadblock so he rolled down his window and pulled out his badge. An officer stood in front of his car, his weapon at the ready.

"ID please, sir." The officer was very cautious, following The Book to the letter. For several minutes he grilled Kurt about his boss, Captain Won, and his partner, John who was busy on his cell-phone, "Thanks, for your cooperation, sir."

He slapped the car in drive and stayed in the emergency lane. He handed John his ID and noticed the look on his face, "What's wrong, Partner?" Expecting a frivolous answer, he smiled and chuckled. "Did you get a hold of Doris?"

John's face could only be described as a mask of wonderment. He nodded, "Sure did."

"Well?"

John took a deep breath and shook his head, "Zane."

"What?"

"Jolene's last name is Zane."

Confused, Kurt asked, "Like in Harold Zane?"

"She thinks Harold Zane is her father-in-law."
"Where's her husband?

"Dead, killed in the Army." John looked as if he were either in shock or trying to make sense of something he could not believe.

"Zane's The Baker?" Kurt inquired.

Looking confused and exhausted, John leaned back in his seat and ran his fingers through his carefully combed hair, "I just don't know, Kurt." He turned and asked, "How can this be true?" He

paused, "So if Filman faked the Ortiz killing."
Again he hesitated, "That means he probably got
the info from Jolene?" pause, "Right?"

"Yeah. I suppose so." He took an exit putting
them on the street about two miles from Doctor
Bick's home. "But what does Jolene have to do
with Filman?" Kurt whistled, "Got any good
answers?"

"Search me." John shrugged.

The silence in the unmarked police car was
accentuated by dispatch messages which did not
apply to them, lights from the instrument panel,
and the outside noises of city traffic.

Kurt sniffed and narrowed his eyes, "Okay. Let's
say that Carla told her father-in-law about the
killings. Wouldn't he get suspicious, if he were the
Baker?"

"Nope! He would just think she was a girl talking
about what she heard from her friend who was an
assistant to an ME." John reached up and used his
hand to rub his beard. "On the other hand" He
hesitated to collect his thoughts, "IF Carla
happened to be 'friends' with Filman, she could
have told him and not thought anything about it."

Kurt rolled his eyes, "That is some reach, man."
He laughed, "You want me to believe that Jolene is
some kind of a pivotal person in this?"

"Hey, could be. What if The Baker doesn't know Carla is seeing Filman and Filman doesn't know she knows The Baker?

"One in a million;" Kurt shook his head in disbelief, "Never happen." Dismissively, Kurt pursed his lips and said, "We should be at Bick's pretty soon." He mumbled, "Pretty farfetched."

John shrugged, "Farfetched, perhaps, but it could explain a lot."

Tolerantly, Kurt rolled his eyes and asked, "So, in your story, does Jolene know that her father-in-law is a killer?"

"That part I don't know, but I don't think she knew that."

Kurt hesitated, as if sifting through his thoughts. He realized John had good instincts, "Doris said Zane baby-sits for Jolene."

"Christ's sake, John. He's not going to hurt his own grandkids."

"I wouldn't say that too fast, Kurt. I've seen it done before."

Memories and scenes flashed in from of Kurt's eyes, "Yeah, so have I." Kurt cleared his throat as if to change the subject, "So what does this have to do with Filman?"

"I know you're concerned about Doris, but maybe the two cases are related."

Kurt considered what John had said. *Of course it was possible, but even if it is possible what is the best move to protect Doris?* He turned to John, "Check the address on this paper." Kurt handed him a sheet of paper with the home address of Doctor Bick.

"Should be about four houses on the left"

Kurt slowed down and checked to make sure his coat was unzipped so he could reach his weapon. Not wanting to alert anyone, he continued past the house, "I don't see any tracks to or from the house. Do you?"

"Na. No one has been here unless they dropped in by parachute."

Kurt struck the steering wheel and cussed. "Call this one in and ask for a patrolman to watch this place. Use your cell."

John picked up his cell-phone and called the station.

Kurt stopped and studied the house of Dr. Bick, "Sure is a big place," he mumbled.

"It'll be a couple of hours before they can break anyone loose, Kurt: lots of accidents." The only sound answering him was the hum of the engine, "You suppose this guy tried to have Doris bumped off so he could collect on her key-man policy?"

"It's a safe bet, but we may never prove it unless we can find that Filman character." Kurt whirled

and looked at John, "If he did Ortiz for
Angelino…" His voice trailed off, "Maybe
Angelino owed him a favor." Kurt made a face
displaying a huge question mark.
 John thought for a second, "Angelino's place isn't
far from here. Let's check it out."

Chapter sixty-two:

   Since he left the dirt road, Morton Filman had
not seen the car behind him. His first thought was
to stop and get gasoline before he ended up stuck
somewhere. He coasted into a 7-11 convenience
store only to find out the gas gauge had been
broken; he could only put four gallons in the tank.
He left his ten-dollar deposit with the cashier and
drove off toward the home of Enrico Angelino.
The closer he got to the Angelino home, the more
concerned he was because he didn't have a plan.
Killing Angelino could be a big mistake, but NOT
killing him could be an even bigger mistake.
   "I'll make it look like somebody hit the house
looking for drugs and cash. If I kill the old man the
mob will just fill in the slot." He chuckled when he
realized he was talking out loud to himself.

Expecting to see guards stationed in front of his home, Filman was surprised when he stopped about one hundred yards from the house, "No guards?" *Maybe he has dogs. No, that can't be— the front gate is open.*

Filman opened the passenger-side door of the truck, the light came on, but he ignored it. Slipping his pistol under his left armpit, he started moving toward the house. Morton was both confused and amused how someone who was so rich did not have more security around his home. The only lights on were one in the back and one upstairs in the front of the house. From previous surveillance, he knew the room upstairs was Martina's. Without much effort, he managed to make his way to the back of the house where there was a set of wooden stairs which came down the outside. The stairs were painted battleship gray and were almost invisible at night. Enrico often used the stairs when he wanted to sneak out for business or to visit one of his many mistresses.

Not trusting his luck, he pulled the gun from under his arm and held it out in front. Slowly he took several steps and then checked his perimeter and moved up a few more steps. By now he was beginning to feel both the pressure and the anticipation of escaping with Martina. His breath was shooting out of his mouth: he looked like a panting horse on a cold winter's night. With a wet hand he reached for the brass door handle: it was locked. He checked the exterior of the door and discovered an electronic alarm system that must have come with the house; it would be easy to temporarily bypass.

The system was designed to allow a person to enter through the door, this would trip the alarm: the person would then have thirty to forty-five seconds to disarm the alarm with a code before the alarm would sound. Thirty seconds was more than enough time to grab Martina and get back to the door. With any luck he would get forty-five seconds. With her as a hostage they would not dare to shoot at him.

He took several deep breaths while he again checked to see if anyone was watching him. Quickly he trusted his knife blade alongside of the door and tripped the door latch. The alarm count would start when he separated the two pieces of the magnetic sensors. He opened the door and closed it as quietly as he could. Swiftly he moved to Martina's door and turned the knob.

"Who the hell are you?" she asked. (Ten seconds gone) She was not afraid, after all her father was a man to be feared. Dressed as if she were going out to some nightclub, she held a wooden hairbrush in her hand: she shifted it to a defensive position. Her eyes were narrowed and she scowled at him. A flicker of recognition gleamed in her eyes, "You're that sob who killed Paulo." She straightened up as if she were going to yell. (Twenty seconds gone) She reached out and grabbed at him, she tore his coat pocket.

Without any hesitation, Morton used the butt of his gun and hit her across the side of her head: she went limp, "Put the finger on me, huh, well you're gonna pay plenty, little girl."

Before she hit the floor, he grabbed her and flipped her into a fireman's carry over his shoulder. Grabbing the quilt from the bed he threw it over her and rushed for the back door: thirty seconds gone, but no alarm. Opening the door at the top of the outside stairs he took the time to carefully close the door--- quietly. *Maybe no one set the alarm.* With one hand on the railing he was at the bottom of the stairs and running for the main gate, still no alarm. He should have been able to feel her weight, but by now his heart was pumping adrenalin throughout his frantic body. He could feel her body bouncing on his shoulder; she was beginning to become heavy. He reached the pickup truck and attempted to throw her into the passenger seat, but he was feeling too weak to pitch her that high so he had to settle for pushing her onto the floorboards: (Still no alarm!)

Not believing his luck, he pulled from the curb
and headed down the opposite side of the street;
driving as if he lived in the neighborhood. He
glanced at the bundle laying to the right of his feet.
A surge of self-confidence overcame him, he had
stolen the daughter of one of the most powerful
bosses in town and nobody even knew it. This last
thought disappointed him: he wanted Enrico to
know he did it and got away with it.

At the next intersection he turned toward the bay
where he had a chartered powerboat waiting for
him to escape to Mexico. He giggled, the floor
moved and Martina moaned. He whacked where
he thought her head was: she stopped moving.
Morton was feeling so proud of himself he was not
even aware of the car following him.

* * *

Harold Zane had arrived at the home of Enrico
Angelino in time to see Morton Filman rush across
the street carrying a girl: he guessed it was Martina
Angelino. Harold's first instinct was to stop
Morton and make him tell where Carla was: that
could be risky. But then, he decided that, maybe
he was taking the girl to where Carla was--it was
worth a chance. If Carla was dead there was
nothing he could do about that now, but if she
were alive then he could rescue her and still kill
Morton. As far as Zane knew, Morton had no idea

of who he was or what he looked like: this could work for him.

Chapter sixty-three

By only a matter of minutes, Kurt and John missed the abduction of Martina. Putting the dome light on top of the car, they drove up the driveway and walked up to the front door. Before they could ring the bell, the door was opened by a two hundred and fifty pound man; behind him was another man who could have been his twin. Mrs. Angelino was standing by the door jamb leading to the kitchen; she was wiping her hands on a red and white checked towel.

Surprisingly, the doorman's voice was like that of a Bostonian Lawyer, "Are you gentlemen from the police?"

Kurt nodded at Mrs. Angelino, "Yes, we are." She did not return the gesture.

Extending his hand he asked, "Your identification, gentlemen." He displayed a polite smile, "Please."

Cold enough they would like to warm their hands and stamp their feet, Kurt and John held out their identification for the 'Bostonian' to examine.

Satisfied, he nodded and said, "What can we do for you, officers? Mr. Angelino is out for the evening."

Cortina said something to the man standing by her and he addressed the doorman, "It's okay, you can let them in."

Feigning half of a courteous arm sweep he said, "Won't you come in, please?" He closed the door and then stood behind them.

Standing in the hallway, Kurt said, "We are looking for a man named Morton Filman." John and Kurt checked the faces around them and then said, "We have reason to believe he murdered a man whom your daughter, Martina, was seeing."

Cortina took a few steps closer to the officers, "Yes, officer, you will recall we cooperated and allowed Martina to check your files." She looked suspicious.

Kurt knew the results of what had happened through their surreptitious cooperation, but this was not the time to bring that up, "Yes, we appreciated your help, Mrs. Angelino."

John stepped forward and said, "We think your daughter could be in danger. She identified this man. " He looked over his shoulder at the man behind him, "He was headed this way just a short time ago."

Cortina's eyes flashed as she burst into Italian and looked at the man next to her. She nodded toward the steps which went upstairs; the man went up the stairs two at a time.

Kurt and John looked at each other as they heard a number of doors slamming.

Cortina looked like a pressure cooker about to explode.

Head held down, the man from upstairs rushed up to Cortina's side and whispered into her ear. She exploded, "What do you mean, 'she's gone'?" Viciously she spat at him, "What are you idiots good for."

He held out his hands and said something to her.

Her face seemed to puff up and her eyes almost disappeared into her cheeks, "Off! Off!" She shouted, "She--turned the alarm off?"(she had planned to sneak out with her friends).

Again he leaned toward her and spoke, but this time she opened her hand and shoved her palm into his face. Throwing the checkered towel at the bodyguard, she stomped her way over to confront the detectives. With her index finger she jabbed John in the chest, "You bastard! You caused this!" She poked Kurt in the chest, "You said it was okay for her, now look." She started to cry, "My baby, she's gone." Strangely enough, it wasn't as much of a shout-- as it was some kind of a plea.

The bodyguard behind John opened his Bostonian mouth and calmly said, "Mrs. Angelino, she might have slipped out." He hesitated, "She's done it before." He tried to sound as if he were offering her an explanation which would both calm her fears and excuse their incompetence.

The guard behind Cortina was shaking his head and waving his arms, obviously trying to signal something to the other guard, "Probably, not this time, Bruno. Her quilt is missing and there is some blood in the hallway."

At this statement, Cortina began to wail and head for the stairs. Flailing her large arms, she stomped on each step as if she wanted to crush every one of them to death.

Bruno spoke over John's shoulder, "Yeah, and Martina's pregnant. The old lady hasn't even gotten to that yet."

The other man came over to Bruno and handed him something, it looked like a piece of paper.

Ignoring Bruno's comment, Kurt spoke to John, "Better put out an APB for that pickup truck. Tell them he left from here within the last fifteen minutes or so."

John went to a corner and called in the All Points Bulletin. "I told them to get the CSU team over here. Maybe they can pick up some clues." He moved closer to Kurt and asked, "What'll we do now?"

Bruno made a face as if he were pained in deep thought. Jerking his head toward the other man he said, "He found this in the hallway. It might be where she was intending to go, but it also might be nothing. Either way we can't leave here now." He held it out to Kurt.

Whispering, Kurt said, "I haven't the slightest idea, but let's get out of here before the old lady comes down those stairs and orders these two goons to kill us."

Standing outside on the expansive front porch, John and Kurt looked up and down the street. "Where would you go?" asked Kurt.

"You think I think like this crazy?"

"No, John, I don't" he replied tersely, "But I'm fresh out of ideas. I don't think she escaped to one of her haunts." He fumbled into his pocket and took out the piece of paper Bruno had given him. He regarded it suspiciously. It might have been meant to throw them off of the girl trail.

"Well, he just kidnapped the pregnant daughter of one of the most powerful gangsters in town." John paused and blew out a column of vapor, "Where would you go?"

Kurt laughed and said, "As far away from here as I could get." He moved the paper into the light.

"Yep…me too; Planes are out, unless he charters, but then the pilot is either dead or talks." John thought a second, "He can't take a bus. A car is really risky because of the road blocks and a troublesome teenager."

"If he holes up he is dead meat within forty-eight hours."

"Okay, no plane, except charter, trains are out, and automobiles are too risky."

Scowling, Kurt muttered, "So what's left?" He paused, "Boats?"

"Too risky! If she starts screaming or making noise…"

"Charter boat;" He punched John in the arm with his elbow, "Charter boat!" he paused to face John, "It could work! Look at this, a soggy matchbook with the name of <u>The Breakwater Charter Service</u>.

John shrugged, "Okay, let's say you've got something." He raised his eyebrows and dropped his chin, "Which marina?"

"Call it in and we'll have all of the marinas tell us if they have had any bookings in the last week."

"So, what if he borrows a boat or owns one?"

"Jesus, John, give me a break. How would I know? You got something better?"

Muttering to himself, John started down the stairs toward their car.

Moving around to the passenger side, Kurt got in
the car and picked up the radio mike, "We'll have
them check marinas, private aircraft, and alert the
Coast Guard." He keyed the mike, "How's that?"

John started the car and slowly pulled out of the
driveway.

Kurt pointed up the street, "Turn right up there, if
the street goes through it will take us toward that
Marina off 22nd Avenue." Kurt's boat was berthed
in the same vicinity.

"Feeling lucky?"

Kurt shook his head, "Nope, just run out of
options." He sighed as he said, "For the kid's sake
I hope we're lucky. This Filman is a real first-
grade loony."

Chapter sixty-four:

It was like some kind of a nightmare where some
bad guy is charging toward you and you try to pull
the trigger on your gun, but you can't seem to get
the right grip to prevent your own death.
Everything was cold and dark, and the dream
turned to one of drowning. Carla's ears were
ringing. She knew she was under water, but she

had no choice, she had to open her mouth to breath. Something swam into her mouth, no doubt it was going to kill her, she bit down as hard as she could, tearing at it with her teeth, the animal began to fade away and she felt cold fresh air surging into her lungs. She had ripped a hole in the plastic bag over her head.

Gradually her mind turned to other priorities. Where was she? It was so cold and dark. What was she doing here, and how did she get here? As her mind cleared she realized her hands were tied behind her back. Her feet were taped together, and there was a piece of loose tape hanging from her mouth. She began working her hands down toward her feet.

What happened to Morton? She asked herself. *We must have been mugged, but where is Morton?* She called out, "Morton?" No answer, no movement.

She pushed off her shoes and her hands cleared her feet. She felt around the car trunk, but there was no one else. Her stomach felt as if someone had punched it with a sledgehammer. Her ears were still ringing and the smell of gasoline was becoming prevalent.

Using her hands she reached to remove the rest of the piece of tape from her mouth, but instead she discovered there was a piece of plastic in the way. *I have a plastic bag over my head.* Instantly she began to panic. She clawed away at the bag as if fighting for breath. Ripping the bag until it was reduced to pieces that looked as if it had gone through a limb shredder; she pulled at the plastic tape on her mouth and around her neck.

While continuing to peal herself free from the tape, Carla began calling, "Someone! Anyone! Help me! Again and again she repeated her pleas.

When she had finally removed all of the tape from her ankles, wrists, neck and mouth, she lashed out with her feet: attempting to make noise and hoping to open the trunk of the car.

As time passed she stopped, her voice hoarse, her head aching, and her legs beginning to weaken, she laid back and tried to rest. Weakly she continued to voice intermittent cries for help. In an attempt to stretch out and maybe even sleep, she put her head toward the opening of the trunk and stretched out her legs toward the front of the car. Carla could feel her energy draining, her senses becoming weaker by the minute. Her mind was alternating between concern for Andrew and Amy and her frustration at being trapped in this space which seemed to be progressively growing smaller.

Minutes passed and Carla awakened. She had fallen asleep. Her feet felt numb from being cramped in one position so long. She moved her head to peer though the blackness and something caught her eye. She looked again; it was a sliver of light just to the left of her left leg. Her hopes surged as she pulled her knees into her chest and, with all of her remaining strength, propclled her feet toward the amber-sliver of light. The backrest moved. The sliver of light now seemed more amber, and it was now larger. She could make out a glow coming from a streetlight.

Her ankle hurt, but she pulled her knees to her chest and again she shot her feet at the beam of light, the back folded down so fast she slid down and bumped her head on the floor of the trunk. If she were right, there was a partition in the back seat, it allowed people to lower this section and even put a pair of skies that reached from the inside front of the car to the trunk: some called it a door, others called it a hatch. Again she muttered pleas for help.

She stretched out her legs and rested. Her breath was coming fast and labored, but she smiled while she gathered her strength, *it had a cargo hatch, thank God it had a cargo hatch.* The tingling in her legs was growing stronger as blood was returning to her limbs. Using every ounce of power she could muster, she worked her way into the backseat of the car.

Exhausted, she flipped up the cargo door and lay on the backseat. Quickly her breath was steaming up the car windows. The cold felt good to her heated and worn out body. "I've got to get to the kids." She struggled to sit up but no matter how hard she tried she just couldn't find the strength. Rattling around in her mind were the words: *Jolene had an accident.* She passed out, still whispering cries for help.

Chapter sixty-five:

Thelma had regained consciousness long enough to see Richard was holding her hand. She smiled but didn't speak. She moistened her lips and Richard held her water jug while she sipped from a bent straw. Even now he could see the gentle sparkle in her eyes. For anything, he would have traded places with her, "You're going to be fine, Thelma. You got lucky."

She squeezed her eyes together and continued to smile, and then she drifted back to sleep.

Richard's chest hurt from the bruise the bullet had caused. It had been a good shot: right at his heart. Had he not had on his Kevlar undershirt, he would have been dead on the spot instead of nursing a bad welt on his chest.

With only a slight effort, he got up from his wheelchair and started to pace the floor. By now a surging cauldron of hate was bubbling in his being. If Filman were in front of him now, he would strangle him with his own bare hands.

"What are you doing up?"

The voice was familiar, "Well, Doris, I'm just tired of playing the cripple." He turned and faced her: he gave her a fatherly smile. "I've milked it about as much as I care to."

She walked up to him and put her hand on his arm, "How's the bruise?" Her tone was that of a physician.

"It's doing fine; it's my <u>chest</u> that hurts." He rubbed the spot and chuckled at his own joke. "Where are the officers?"

"Kurt and John?" She wasn't sure what to say. Kurt had updated her on their hunch to check out the marina traffic, but she didn't want Richard gallivanting about.

"Yes." Richard hesitated, "I have something to tell them about Filman and a boat he chartered." There was an edge in his voice as he glanced toward Thelma. "More accurately, it is a boat he has planned to 'borrow'."

"I can call Kurt on my cell phone, what should I say?" She wanted the information, but without giving away that the men were headed in that direction.

"The boat is at a marina called the Southern Gulf Club." Richard took a deep breath and turned to Doris, "I need your rent-a-car."

"Why? You're injured. You shouldn't be going anywhere." Doris was frowning like an angry housewife, "Give me the rest of it."

Richard rolled his eyes and tried to control his desire to leave, "No!" He seemed to be in deep thought, "I want this guy—myself." Again he looked at Thelma.

Knowing she needed to keep her voice down, she nodded toward the door to the hallway, "Let's talk."

Richard stalled. He smoldered as he cast casual glances about the room, "Okay, but I want your car." Wincing as he turned he said, "We haven't much time."

By the time they had found a spot where they were not likely to be overheard, Richard was beginning to boil.

He was close to pushing Doris against the wall and taking her car keys. "I want him and I'm not saying anything else until I have him."

Seeing that he was beginning to act desperate, Doris offered a compromise, "Okay, you can have my keys. It's parked in A-14, North lot." She pulled the keys from her black purse. "But—I want you to call Kurt as soon as you are at the marina, --agreed?"

Glancing at his watch, Richard concluded he would agree to anything, "Okay, it's a deal." He snatched the keys and involuntarily he winced.

Releasing the keys, she said, "Hurts. Huh?"

"Damned right it hurts, but not as much as seeing Thelma in that –bed." He turned and executed a quick walking pace as he headed for the elevator.

Doris watched him as the elevator doors closed: then she speed dialed Kurt.

An irritated voice answered the phone, "Yeah?"

Without preamble, Doris said, "Richard said Filman has a boat chartered at the…" She faltered, "Oh, God I can't remember."

"Remember what?"

"The name of the Marina."

Kurt sounded amazed, "He knows the marina?"

"Yeah, he told me."

"Well?"

Panicked, she stumbled as she was on the verge of crying, "He told me. I just can't remember."

Kurt tried to sound calm, "Well, ask him?"

"I can't," She sounded apprehensive.

"Can't?"

Sheepishly she muttered, "He's gone."

Kurt was confused, "Gone? Where? He's injured."

By now Doris was beginning to turn from humiliation to anger, "He left." She took a fast breath, "He's got my car and he's headed to the marina."

Feeling exasperated, Kurt closed his eyes and asked, "Which marina?"

Irritated, Doris launched a defensive attack; "I didn't write it down, okay?"

"I understand, Doris, but were there any words that struck you?"

She hesitated and then she furrowed her brow, "Yeah, as a matter of fact, he said something about a gulf club."

"Golf club?"

"Yeah, gulf club."

Making a face he looked at John, "She says the marina has the name of golf club in it."

John nodded, "The Southern Gulf Club." He flipped his head as he made a left turn, "It's a play on words."

Kurt shot him a confused look.

"You know… g-o-l-f and g-u-l-f, **club**." John did a quick nodding, "Southern Gulf Club."

Kurt spit back to Doris, "Southern Gulf Club?"

Excitedly, she screamed, "Yes! That's it!"

"Okay, sweets, we are on our way." Kurt hung up.

Doris stared at her phone. He had hung up before she could tell him of Richard's intention to get Filman himself. For only a split second she considered calling back, but then she decided she weathered enough interrogation for one day. She turned right and headed for Jolene's room.

Chapter sixty-six:

Painfully, Richard slipped out the front entrance of the hospital. The doctors had cautioned him that the bullet, although it had not penetrated his skin, had sent a shock wave which had 'upset' his heart.

The car was parked exactly where she said it was: North lot, A-14. He slipped behind the wheel and fired up the engine. By habit he checked the instrument panel. While the information seemed a bit blurry, he concluded the car would make it to the marina. He backed out of the slot and crunched into a parked car on the other side of the lot. His temper flared, but he disregarded the incident and put the car in drive.

Following several close calls, he managed to get on the south freeway and into the fast lane. Not knowing where Kurt and John were, he rushed to make sure all they could do was function as back up, or pick up Filman's body. His head was beginning to hurt and all he really wanted to do was to lie down and sleep.

Floating between the white lines of his traffic lane, he leaned forward almost to the point of putting his chin on the steering wheel. He was forced to squint in order to maneuver the small car in between the cautious traffic and read the overhead exit signs. He fought to keep his eyelids from drifting down and closing; they seemed to be drawn together like a set of black and white Scottie magnets.

Overhead he read the exit sign for Southern Harbor: two miles. Too weak to care about surrounding traffic, he cut to his right and clipped the front end of a small foreign car. Undaunted, he kept going right until he reached the exit lane. A minute later he was barreling down the exit ramp. His mind seemed as if it were on automatic, but he could not remember which way Filman had gone the day he followed him to the marina. Gambling on a fifty-fifty chance, he turned left not realizing that the light was red.

The traffic was light and all the damage he did was to scare the Hell out of several late night drivers coming home from a nearby bar. To his right he could see the masts of several types of sailing craft. He slowed down and began reading the signs for the various exits to different slips at the marina.

Richard straightened up when he read a sign with an arrow and words that read, "POWER CRAFT": he followed the arrow. He rolled down the window and inhaled the cold night air. Squeezing his eyelids he forced his mind to recall the slip where Filman had gone. It was; the image would float in and out at his touch, like a piece of drift wood surging in and out with the tide. He would think he had it and then it would float away like some wispy ghost.

He managed a weak grin when he saw the sign for Gulf Club 24. *Yes, it was* pier *24-slip K2, La Senora Justina.* His arms felt like Gumby appendages as he pulled the wheel to the right and drove over the pebble-gravel covered parking lot and coasted into a handicap-parking place. After cracking the car door just enough to turn on the overhead light, he pulled out his Barrett and checked his clip: it was full. He put one in the chamber and got out of the car.

Except for the light on in the guard shack, there was little activity he could see. He swung his head around to check on the parking lot: the swift movements made him stagger as if he were drunk. He shook off the feeling and moved his eyes more slowly: there were only ten cars in the parking lot and two of them were pickup trucks. He assumed one of the ten belonged to the night watchman. Moving from car to car he put his hand on the hood of the cars to feel for warmth: two of the cars were hot and one was warm.

Attempting to put everything in better focus, he took in several deep breaths and savored the cold sea air. Richard could tell the wintry night was beginning to clear his head. Slowly he moved toward the guard shack, not yet sure what he would say in order to gain access to the pier. He did his best to not appear as if he were drunk. Shoulders back stomach in; he set his face toward the shack.

A set of headlights swept across his body as another car pulled into the parking lot. Thinking this could be his chance, he ducked into a large hedge of bloomless-bougainvillea and waited to see if the man would punch the entry code into the access pad at the top of the gangplank to the pier.

Richard was feeling better, but he could tell his faltering heart dulled his senses. He knew it wasn't serious, but for now it was interfering with his ability to move about. He watched as the man clad in blue jeans, a heavy wool shirt, and white sneakers reached for his wallet, undoubtedly to find a piece of paper that would give him tonight's code. The crunching of the gravel under his feet and the vapor seeping from his nose presented a strange image. The man stopped and consulted his paper; he had to reposition it according to the rustic lighting from nearby poles. Richard watched as the man punched in the numbers and while the buzzer sounded, he replaced the paper into his wallet.

Richard moved quickly, he pulled out his wallet and shouted to the man, "Hold on there, please. I seem to have misplaced my reminder sheet."

The man in the sweater laughed, "Happens to me all the time." Under a brighter light Richard could see the man had a full bead, specked with gray. When the man smiled he had a beautiful set of once white teeth, "What slip are ya?"

A cautious man, Richard thought. "I'm visiting a friend in K2. He gave me the code, but, as usual. I misplaced it." Richard laughed and the man seemed to relax.

"Come on and I'll walk you part of the way." He paused to extend a hand, "Paul Vector"

"Richard Price here. Thanks for the help."

Paul slapped Richard on the back and said, "It don't do well to bother Angus anyway." He stopped talking in order to set up his punch line, "It'll interfere with the watching of his soap operas, or whatever he seems glued to."

Richard listened and nodded as Paul Vector went on about how the boat club had gone downhill in recent years. Paul was considering moving his membership to a club with more serious clientele. At slip 'D', Paul peeled off and sauntered into the orange light streaming from the overhead, yellow bulbed, pier lamps.

Casually casting a look around he began to pick up his pace. Of all things he didn't want Filman to cast off and get away. The sea was calm behind the breakwater but there was no doubt the water was freezing cold. Winded, he reached slip 'K' and studied the sign to see in which direction he should go in order to find slip K2. The sign said that K1 through K10 were on the right. Richard took a deep breath and fingered his pistol. K2 was the first boat on his right; it was about thirty-five feet long and had sleek lines. A sign on the side said it was a Bayliner 3520. There were lights on inside and voices whivh alternated between normal and calming, and then angry and loud. Richard bent down and tucked the end of the bowline so it would be awkward for a quick get-a-way.

Cautiously he stepped on board and headed toward the loud voices.

Chapter sixty-seven:

Bruce Kaminski of the Crime Scene Unit was busily working with his computer, pausing only long enough to refuel from his large, thirty-two ounce 'Raiders' cup. He was already to the stage where he had to shake the plastic cup in order to get the last smidgen of liquid from the bottom. Without interrupting his typing, Bruce glanced up as he heard a door open, "'evening, Captain."

Captain Won was pulling off his Macintosh coat as he headed for his office, "What brings you out of the woodwork tonight?"Responding with a fake cough, he said, "My captain asked me to be here."

Snickering, Captain Won said, "Was that tonight?"

"All right, Cap, what's so important?" ignoring the question, Bruce kept typing.

"Kurt and John are chasing down a murder suspect." Captain Won was now in his office; he raised his voice so that Bruce could hear him, "The bathtub lady." There was a rattling of papers and he asked, "Got anything new from forensics?"

Bruce stopped typing, "Yep." He was baiting the Captain.

"Well? What!" His voice sounded flat even though the room was almost empty.

"Thumb print off of the crust of the bread jammed into her throat." To antagonize the Captain, again Bruce began typing.

Captain Won came out of his office and walked up to Bruce's workstation, "Got a match?" he asked expectantly.

Bruce nodded and started to reach in his pocket, he was controlling the smirk on his face.

Won laughed, "Good one." He moved to where he could look Bruce in the eye, "Now tell me if you got a match **of the fingerprint** against any of our files."

"Military." Bruce stopped typing and folded his arms across his chest, "Name's Zane: Harold Carlton Zane. Address unknown, but he has cashed several checks that came from a military surplus shop downtown: owned by a Pete Corbin, also a vet."

"John and Kurt think this guy is The Baker. Just changed his MO." The statement was more of a question then it was a proclamation. "Did you tell dispatch to send a car over to that surplus store.... see what they can find out."

Bruce nodded, "Yeah… my boys and I think there might be something to that change of MO theory."

Captain Won parked his bottom on the desk in front of Bruce, "Look, Bruce, I don't need to tell you that we are only four months away from another election cycle." He offered a fatherly smile, "We need this one, Bruce." The Captain picked up a stapler and maneuvered it in his hands as he said, "The Commissioner has been on my butt about this Baker guy." He set down the stapler and added, "If we get this guy, the Commissioner will be really grateful, and so will I." He paused as if he had just completed a campaign speech and was waiting for the applause.

Exercising tremendous will power, Bruce focused all of his attention on the Captain and said, "Anything I can do to help. I'll be glad to help out, Captain."

"Good, good." He looked like someone fishing for 'The Mister Congeniality' award. "So, is this The Baker?"

Kaminski blinked and said, "Sir, he's whoever you'd like him to be." Bruce paused, "But we think he's the genuine article." He leaned back in his chair, and intertwined his fingers behind his head, "Mister Baker man himself."

The captain started to go back to his office, "Sorry about wrecking your evening, Bruce, but I've got a late night dinner with the Commissioner and I wanted to give him the good news."

"Does that mean I can go back home, sir?' Bruce was picking up the phone and talking to the dispatch to send a squad car over to Pete Corbin's War Surplus Store.

"Certainly! Just check in with whoever is filling in for Doctor Mercer before you go home. We'll want the Doc on board too, you know."

After completing his call and knowing that it would cost him another hour, Bruce Kaminski pushed in his keyboard and turned off his desk light. "Oh, by the way, sir, Millhouse and Miller think they have traced that Morton Filman to the Southern Gulf Club pier."

Scrunching up his brows and wrinkling his nose, he asked, "Filman?"

"The Ortiz killing, sir;" The captain still looked puzzled, "The Hispanic , err, dating Enrico Angelino's sixteen year old daughter."

Taking a deep breath and nodding, the Captain blinked his eyes, "Oh, yeah, now I remember." Acting only slightly interested he said, "Keep me posted if you hear anything more, can't have these gangsters taking the law into their own hands."

Bruce had to keep from laughing. Everyone knew the Captain was following the Ortiz killing because Enrico Angelino was a big campaign contributor. Shaking his head, Bruce headed for the elevator and punched the button for the basement, maybe he would get lucky and the ME would be too busy to talk.

Chapter sixty-eight:

In spite of his battle scared face, Amy and Andrew never felt nervous around 'Uncle Pete'. He liked to play with the kids. Their favorite game was to play hide and seek among the shelves and clothes racks.

It was Pete's turn to hide and he chose to squeeze in among a floor display of paper filled duffle bags. Amy and Andrew were waiting for the signal he was well hidden. Pulling a small piece of canvass over his head he yelled, "Ready!"

Andrew hesitated and started patting his pockets, he glance up at Amy, "I—can't-find—my inhaler." His face was wet with sweat and his heart was already pounding.

Amy watched as she saw his face and lips turning blue. She checked out Andrew's pockets. She called out, "Andrew is having an asthma attack!"

A muffled reply came from within the duffle bags, "What?"

"Andrew needs his inhaler, Uncle Pete." He's already wheezing." She sounded calm for what seemed a serious situation.

"You wouldn't try to kid an old kidder would ya, sissy?" He chuckled thinking the kids were trying to trick him in revealing where he was.

Amy helped Andrew lie down on the cold, checkerboard-tile, "Hurry!"He's turning blue!" No matter how often she had seen Andrew have an asthma attack, she was always worried when Mom was not around, "Call Mom! Hurry, he needs his inhaler."

Convinced Amy was telling the truth, Pete jumped out from among the smelly duffle bags, "Where's his what 'cha ma thing?"

"Inhaler!" She pulled at his sleeve, "He needs his inhaler, Pete!" She was beginning to mist up, her fear contagious.

He knelt next to Andrew and checked his eyes. "He needs help, Amy. Where is his –inhaler?"

Andrew was making a conscious effort to suck in a big breath of air, "Glove box---Mom's car!" He looked from Amy to Pete and back again. He sensed there was something wrong.

Pete didn't seem to understand the real problem, "Your Grandpa has the car, Andrew." Pete sat back on his heels. He looked up at Amy, "What'll we do?" Pete was not reassured when he saw the panic in Amy's eyes.

She wiped tears of concern from her eyes; "Mom always took him to the hospital." A mask of relief seemed to come over her face, "That's what we should do, Uncle Pete. Let's take him to the hospital."

As if he were once again on the battlefield, he scooped up Andrew and rushed for the door, Amy was running to keep up with the old war veteran. Before he reached the front door, two police cars pulled up in front of his store they pulled up on the sidewalk blocking each side of the door opening.

Assuming they were there to apprehend a vicious serial killer, their guns drawn, they rushed the door. What the officers thought they saw was a vicious killer kidnapping a small boy and a little girl.

The glass front door flew open, "Alright, you, put down that kid and get your hands in the air!" One policeman had moved to Pete's right, the other to his left.

Thinking that the police were there because he sometimes sold illegal weapons, he was panicked and didn't know what to say. He made several attempts to open his mouth, but he either stammered or the policemen kept waving their guns and telling him to do something.

Amy couldn't believe her eyes, her brother was fighting for his life, and these men wanted Pete to stop. She rushed around Pete, thinking she could get the officer's attention.

Smiling, and calling her to himself, one of the officers said, "That's right, little girl. Come over here. You'll be safe!" He moved toward Amy and scooped her into his arms; her face was against his heavy wool jacket.

Amy struggled and screamed, "He's my uncle!" She beat on the officer, "He's trying to help my brother."

Brushing off her comments as those of a confused kidnap victim, the officer yelled, "Get her out of here!" He kept his eyes on Pete and waved for a third officer to join them in surrounding Pete Corbin.

By now Pete was beginning to have flashbacks about his time in the killing fields of Vietnam. His nostrils flared and his eyes took on the look of a cornered animal. He looked down at Andrew; he was unconscious, sweating, and breathing shallowly, "The kid needs help. He needs—a – doctor." As if to prove his point he held out Andrew and showed the police how the boy was sick. He got an unexpected response.

From behind him one of the officers hit him on the head. It was a peculiar sound because he hit Pete right on his 'metal' plate. It still got the desired result because Pete, struggling to hold onto Andrew, fell backwards and hit his head against the concrete floor covered with one layer of checkerboard tiles.

"The SOB has hurt the kid. He looks bad. Better get him to a doc." The officer looked closer and said, "Take the squad car, I'll call an ambulance for this ugly…." "And take the girl with you." He flipped open his phone and called for an ambulance. Outside the squad car was pulling away from the curb: Amy pounding on the window of the back seat.

"Let's check around and see if anyone else is here" Putting away his cell-phone, he said, "I wonder where he was holding the kids?" Swiveling his head around he saw where the duffle bags had been knocked over, "Looks like we got here just in time, he was either putting them into or taking them out of those there duffle bags."

The other officer was turning his head and shifting his eyes all over the display area, "Yea, the kids might have just been making a break for it!" Pursing his lips and nodding, he said, "Yep, The Chief is going to be milking this one clear up to election time."

They laughed as they considered the accolades that were bound to be theirs.

"Okay, let's take a look in the back."

"Don't we need a warrant or something?"

"Na, we got the kids, --we got probable cause." Pulling out his flashlight he headed behind the blanket that served as a divider to the back room. In the distance they could hear the whining of an ambulance. "Those boys are really on the ball."

* * *

Before they reached the hospital, Amy had been able to convince the officers her brother had acute asthma and needed his inhaler. Their minds still refused to believe the ugly man they had seen was actually their uncle and was taking her brother to the hospital. To assume she was right was to place their careers in serious jeopardy.

"We'll get your brother to the doc and tell him what you said, little girl, but you had better not confuse everyone with your 'Uncle' story." The policemen looked at each other, "It might slow up your brother's treatment." He paused to let it sink in, "You know. They'll waste too much time asking too many questions. You don't want that to happen to your brother, do you?"

Stupid, Amy wasn't, she knew what was going on, it was like when someone lied at school in order to keep the teacher from getting in trouble, "Sure. I understand." And Amy went quiet as the patrol car pulled up into the emergency entrance. She could wait, but could Andrew?

Four people pushing a gurney rushed at the patrol car. They opened the car door and looked at Andrew, "Jesus!" They slipped an oxygen mask over the pale-white face. His lips were almost purple and his body was completely limp. As they sped him away, Amy could hear the gurney team talking, "How's it look?"

A crisp voice said, "Fifty-fifty, I'd say." He adjusted Andrew's mask, "He don't look too good." They were still mumbling, but she couldn't hear them.

"You'd better come with us, little…."

"Amy!" She scowled and jutted out her chin, "My name is Amy!"

Surprised by her aggressiveness, "Okay, --Amy." The officer offered a benevolent smile, "Where are your parents?"

Cocking her head to one side as if she were not sure the man before her would understand, she put her hands on her hips and narrowed her eyes, "My

Daddy's dead. He died in the war." She gave that information some time to sink in. "My Mom is out on a date with her boyfriend. My Grandfather left us with Uncle Pete until he could find Mom."

The officer didn't want to ask the question begging to be asked, 'you mean that man was your uncle?' but instead the officer took her by the hand and led her into the emergency ward. Answering his own question he satisfied himself by thinking, *even if he is her uncle, he is still a criminal.*

Pete muttered to the EMTs, "Where're the kids?"

Ignoring Pete's ramblings, "He's got a concussion, but I don't think it's too serious."

"Okay, let's thin the blood and watch his vitals." There was a scurrying about and then one of the men said, "Give him a little something to calm him down, will 'ya?"

The ambulance pushed its way through the snarled traffic and angry citizens. In the back an attendant sat and watched the marvels of modern medicine as they provided read-outs about Pete's physical condition. He knew he should be thinking about something, but he couldn't imagine what it was. Closing his eyes, Pete could hear the roar of shells bursting around him. A radioman was talking, but it was unintelligible. There was the acrid smell of blood and burning flesh, "Hey, man, are they going to be able to bring the chopper in?"

Pete yelled as he moved his arm to grab the medic, but something was holding his hand onto the stretcher. He didn't realize he was handcuffed.

"This guy thinks he is on a battlefield."

The driver leaned to his right and said, "Yeah? Probably seen too many war movies;" He slowed to pace with the traffic. "I was in 'Nam in '70 when we hit Cambodia, it was hell, buddy boy."

The attendant's voice shifted as he said, "Hey, Hank, what's The Congressional Medal of Honor look like?"

The driver thought for a second, "I think it's blue with a bunch of stars." Again he turned his head, "Why'd you ask?"

The attendant's eyes misted up and he said, "Look at this guys body, he's got bullet holes and burns all over him."

"So?"

"He's also got this around his neck." He pointed to a wide blue band with white stars on it."

"Oh, Jesus!" A sense of urgency and respect rocketed into his voice. The driver hit the siren on the ambulance, "OH, JESUS!" He mashed the accelerator.

***

Doctor Hulbert Bick, M.D., put down the phone. In front of him was an eight and one half by eleven inches sheet of paper, on it was scribbled a bunch of numbers representing his debt to a gambling syndicate. Pangs of despair seemed to come from everywhere. He leaned back in his high-back white leather office chair, a mark of better days. He was trembling, not just with fear, but also from too many drugs and the realization there was probably no way out of his mess.

His creditors wanted money, his bookie wanted money, and now, unless he coughed up some cash, Filman had threatened to send an anonymous note to the district attorney's office implicating him in the attempt on the life of Doris Mercer.

He pulled out the file drawer on his mahogany desk and stared down at his bottle of twenty-five year old Scotch. Next to it was a brandy snifter of cut crystal. *Nothing but the best*, he reflected.

From his cashmere jacket he pulled out a bottle of five hundred grain Darvon, and popped the top off of the bottle: it flew about ten feet and landed on his South American Cherry Wood floor, and then it rolled toward his sixty-inch plasma TV screen. With a ceremonial flourish, he filled his brandy snifter and replaced the bottle in the file drawer.

Into his left hand he emptied the bottle of pills, and then he tipped his head back and dropped them into his mouth. Doctor Bick picked up the snifter full of Scotch and inhaled the bouquet he had always enjoyed. Raising his glass in a final salute to life, he then filled his mouth with the fiery liquid. As if savoring the flavor of the burned charcoal oak, he gradually floated the pills down into his empty stomach.

Where there had been fear and anxiety, there was now a soft humming throughout his body: perhaps even a sense of floating in warm water or on a soft cloud of tropical air. As his eyes began to shut and his consciousness dart in and out, he thought, "*of all the dumb things I've done, this has got to beat all.*"

He was not aware as his nervous system stopped firing and his lungs and heart ceased to work. Doctor Bick, the physician who had sworn to save life had just ended his own. No one knew that his final thought was, *I'm dying and nobody will even care.*

Chapter sixty-nine:

A shattering of glass awakened Carla. Little chards of safety glass showered her, but she didn't care. Cold air seemed to float into her lungs and she felt a stinging sensation as she tried to take a deep breath.

A man's voice was asking her something, but it was like trying to tune in some radio station that just wouldn't cooperate. "You all right?" The man knew it was a stupid question. If he had thought she was all right, he wouldn't have broken the glass.

Keeping her eyes closed, Carla rolled her head and asked, "What'd you say?"

"---All right?"

She snorted, and attempted a smile, she was alive, but was she all right? Good question, "—Think so."

After pulling up the door lock he opened the door and spoke in a nervous tone, "My dog must have sensed you were in here." He reached in to help her out of the car, "He wouldn't let me finish his walk." Nervously he laughed and carefully guided her out of the car.

She realized the man speaking to her had a European accent. Carla struggled to control her vision, "Where am I?" Her words sounded slurred.

"Next to Kennedy Park;" He spoke as if he didn't understand why she didn't know where she was. "I think you need to see a doctor."

"Yeah." She agreed, "Yeah, a doctor." She sagged against the car. The man was talking to someone, but she couldn't see anyone else. There was a strange sensation on the back of her left hand, she looked down and smiled as she watched a standard Black Schnauzer licking her hand.

The man with the funny accent was talking again, "I've called 911 and they are sending an ambulance to take you to a hospital." He leaned closer to her and said, "Gunther and I will stay with you until the ambulance arrives." Gently grabbing her hand he said, "This way, they said they would only be a few minutes."

Weakly, she flipped out her fingers and attempted to pat the dog that had possibly saved her life.

The man walked her to a bench and supported her back as he helped her to lie down, then he removed his winter coat and folded it to use as a pillow for her head. "Just a few minutes, miss." He stroked her forehead.

There were so many things that she wanted to say, but forming words was just too much of an effort, She lifted her hand and placed it on top of the man's hand, "Thanks," was all she could manage. Her mind was drifting from one thought to another, *I wonder if Morton is all right? Were we mugged? How are the kids?* Feeling herself slipping into unconsciousness, she tightened her grip on the man's hand, "My kids—Andy, Amy?"

"I'll see what I can find out for you." Pushing the hair back from her forehead, he asked, "What's your name?"

Carla licked her lips and blinked her eyes; she could barely make out the face of the man who was helping her, "Carla." She took another deep breath, "Zane"

The man looked confused, "Zane?"

She nodded her head, but her eyes were closed.

He knew where he had heard that name; it was on the radio, an all point bulletin for a man called Harold Zane. "Is your husband Harold Zane?"

She rolled her head from side to side, "Grandpa-- kids."

In the distance he could hear the screech of an approaching ambulance. Now the foggy looking lights were beginning to show, the red, white and blue lights could barely pierce the cold winter air. He looked down at the slumbering girl and moved a single strand of hair away from her closed eyes. He glanced down at Gunther and said, "She's a pretty one, old boy." He patted the dog on the head and smiled, "Good job."

The whole procedure of getting his name, while the team checked her out and placed her on a black gurney, struck him as sterile. But then, he realized they did this sort of thing all the time. He corrected himself. *No! Not all the time, she was too special.* Holding his leash, he patted the dog.

"They'll want a statement from you, mister." The driver announced.

He unfolded his coat and took out a small gold case, "Here's my business card."

The driver glanced at the card and snorted, "Well, doesn't this beat all." He closed the doors and continued, "A lawyer, uh?" Starting his way around the ambulance he said, "I've heard of ambulance chasing, but this about beats all." When he jumped into the driver's seat the lawyer could hear him saying, "You're not gonna believe this."

The man grinned, he too appreciated the joke, but then he was not in that kind of law, his specialty was criminal law. "Gunther, I think we had better go home and line up some calls for tomorrow." The dog looked up at his master. His eyes gave the impression he was going to say something important, but instead he just barked.

He pulled on his coat and whistled as he briskly walked toward his 2003 Bentley sedan.

Chapter seventy:

Enrico Angelino wanted to kill someone, right now he didn't care who. Furiously, he was pacing his office at home. He had already had to send for a doctor to give Cortina a sedative before he knocked her out. The yelling and screaming had become more than he could handle. The expression on his face was one of murderous contempt, "How in the Hell could you let her turn off the alarm?" His voice was so loud and his hand gestures so violent, he was slopping whiskey from his glass: small spots of brown created a breadcrumb like trail as he moved about the room.

Bruno knew better than to say anything, he had seen what happened to people who talked too soon. His partner, Michael, not sure they were even going to live through this, was taking his clues from Bruno.

Enrico squeezed his lips so tightly they seemed to disappear and turn into a thin blue line where his mouth was. He threw his glass of whiskey into the fireplace, the flames jumped. He flipped back the lapel on his jacket revealing a revolver in his shoulder holster. His hand moved to the weapon and his fingers began to drum on the blue-black piece of crafted steel. He turned his back to Bruno and Michael.

It was almost time to talk, and Bruno began to search for the words that would keep them, well at least him, alive. "Boss, we'll get Martina back."

"Damned right you will!"

As softly as he could, Bruno continued, "I thought this Filman guy was dead."

Enrico whirled around and smashed his balled fist against his desk, "Thought?" his face contorted in distain, "You thought? That's a hot one." He went silent and in a display of exhaustion, dropped into his brass pined, red-leather, high-back, office chair. Breathing in short bursts, he passed his fingers through his thinning hair, "Okay—okay, we all thought he **might** be dead, but that cop thought Filman just faked it." His voice was tense, but he was beginning to move from dangerous to just on the edge. Rubbing his stubbled beard, he demanded, "Get me a drink!"

Bruno nodded to Michael and he went to Enrico's bar. The room was hushed and only the sound of the whiskey flowing into a glass broke the silence. Michael looked as though he were carrying a glass of nitro-glycerin as he walked across the floor and cautiously placed the container on Enrico's desk.

In a breathy, but calm voice, Enrico said, "I want that bastard dead." He looked Bruno in the eye, "Dead! No messing around, no fancy stuff, no torture, just dead." He was playing with his letter opener, "This guy steals my daughter, and besides he knows too much." He shifted his fiery eyes to Michael, "Dead!"

Both Bruno and Michael nodded and hoped this would be where Enrico would tell them to get out, but instead he was breathing like a runner who had just finishing a sprint. Picking up his glass he took a substantial gulp. He wiped his chin and waved for them to leave.

In his haste to leave, Michael almost bumped into Bruno as he slowed to open the large oak door. They exited and Bruno carefully closed the office door and leaned against it, happy to be alive. "I thought we had it, Mickey." Nodding toward the other side of the door he muttered, "That guy's a basket case."

Feeling brave now that they were not in the same room, "Yeah, well, I thought the least you could do was stand up for us." A subtle pout appeared on his lips, "It wasn't our fault, Bruno. That little-----, was always slipping out going someplace." He waved his hands toward the upstairs where Cortina was now asleep under the influence of some sort of medical injection, "Is everybody nuts in this place?"

Ignoring Michael's tirade, Bruno, shook his head, and said, "No doubt about it, buddy. We're just glorified babysitters." He lowered his voice, "But what bothers me is…" He looked around, "---I haven't got a clue as to where we should be looking for her."

Michael rolled his eyes and started toward the door. At the front door he grabbed his coat and turned to Bruno, "If the cops get to either of them first, this place is going down, Bruno."

Motioning for Michael to keep his voice down, Bruno said, "Okay! Okay, let's get the hell out of here. We'll start by checking out the bars and that crazy doctor that Martina goes to."

Opening up the door Michael announced, "I'll drive."

Chapter seventy-one

Richard moved closer to the voices. He tried to see through the windows, but the small, mustard-gold curtains were pulled tightly against each side.

For the first time he noticed the smell of the sea air: not fishy, but a mixture of water plants and salt. In various parts of the marina boats were starting, leaving, and docking. A large forty-five footer was having some sort of celebration and the music was moving across the water as if the band were playing from the dock behind him. The boat moved slightly as he worked his way toward the main door to the cabin.

A harsh male voice was snarling, "Watch your mouth, little girl." There was a sound like someone being slapped, "Your daddy isn't here to protect you now." He mocked her attitude.

Richard expected to hear a cry, but instead he heard a string of cuss words and the boat moved as something moved to the starboard. There was the sound of glass breaking, and furniture crashing. He used the cover of the noise to move to the door and grab the handle. Slowly he turned the knob and peeked through a narrow opening. There were pieces of glass and wood scattered all over what looked like a dark oak main room. Beyond, he could see a set of stairs which went down toward the bow: it was from there the noise was coming. A woman in a dark, what looked like an evening dress, and a man in street clothes were going from one side of the boat to the other as they tussled back and forth. She was screaming obscenities at him and he was yelling at her as he attempted to pin her flailing arms. The result was a rocking motion to the boat.

He was considering how to best enter the cabin and be unobserved when he felt a presence behind him. Richard froze and considered, should he rush forward or turn and confront what might be a person. Instead he felt his head move forward into the door jam. He heard a kind of popping in his neck as he slowly slid down to the cold, wet surface of the deck.

* * *

Harold stood over the unconscious man and looked at his face, but he didn't recognize the old man. *What is he doing here, maybe he's a cop.* To him it really didn't matter, he needed to find out where Carla was. He peeked through the door and observed the scuffling. Without any hesitation he shifted his gun into firing position and opened the door, the two people were too preoccupied to notice him. He stopped and squatted to see if the girl was Carla, but just at that time Filman managed to pin the girl across the table in the galley.

With the man's back exposed to him, Harold Zane yelled, "Carla?" He bobbed his head to try to see who the girl was, "Carla?"

Morton Filman stiffened, "Carla?" He looked at the defiant sixteen-year old who was spread-eagled on the galley table. He blinked as if believing she would change into Carla, but she couldn't change into Carla, he had killed her and left her in the trunk of a car.

Harold yelled at Filman, "Let her go!" Being careful not to hit the girl, he fired a warning shot that just missed Filman's right ear. The sound was nothing short of deafening.

Releasing Martina, he dodged to one side and pulled his pistol. Blindly he fired up the stairs toward the main cabin. Again the echo was so penetrating that it could be felt in his head. Martina grabbed her ears. "There ain't any Carla here, mister!" Sensing, rather than seeing Martina move, he shifted his gun to cover her. "Stay where you are." he hissed at her.

Martina responded by sticking out her tongue and sliding off of the table toward the kitchen sink. Her eyes shot toward a butcher-block knife holder: it was full.

Shifting to his left, Harold put a table top in front of himself and craned his neck to look below, "Filman! All I want is Carla and I'll go away." He tried to sound sincere.

Keeping an eye on the whereabouts of Martina, he sneered, "How should I know?" Morton retorted. "I don't know any Carla." *How does he know my name?*

With a voice seeming to come from beyond the grave, Martina yelled, "He killed her. He just told me he would kill me too if I didn't cooperate." She ducked down and grabbed her knees, "Help me, mister." Her voice muffled by her face pressed against her thighs.

Not wanting to believe Carla was dead he said, "Look, Filman, all I want is Carla. Where is she?" Skidding the tabletop closer to the top of the steps, he looked down and saw Filman cowered against a door that probably led to the bathroom. If he took a shot now he might kill him: for Andy and Amy's sake, he needed to find out what happened to Carla.

Unaware that the door behind him was bouncing open and closed, Harold eyed Filman and decided to take a chance by shooting him in the kneecap. He rested his gun and steadied it against the side of the table. He took careful aim. Behind him he heard the crushing of glass: someone was behind him. If they were armed they were after him, if they were not armed he would need to confront them. With lightening speed, he flopped to the ground. From lying on his back he rolled to avoid any bullets coming his way; he didn't really have time to aim. He pulled the trigger, but at that moment his left elbow struck the base of a broken glass. In spite of his years of training he flinched to the right and missed the man who had ducked to a squatting position.

Kurt heard the bullet whine past his chest, and thud into the wall behind him. The situation was just like at the qualifying range. He rapid fired five rounds at the man on the floor and moved to his right and behind a tipped oak coffee table.

His throat choked up with the smell of cordite, he asked, "You Zane?"

The man made a gurgling sound as he struggled to speak, "Who's asking? You a cop?" He blinked his eyes and said, "Carla. Where's Carla?" the words were weak and sounded incoherent.

By now John was watching through the open door. Kurt signaled him to stay where he was and to look toward the steps to the galley. "Yeah, I'm a cop." He pushed in a fresh clip and began replacing the five rounds into the one he had just removed. "Are you Harold Zane?"

Harold let his head flop to his right so he could see the top of the stairs that went down to the galley where Filman was. "I'm Zane." He almost sounded apologetic. "Heard you're after me;" Blood was starting to seep from under his body; an ever-widening stream seemed to be making its way toward the spot where Kurt was behind the coffee table.

Ignoring his words, Kurt asked, "Who's here with you?"

He was too weak to sound venomous, but he tried, "Filman."

John, his voice excited, said, "Nice try, Zane, but hc's dead."

From the galley came a banshee-like scream, "He's here!" Then her voice went muffled like someone had put a gag in her mouth.

Miller looked at Zane and picked up his cellphone and called for backup and an ambulance. He placed his fingers on Richard Price's neck and felt a weak but steady pulse. "Come on out, Filman. There's no way out of here except past us."

Chapter seventy-two:

From all appearances, Harold Zane had passed out or died. The boat had suddenly become quiet as John moved in to the cabin, just to the left of the galley steps.

Distain dripped from Morton's words, "All right, bright boy, but I got Angelino's daughter down here." There was some kind of scuffle. "I'll kill her if I have to." The fracas resumed. Glass was breaking, wood was shattering and Filman was cussing.

John and Kurt exchanged looks; Kurt shrugged and then moved toward the head of Harold Zane, he intended to remove the weapon still lying in his right hand. "Well, if we don't get you, her father will!"

Filman let out another string of cuss words, and said, "I'm coming up. The girl is in front of me, so put down your guns." It sounded more like an order than a negotiation.

John shot back an answer, "No can do." He hesitated as he watched Kurt creeping up on Zane. "Send out the girl and then we can negotiate your surrender."

"You're kidding. Right?" he said shoving Martina forward so her face was visible. The fright in her eyes was masked by a sneer of hatred and defiance. She stretched out her arms in order to maintain her balance. "So who kills her? You or me?" Somewhere in Morton's memory he could recall a movie he had seen, a smell of popcorn passed into his widened nostrils. "You aren't gonna take me alive, you dirty rats!"

Kurt looked at John and mouthed, "Who does this guy think he is, James Cagney?"

In spite of the situation, John grinned and shook his head.

Filman pushed Martina up to the next step: his face was visible, "I'm going out of here and none of you dumb coppers are gonna stop me. Ya hear?"

Martina was rolling her eyes and looking back at the lunatic who was threatening her life, she mumbled something that sounded like, "Shoot him!"

Both John and Kurt were looking for a clean shot without harming Martina, but they were thinking Filman would take one more step up and then they could shoot. Instead, Filman turned and ducked down the stairs leaving Martina standing alone.

Cautiously, John moved forward to grab Martina and pull her to safety, but she turned and jumped down the stairs. John rushed after her.

Martina reached under her cocktail dress and from her garter belt; she pulled out a boning knife. The long thin blade flashed as she lifted it into the air.

Morton Filman had flipped open the forward hatch and was about to pull himself up and onto the forward deck. He stretched up his arms and grabbed the wood frame that kept water from entering through the forward hatch. With an adrenalin-assisted pull, he began to take himself toward freedom.

Screaming like a witch from some horror film, Martina sunk the boning knife into his out-stretched back. Again and again she struck, her left hand adding force to her right.

His body seemed as if it were tied to the opening above, he squirmed, but refused to let go. He twitched and gasped, but continued to try to pull himself up. There was no pain now, only the feeling of being struck and held back from his door to freedom. Slowly his iris began to dilate. The last thing he remembered was the smells of the movie theater and the aroma of fresh popcorn.

She was beginning to feel weak from all the times she had stabbed him, she fell to her knees and continued thrusting, sometimes missing other times striking only his feet. As she weakly raised the knife for one more blow, John grabbed her wrist and took the knife from her blood-covered hand. She slumped to the floor, sobbing and muttering unintelligibly.

Kurt had checked the carotid artery on the neck of Harold Zane, there was no pulse, "What's going on down there? Is she all right?" It sounded like an afterthought, "How is she? Where's Filman?"

The smell of blood and the body looking like it was hung up for field dressing was too macabre for words, "She's okay!" He watched as the body slipped out of his coat and sagged to the bunk below. "He isn't!"

"I'm gonna check on Richard. The ambulance should be here any minute." Kurt headed for the main door to the cabin. As he pushed open the door he looked down at the deck. He looked forward and aft, "Where did you put Richard?"

John was helping Martina up the stairs; her face was chalk white, but covered with blood. The scene reminded Kurt of the movie <u>Carrie</u>. Her cocktail dress was torn and covered with stains. She was barefooted and seemed totally mute. "What do you mean, 'where did I put him'? He's right outside the door, I was afraid to move him until the medics got here."

"He's not here!" Kurt insisted as he continued to look around.

"He's got to be!" He set Martina on a couch and went to help Kurt. "He was right there." He pointed to the spot. "You go forward and I'll go back here."

Together they searched the deck of the powerboat, but it didn't take long. John finished first and rushed forward to see if Kurt found anything. Kurt was walking toward him, he was holding up a black overcoat, "I think this is Richard's."

"Where'd you find it?"

"Up by the forward hatch where Filman was trying to escape."

Bewildered, he asked, "He was there?" John wrinkled his face. "What was he doing there?"

Kurt tipped his head to one side and said, "Keeping Filman from escaping?" He paused as they heard the sounds of police and hospital vehicles approaching, "What I can't figure out is...where is he now?"

John blinked, "On the dock?" He didn't sound convinced.

Kurt's voice turned philosophical, "I rather think we'll find that answer back at the precinct."

"You checked him out?" John sounded surprised, "I know you said something about that, but I thought you were kidding."

"Not where Doris is concerned." The backup crew and the medics were making their way past the night watchman and down the inclined gangplank. The crime scene team was pulling up in the parking lot.

John sighed and asked, "What do we tell Thelma? For all we know he fell overboard, Kurt."

Kurt grinned, "I think that's what he had in mind, Partner."

"Huh?"

Kurt headed back into the cabin, "Disappear." He mumbled as he looked around.

John asked as if it were incredulous, "Disappear?" He snorted, "You think he is faking his own death?"

Kurt shrugged, "Possibly."

"So what makes you think he has something to run from?"

Kurt didn't answer.

The medic and the back-up team had arrived. They took one look and put Martina on a stretcher while one man went back for two body bags: one for Morton Filman and another for Harold Zane.

John glanced over his shoulder and eyed the ominous looking body bags, "One for the butcher and one for the baker" he raised his eyebrows as he nodded toward the zippered shrouds.

"We haven't proved that yet, John." He lowered his voice, "But I think you're right." Kurt approached the CSU team and gave them a run down on what had happened. "We're going to follow Miss Angelino to the hospital for a checkup and then we'll find out what this whole thing was all about." Pulling the team leader aside he said, "We think these two guys are suspects in some of our local killings, so take extra precautions with the evidence."

When they reached their car, they both sat down and breathed a sigh of relief; John looked at Kurt and said, "Why do you suppose that Zane guy was at the boat?"

Kurt scrunched his mouth as he thought, "He asked me, 'where's Carla?'"

John nodded, "Yeah, Carla Zane, his daughter-in-law."

"But why would he be asking me where she is?"

The car started moving forward, "Did she come with Zane, or was she supposed to be on the boat?"

John turned onto the freeway, "He was probably delusional."

"Could be, but he sure looked worried." Figuring if he called Enrico Angelino, he would end up being stuck on the phone, Kurt called the dispatcher and told him to ask the Angelinos to meet them at the hospital.

There was a short silence as they maneuvered through the nighttime traffic; stalled cars and accidents were a common sight. "You gonna tell Thelma?" John's voice was distilled to concern for the aging woman.

"Tell her what?" he paused and said, "What do we really know? He was lying on the deck, unconscious, then a few minutes later we find his coat and he had disappeared."

"Awe, come on. She has to be told something." He turned in the seat and his face was bathed in alternating light from the traffic around them, "She's going to ask, you know."

Speaking very slowly Kurt said, "You remember the Margaret-Goldstein-Wentworth case?" He waited.

Tenuously, John replied, "Sure. The one Captain Won was bothering us about: the rich guy's wife, Thurman Wentworth, right?" He raised his voice, "So why are you changing the subject?"

Kurt shook his head, "I'm not." He glanced at John, "I did a lot of research on that murder. She was supposed to have witnessed a crime, a robbery. Well, she told us about it and then the man who committed the robbery murdered her, supposedly. You know…an endangered witness thing." He paused and then blurted out, "You know…you set up a situation where a person is a witness to a crime, and then, when you kill them the police will think it's to keep you from testifying. Actually, it's a contract hit…just a set-up."

"Sounds logical…it could happen. She was a witness and she supposedly is in danger. He wanted to shut her up."

"There was more to it than that. She headed an organization that solicited pregnant teen-age girls, helped them to get secret abortions and then forced them to work off their debt by being prostitutes."

"Okay?" They were approaching the turn off toward the hospital, John pulled to the right lane, "And where does Richard Price fit into all of this?"

"Now mind you, right now I'm guessing, but I think he has been a contract killer for a long time. He specialized in killing off rich people who were doing evil things." Kurt took a deep breath to relieve his tension, "It wasn't just because he hated evil people, John: he made a bundle providing his services."

They were pulling into the hospital parking lot, "So you're saying the file you've been working on has led you to believe Richard is a hit-man?" Slowly he guided the car into a parking spot, "Are you sure?"

Kurt opened his door and it hit the car next to him. He cringed, "As a matter of fact, I'm not, least not so as I could prove it in court. Even his travel plans and relationship to the victims has been hidden, but there is a very thin financial paper trial that **could** peg him as at least being involved."

Their feet crunched over the frozen patches of snow, "Kurt, a defense attorney would have a skeet shoot with that kind of case."

"Boy, do I know that, but you know how hunches sometimes check out."

Inside the building John grabbed Kurt by the arm, "So what are you going to tell Mrs. Price?" He widened his eyes in expectation.

"What can I tell her? For all I know, she already knows about him."

"Knows what? You said yourself you don't have anything that would hold up in court." John stopped. "Are you going to pursue the investigation?"

Kurt thought for a second and then said, "What case? I haven't been assigned anything. And we don't know if he is dead or alive."

"Well, if he's as clever as you say he is, and he believes the Great Kurt Millhouse was on to him, he probably did take a powder." His voice was mirthful as he said, "Heck, Kurt, he probably knew the second you started checking up on him."

Rolling his eyes, he responded with a forced laugh, "Sure. He was scared to death." Playfully, he punched John Miller in the arm and said, "But---but, I'll bet you that---one day, Thelma will get a mysterious post card and then disappear to some non-extradition south seas island." He turned and said, "I'm going to check on Doris and Jolene. I have a few questions I need to ask her about Carla."

John was conjuring up the scene of the old couple basking in the sun on some distant South Seas island. In one sense he thought of it as romantic, but in another he didn't like the thought of a killer, even if he did kill 'bad people' untouchable by the law, getting away with it." He shrugged, resigned that, at least for now, it was out of his hands. He checked his watch; it would be light in another

three and one half hours: he would check on Max
then.

Chapter seventy-three:

Even Richard Price would have been astounded
by the evening. Jolene, Thelma, and Carla in the
same hospital and Andy there because of his
asthma attack.

Martina Angelino had just arrived and would
soon be home dealing with her troubled parents,
after she finished telling the police how her father
had Paulo Ortiz, the father of her child, killed by
Morton Filman.

Of course Price would have understood the
connection to all of the parties and explained the
thin and thick threads of the web that had been
spun by Morton Filman: a different kind of
Spiderman.

Before entering Jolene's room, he nodded to the
on duty officer and glanced into the window. Doris
was sitting by the bed, and they were talking a blue
streak. As he pushed open the door they both
stopped talking and looked at him, "Well, don't we
look better." He quipped.

Without preamble, Doris said, "Jolene just got a
call. Carla's in this hospital, and so are her kids.

They brought in Andy for an asthma attack, but he's going to be okay."

Looking confused he said, "Andy, is that Carla's kid?" He looked around the room as if he expected someone else to jump out of the bathroom or from under the bed.

Jolene and Doris exchanged looks and Jolene gave her a nod. With excitement in her voice Doris lowered her volume so that it sounded conspiratorial, "Someone tried to kill her." She waited for his surprised expression… then continued, "She was hit on the head, hands and feet taped, and a plastic bag taped over her head." She reached out and grabbed his arm, "And then they left her in the trunk of a car."

Tipping his head he gave her an askance eye shift and said, "Who? Carla? And she's alive?"

"Yep, bit her way through the plastic bag and kicked her way out by punching out that little thingy where people put down the back seat to put their skies in short cars."

Not sure but what he was having his leg pulled, he said, "Cargo door?"

"Something like that, but the best thing is she met a man." Doris was practically jumping off of her chair, "He's a nice man who was taking a walk with his dog. The dog heard her in the car and the man helped her out of the car and he called an ambulance."

Trying to put together her shift in subjects and excitement, he registered an expression of confusion and pain, "How did you just make that shift." He threw up his hands.

Surprised, Doris looked at Jolene who scowled in bewilderment.

"You were just talking about her near death in the trunk of a car and the next thing you're talking at record speed about a man and his dog."

Jolene and Doris both rolled their eyes and shook their head, "She met a great guy. He's a lawyer."

Kurt pulled up a chair and muttered; "Now that's an oxymoron!"

Doris frowned as she produced a painful expression, "She's real worried about her boyfriend. He was just going to show her something in the trunk when she got hit from behind. She thinks he might be hurt or even dead." She looked over at Jolene, "Poor Morton."

Kurt's head snapped up as he asked, "Morton?" his eyes shifted from Doris to Jolene. "Morton Filman?"

Thinking Kurt might have heard of the murder of Morton Filman, they looked both surprised and concerned, "You know him?"

He shifted his eyes from Doris to Jolene and back again, "We think he was the guy that rigged your car, Doris. He was doing a job for Dr. Bick: for the insurance money." Since no one said anything he continued, "Tonight he had kidnapped a sixteen year old girl and had taken her to a motor boat. We think he was planning to leave the country."

"What happened?" The ladies asked in unison. They looked as if they had found out that the seven dwarfs were lechers.

For the next ten minutes Kurt kept the ladies spellbound as he put together the pieces which happened that night. He was delighted by their expressions of fear, anxiety, and suspense. "What John and I are having a problem with is what to say to Thelma Price. We just don't know how much she knows about Richard's activities, if my suspicions are true."

Doris scowled at him, "But you said all you have for now is speculation. Didn't you?" Her tone was challenging.

Thinking discretion was the better part of valor, he nodded and slowly replied, "That's true, dear, but I still have to tell her something. After all, he has disappeared. He could even be dead."

"Well, I don't understand why he even went to the boat? Jolene managed to mouth.

"Best as we can figure it out it was because Filman had shot Thelma. He was mad and wanted revenge, but as far as we can tell, he must have been hit on the head and left above deck: probably by Zane."

For a few minutes everyone was silent, but the emotions were still running high.

Kurt closed his eyes and almost began to fall asleep, "Dot, why don't I take you to your place? The CSU boys should be gone by now and I need to get back to my place." He sighed and shook his head, "We're gonna have a load of reports to file and I don't look forward to Captain Won's response to my speculations about Richard."

Doris stood and leaned over to give Jolene a gentle hug and a cheek kiss, "Hurry up and get well. I'll miss you at work." She grabbed her handbag and started following Kurt out the door, "And keep me posted on Andy and Carla."

John saw them when they reached the lobby, he was sipping a cup of coffee and engrossed in rapid conversation with the night nurse, "I'm dead on my feet, partner. I think I'll drop by and see how Max is doing and then I'm going to catch about a month of shut-eye."

"Need a lift?"

"Na, Carol is going off shift in fifteen minutes; I'll hitch a ride with her." He gave Kurt a knowing wink, "She loves dogs." He grinned, "And cops." He gestured with his cup of coffee, "You two go on, and I'll see you in the morning."

Settled in the car, Kurt turned to Doris, "You had me scared. But now the night's like some kind of blur."

She leaned over and gave him a soft kiss, "You're not the only one scared." Turning to look out of the front window she said, "So where do we go from here?"

The silence was so complete they could hear the lingering, subtle noises of the cooling engine. He turned on the ignition and said, "Well, I've been doing a lot of thinking about that." Looking awkward and unsure of himself, he muttered, "How does Mrs. Millhouse sound to you?" He sat still as a snowman while he waited to hear her answer.

"You talking about your mother?" She teased.

"All right, don't make this more difficult than it is." He turned to face her. His words were slow and deliberate, but still awkward, "Would you consider marrying me?" He cringed, preparing himself in case she should say 'no'.

Doris sat up straight and said, "I don't know about being proposed to in an automobile in the middle of a cold hospital parking lot, but the rest sounds great to me."

Kurt frowned, "Is that a yes? " He closed one eye and said, "You're not going to go all weird on me now, are you?"

Doris grinned and stuck her tongue into one side of her cheek and crossed her eyes, "Now that all depends, Lieutenant Millhouse." Looking him straight in the eye and using her gloved index finger she poked him in the chest, "Just remember you're marrying a Medical Examiner, you know what I do for a living." She leaned forward and gave him a cheek kiss and then whispered in his ear, "If you ever cheat on me you're gonna find out how good I am with a knife." Pulling back and wrinkling her nose, she sported a malevolent smile and said, "And I know where to start, officer."

Accordingly Kurt smiled and gulped, "Any more warnings?"

"Oh, not a warning, dear…a promise;" She grabbed his tie and gave him a bridal kiss. Quickly her tone tuned to business, "Now let's talk about the reception."

Chapter seventy-four:

Thelma took the news about Richard in stride. Four months later, after she had purchased a tropic wardrobe, she disappeared without leaving a forwarding address; there was much speculation she would be joining Richard.

After receiving an anonymous phone call, Pete Corbin sold his business and moved out of state.

Carla was charged for her involvement in passing along sensitive information to Morton Filman about the M. O. used by The Baker. However, because of the skills of her high priced criminal attorney, she got off with six months probation in the custody of her smiling attorney. Both Andrew and Amy love the Schnauzer, Gunther.

Jolene and Carla have made up and Jolene is now attending night school working on her pre-meds.

Enrico Angelino is spending a lot of money bribing the appropriate officials to continue to postpone the hearing on the death of Paulo Ortiz. The complainant, Martina, seems to be on vacation in Sicily.

John and Max are constant companions, but nurse, Carol Winfred, is working hard to make it a threesome: she's meeting very little resistance.

Kurt Millhouse and Doris Mercer, now Mrs. Millhouse, were married last November. Now that the summer heat is upon the city she has two complaints, the heat and the fact she is having difficulty standing close to the operating table. They are expecting a boy in late August.

The End

Other Books by Raymond Lee Hegstad

The First Manuscript

The Blue Fin

Chockalet Sleuths (Three books)

Rescue By Death

Endangered Witness

The Phantom Director's cut

www.ingramcontent.com/pod-product-compliance
Lightning Source LLC
Chambersburg PA
CBHW071248220526
45468CB00001B/38